BEST DOG HIKES
ALABAMA

BEST DOG HIKES
ALABAMA

Joe Cuhaj

FALCONGUIDES

GUILFORD, CONNECTICUT

This book is dedicated to the inseparable bond between dogs and their human friends and the adventurous spirit of that bond.

FALCONGUIDES®

An imprint of The Rowman & Littlefield Publishing Group, Inc.
4501 Forbes Blvd., Ste. 200
Lanham, MD 20706
www.rowman.com

Falcon and FalconGuides are registered trademarks and Make Adventure Your Story is a trademark of The Rowman & Littlefield Publishing Group, Inc.

Distributed by NATIONAL BOOK NETWORK

Copyright © 2019 The Rowman & Littlefield Publishing Group, Inc.

Photos by author unless otherwise noted
Maps by Melissa Baker

British Library Cataloguing in Publication Information available

Library of Congress Cataloging-in-Publication Data

Names: Cuhaj, Joe, author.
Title: Best dog hikes Alabama / Joe Cuhaj.
Description: Lanham, MD : FalconGuides, [2019] | Includes index.
Identifiers: LCCN 2018043846| ISBN 9781493033942 (paperback) | ISBN 9781493033959 (e-book)
Subjects: LCSH: Hiking with dogs—Alabama—Guidebooks. | Trails—Alabama—Guidebooks. | Alabama—Guidebooks.
Classification: LCC SF427.455 .C84 2019 | DDC 796.5109761--dc23 LC record available at https://lccn.loc.gov/2018043846

∞™ The paper used in this publication meets the minimum requirements of American National Standard for Information Sciences—Permanence of Paper for Printed Library Materials, ANSI/NISO Z39.48-1992.

Printed in the United States of America

CONTENTS

THE HIKES

Gulf Coast Region

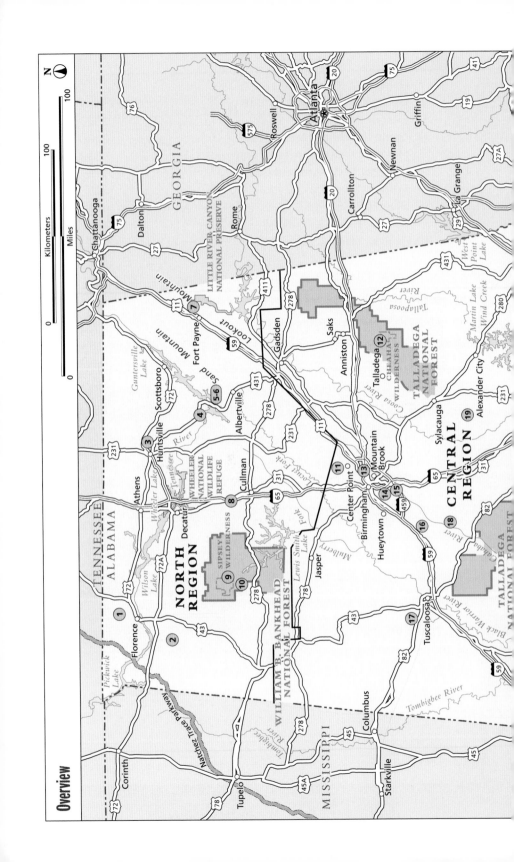

Overview

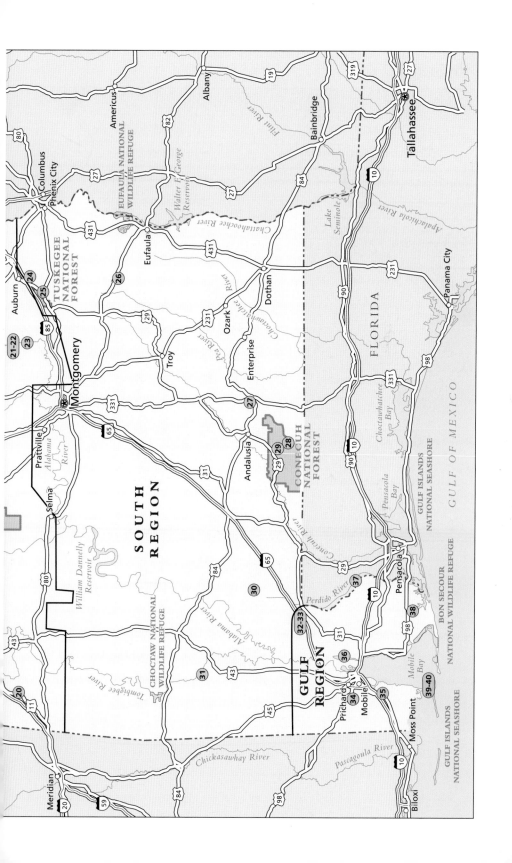

Map Legend

Municipal		Symbols	
═〈65〉═	Interstate Highway	🛋	Bench
═〈431〉═	US Highway	‖‖‖	Boardwalk/Steps
═〈27〉═	State Road	⌣	Bridge
═〈906〉═	Forest/County Road	⊼	Campground
═ ═ ═	Unpaved Road	†	Cemetery
•–•–•	Power Line	⌶	Gate
─ ∙ ─ ∙ ─	State Border	🛏	Lodging
		🄿	Parking
Trails		▲	Peak/Mountain
------	Featured Trail	🄰	Picnic Area
- - - - - -	Trail	■	Point of Interest
		🚻	Restroom
		🔻	Scenic View/Overlook
Water Features		🗼	Tower
⬭	Body of Water	○	Town
⬭	Marsh/Swamp	①	Trailhead
∿	River/Creek	❓	Visitor Information
⌢	Intermittent Stream	🚰	Water
≋	Waterfall		
∥	Rapid	**Land Management**	
⌒	Spring	▭	National Park/Forest
		▭	State/County Park/Preserve

MEET YOUR GUIDE

Growing up on a mountainside in New Jersey sparked my lifelong passion for the outdoors. The Appalachian Trail was virtually in my backyard, so it was no wonder that I would take to the trails. My dad had an old beagle, Lady, who loved to tramp through the woods with me. She would smell every wildflower we passed, earning her the nickname Ferdinand.

Almost forty years ago, after a stint in the US Navy, I moved to Mobile, Alabama, with my wife, Maggie, who was originally from the area. My love of hiking and the outdoors only grew as I discovered the largely unknown (at the time) adventures the mountains, canyons, and rivers of the state had to offer.

It was a huge move for me. I was a radio news anchor and disc jockey at a station just outside of New York City. It was hard going from the No. 1 market in the country to the

eighty-fifth, but I quickly found my footing, working as program director, music director, producer, and on-air talent on the Alabama Gulf Coast. During that time my daughter Kellie was born and became a true "radio brat" (really, that's a good term).

In 2005 I became involved with the Alabama Hiking Trail Society, a statewide trail building and maintenance organization, serving as president of their Gulf Coast chapter in 2006. That year I was honored by the American Hiking Society as the South Region volunteer of the year.

Today, I work by day in software programming, but every spare minute revolves around my writing. I am a freelance writer and author, having written for a variety of online and print publications. My books include four for Falcon: *Hiking Alabama* (now in its fourth edition), *Hiking the Gulf Coast*, *Hiking through History Alabama*, and *Paddling Alabama*. I have also coauthored a book on the history of baseball in Mobile. I am currently working on two new titles, a historical book about July 1969, when man first landed on the moon, titled *Everyone's Gone to the Moon*, and a collection of humorous short stories, *Living in a Banana Dream*.

And as all of that is going on, my rescue Labrador, Archer T. Dog, and I always manage to find time to hit those trails.

JOE'S FIVE TIPS FOR HIKING WITH YOUR DOG

1. When you have your dog on leash, it is best to use a harness instead of just hooking it onto a collar. If your dog pulls suddenly, the force on the collar can cause serious throat damage.

2. At some time you will be attacked by little yellow demons: yellow flies. They bite with ferocity around the head and neck, and dogs are prime targets. Use a nontoxic spray with the active ingredient pyrethrum.

3. I can't stress this enough: The combination of summer heat and humidity in the state can be oppressive. At least double the water you take for both you and your pup on these days.

4. Just like people, dogs can sunburn, too. Get a sunscreen specifically designed for dogs. Apply to the nose, around the lips, tips of the ears, groin, and belly throughout the day and after swimming. Be careful not to get it in their eyes.

5. Don't take chances when hiking near lakes, ponds, and wetlands on the Gulf Coast and in the extreme southern half of Alabama due to alligators. Sadly, many dogs have been lost because owners did not heed warnings. Check with land managers about the alligator population on a trail before heading out, and in those areas, keep your pet on leash and close by at all times.

ACKNOWLEDGMENTS

As always, this book wouldn't be possible without a helping hand along the way. My thanks go out to Marion and Emily Campbell, Derek and Mecianne Brown, Joseph and Rhonda Rickard, and Deborah Parrot for allowing their pups to appear in the book. Thanks, also, to Jim and Faye Lacefield with Cane Creek Canyon Preserve, Chuck Yeager with the City of Pinson / Turkey Creek Nature Preserve, Pamela Bradley with the Alabama Forestry Commission, Ursula Cary and Evan Helmlinger at Falcon Guides for putting up with me and my bajillion questions, and the staffs at Alabama's Nature Conservancy, Forever Wild, and US Fish and Wildlife Service. A very special thank you goes to my wife, Maggie, for putting up with yet another adventure (she was a trooper slogging through bogs) and thirty-eight years of bad puns. And I can't leave out the one, the only Archer T. Dog. I'm sorry he had to miss half of the hikes due to leg surgery, but I promise I'll make up for it.

TRAIL FINDER

BEST PHOTOS

2 Cane Creek Canyon Preserve
7 Falls Loop Trail
9 Fall Creek Falls
10 Caney Creek Falls
12 Chinnabee Silent Trail / Lake Shore Loop

15 Waterfall Loop
18 Piper Interpretive Trail
21 Cherokee Ridge Alpine Trail
22 John B. Scott Forever Wild Trail
32 George W. Folkerts Bog Trail
33 Pitcher Plant Loop

FAMILY FRIENDLY

3 Plateau Loop
11 Turkey Creek Nature Preserve
14 Red Mountain Park
16 Tannehill Ironworks Historical State Park
17 Lakeside Trail
20 Lake Trail

27 Frank Jackson State Park
30 Little River State Forest
35 Muddy Creek Interpretive Trail
38 Blue Trail
39 Audubon Bird Sanctuary
40 Pelican Island

FINDING SOLITUDE

4 Honeycomb Trail
5 Tom Bevill Loop
6 King's Chapel Loop
13 Ruffner Mountain Nature Preserve
16 Tannehill Ironworks Historical State Park
19 Flagg Mountain Loop
23 Wood Duck Trail

25 Bartram National Recreational Trail
26 Pines Trail
28 Five Runs Loop
29 Conecuh Trail North Loop
31 St. Stephens Historical Park
34 Glenn Sebastian Nature Trail
36 Blakeley Delta Wetland Loop

WATER FEATURES

1 Shoal Creek Preserve
2 Cane Creek Canyon Preserve
4 Honeycomb Trail
7 Falls Loop Trail
8 Hurricane Creek Park
9 Fall Creek Falls
10 Caney Creek Falls
11 Turkey Creek Nature Preserve

12 Chinnabee Silent Trail / Lake Shore Loop
15 Waterfall Loop
21 Cherokee Ridge Alpine Trail
24 Chewacla State Park
28 Five Runs Loop
37 Perdido River Trail Section 1
39 Audubon Bird Sanctuary
40 Pelican Island

TOP FIVE HIKES

1. Caney Creek Falls: You will be hard-pressed to find a more beautiful waterfall. Caney Creek Falls never disappoints, no matter the season, with its towering cascade (that you can walk behind) into a beautiful blue pool that's a real treat to swim in. It's the most photographed waterfall in the state, and for good reason.

2. Cane Creek Canyon Preserve: This is a hike for everyone with a breathtaking view from "the Point," towering rock walls, deep rock shelters, rainbows of wildflowers, and tumbling waterfalls.

1.

2.

3. Chinnabee Silent Trail / Lake Shore Loop: The Chinnabee takes you past some amazingly beautiful cascades, including the Devil's Den Falls and the multitiered Cheaha Falls, not to mention a great swimming hole. The Lakeshore Trail is the place to view turtles on the wildflower-lined path.

4. Waterfall Loop: In season, Moss Rock gives you multiple waterfalls and a simply gorgeous wildflower-strewn sandstone glade.

5. George W. Folkerts Bog Trail: The Bog Trail is a wildflower lover's dream, with hundreds of different species blooming here in season and what has been described as the "most visually stunning pitcher plant bog in the world," and it doesn't disappoint.

BEFORE YOU HIT THE TRAIL

INTRODUCTION

Welcome to my latest guide to hiking in Alabama. This is one of those books that I was really excited to write. Ever since I was a kid growing up in the mountains of northern New Jersey, I loved taking to the woods to do a hike with my best friend, the family dog. There is just something special about hiking with your dog that to me is almost indescribable.

This guide will take you on forty great hikes (plus six bonus hikes) in Alabama where you can bring your pup to explore canyons, waterfalls, rivers, and beaches, each one selected so that both beginners just starting out and more experienced hikers can enjoy the state's amazing natural beauty with their dog.

I've tried to strike a balance for both types of readers, and within these pages I hope to introduce you to some new hiking experiences across the state and update some of my old favorites.

And before you ask, as many do, yes, a few trails were omitted from the main text, like the Walls of Jericho for example. In the case of the Walls, it isn't that I didn't want to include it, but it is arguably the most hiked trail in the state (however, I did reference it in Appendix E: Bonus Hikes at a Glance). I want to help guide hikers to other lesser known or hiked areas whenever possible.

Believe me, this guide is only the tip of the iceberg when it comes to hiking with your dog in Alabama, and I hope it will inspire you to leash 'em up and explore all of the hundreds of miles of hiking trails within the state.

WHY HIKE WITH YOUR PUP?

Actually, the question should be, why *not* hike with your pup? There are way too many good reasons to bring Fido with you on the trail.

Obviously, it's healthy for both of you. Hiking, no matter the distance or difficulty, gives you both more stamina, strengthens your bodies, and can even help prevent or reduce ailments you both may have.

If your dog has destructive behavior at home, hiking will get that excess energy out of their system.

As you probably already know, dogs are naturally inquisitive. That sense of curiosity will come to life and stimulate them mentally when you take them out on a trail, and in turn, that curiosity and awareness of the natural world that surrounds *you* will be enhanced.

Believe it or not, dogs get bored with the same routine. Walking in the same neighborhood, visiting the same dog park—it all becomes mundane. They need new stimulation,

new smells, new places to explore. They aren't impressed with mountaintop vistas or the Native American history they pass. Hiking gives them what they need to relieve the humdrum.

Then there is the bonding experience. You and your pup will really become best friends as you explore the wilds together. Face it, we are all distracted with life—work, home, you name it—and, as a consequence, the amount of quality time that you spend with your puppy often takes a hit. But out on the trail, you are focused on each other, and you will bond like never before—an exhilarating experience.

ALABAMA THE BEAUTIFUL

Not too long ago, the Alabama Tourism Department had a marketing slogan for the state: Alabama the Beautiful. Those three simple words quite nicely sum up what the state has to offer in terms of its biodiversity. The state is recognized as one of the most ecologically diverse areas in the country, with scientists from the University of Georgia calling it the "country's Fort Knox of biodiversity." The best way to see that beauty and wonder is by taking a hike with your best friend.

The state is divided neatly into four distinct regions: the North (Cumberland Plateau), Central (Piedmont Plateau), the South (Black Belt), and the Gulf Coast (Coastal Plain).

Millions of years ago, the entire area we now know as Alabama was covered by a shallow ocean. As the land began to rise and the ocean receded, ancient shell banks and coral reefs died and dried out, leaving behind limestone bedrock. Over millions of years, the elements began to carve caves, canyons, and rock shelters into the limestone. Today you can visit this karst topography on hikes to Cane Creek Canyon Preserve (Hike 2), Hurricane Creek Park (Hike 8), and Fall Creek Falls (Hike 9).

A little farther south, as the ocean continued to recede, the land was thrust up, creating the Piedmont Plateau, a region where the Appalachian Mountains either end or begin, depending on your point of view.

This is the area where the state's highest mountain, Cheaha, is located. The mountain is in the heart of the Talladega National Forest, where breathtaking views of those mountains can be had from rocky overlooks, swift-flowing streams cascade over rock beds, and glistening waterfalls tumble into gorges. You and your pup can experience all of this splendor on one single hike: the Chinnabee Silent Trail / Lake Shore Loop (Hike 12).

Also in this region, you can visit the southernmost end of the Appalachians, Flagg Mountain Loop (Hike 19). At one time, Flagg was to be the location of a state park built by the Civilian Conservation Corps (CCC), but World War II ended that, and their stone handiwork was left for nature to reclaim—until recently, that is, as the mountain and park are being renovated.

The region from Montgomery to just north of the Gulf Coast is known as the South Region or Black Belt. With its gently rolling hills and notoriously rich soil, this area is a prime agricultural center. The region is crisscrossed with a network of streams and rivers that eventually flow down to our next section, the Gulf Coast.

All or most of those rivers that flow through the South Region end up funneling into the Gulf Coast Region before they end their journey in the Gulf of Mexico. But is their journey really over?

Before arriving at the Gulf, these rivers converge to form the second largest river delta in the country: "America's Amazon," the Mobile-Tensaw River Delta. You'll get to see only a small part of the delta when you hike the Blakeley Delta Wetland Loop (Hike 36).

Finally, we arrive at the beautiful sugary-white beaches of the state's barrier island, Dauphin Island, where you and your dog can visit and frolic in the surf along the Audubon Bird Sanctuary (Hike 39) and Pelican Island (Hike 40) hikes.

FLORA AND FAUNA

Alabama is a tree state, with over two-thirds of it covered in forest, predominantly southern yellow, red, white, loblolly, longleaf, and slash pine forests.

When it comes to deciduous trees, you'll likely encounter hickory, sweet gum, and several different varieties of oaks, including live oaks and scrub oak along the Gulf. For beautiful fragrant species of trees, you'll find the countryside dotted with several types of magnolia, like the bigleaf. Of course, blooming dogwoods brighten the landscape as well.

The trails I have selected for you and Fido are bedecked with amazing varieties of wildflowers, including merrybells, Carolina jasmine, yellow orchid, red cardinal, mountain laurel, native azalea, and—well, I could go on and on.

The state's wildlife is as varied as the wildflowers that grow here. Florida black bears can now be found in most of the state but are largely concentrated in the northeast and the delta region of the Gulf Coast. You may also encounter bobcat, coyote, fox, or whitetail deer. All across the state, there's a good chance you'll kick up a wild turkey or quail from the brush. And in the Gulf Coast and the extreme South Regions, there is one critter you don't want to mess with: the American alligator.

The alligator prefers an eclectic menu of fish, frogs, snakes, turtles, birds, and small mammals—that includes dogs! Recently there have been several incidents in the extreme South and Gulf Coast Regions where owners did not heed warnings and allowed their dogs to play in the ponds, wetlands, and even Mobile Bay, with tragic results.

Please keep your pets and children close at hand near these water features, don't allow them in the water, and keep your dog on a leash around these areas. (See Appendix C: Wildlife Conflicts for more details.)

WEATHER

When it comes to the weather in Alabama, take your pick. There's the subtropical climate along the Gulf and the cold, snowy winters to the north. For the most part when it comes to hiking in Alabama, the weather is pretty much perfect, the exception being in the dead of summer, when high temperatures and humidity can be brutal and hiking is not recommended, or at least it should be limited.

Overall, winters are short-lived even in higher elevations in the northern part of the state. Quite often you will have springlike days scattered throughout January and February. Temperatures here range from 50 degrees in the daytime to 30 degrees at night in January and 90 degree highs, 70 degree lows in July. Colder temperatures are naturally more frequent in the north during winter, and, yes, significant accumulations of snow averaging 5 inches can occur.

Down south, average daytime temperatures range from 60 degrees in January to 90 degrees in July. Cold snaps below 30 degrees, even near zero, do occur, but they seldom last long.

During the summer, keep an eye out for those pesky summertime pop-up thunderstorms. They are widely scattered and short in duration, but the large amount of rain and dangerous lightning can make outdoor travel a challenge—and dangerous.

And we can't forget hurricane season from June through November. Alabama only has a small footprint directly on the Gulf, but it is still a target. Most injuries and deaths resulting from hurricanes and tropical storms are due to flash flooding farther inland as the storm moves up and away from the Gulf of Mexico. Tornadoes often accompany the storms as they push inland.

When hiking during hurricane season, check the weather often, be alert for any tropical disturbances before heading out, and follow the advice of local, state, and federal and emergency officials.

PREPARING TO HIT THE TRAIL: ARE THEY READY?

The most important thing you can do for your dog, even before setting one foot on the trail, is to visit the vet for a complete checkup to make sure Fido is physically ready to hike. There are many people who think that dogs should just be ready to go, but there could be underlying health issues that prevent them from tagging along.

Let the vet know what your plans are: the type of hiking you will be doing and where you will be going, and ask if your pup will need specific vaccinations or preventative medicines to control ticks and other parasites.

TRAINING AND TRAIL ACCLIMATION

What makes a good trail dog? A lot of people think it's the breed. Do a Google search on the subject and you'll find hundreds of articles listing the ten, fifteen, sixty-seven best dog breeds for hiking. They all describe their physical characteristics: they love water, they have stamina. And that is something you need to look at. You need to look at the breeds and compare them with your goals for hiking.

For hiking with a dog, size does matter to a greater or lesser degree. A small dog won't be able to hike longer distances, and very large dogs will eventually have joint problems. Herding breeds will have a lot of energy, while some other breeds may be more laid back.

All of that is to say that the type of hike you take will be determined by the breed you have. But having said that, the bottom line is that all dogs love to walk and explore the world around them. Whether you are looking to get a new dog or already have one, it all boils down to your dog's individual energy, stamina, attentiveness, and personality. How far, fast, and difficult the hike depend on your individual pup, and in the end, your investment of time and training is what makes a great canine hiking companion.

FOOD AND EXERCISE

Always feed your dog before and after rigorous exercise. Puppies are normally fed multiple times throughout the day, while older dogs are usually fed twice a day. Divide one of their feedings in half. Feed them the first half 1 hour before exercising, the other 30 minutes after. This will help reduce the possibility of bloating, which can turn into a twisted abdomen during exercise and create blockage and serious health problems. In fact, once you finally do get on the trail, it's better to divide up Fido's meals into smaller, more frequent feedings during the day.

TRAINING REGIMEN

If you have a young puppy, it's going to take a little time to get it up to speed—not only to hike but also healthwise. If they are under 4 months old, their immune systems aren't ready to greet the big new world. Your vet will give your puppy a series of shots to combat distemper, parvo, and hepatitis beginning at 4 to 6 weeks old, with the final series coming at 16 to 20 weeks old. But don't let this stop you from taking them in the backyard to start exploring and learning that there is more to life than the dog bed or kennel.

Once they are immunized it is a good idea to enroll them in a puppy class. They'll learn to socialize with other dogs and people and learn the basics that make for a great trail dog, like coming to you when you call them or heeling while walking.

Once they become accustomed to a leash and can respond to basic commands, it's time to start building up their stamina and confidence when venturing out into that big scary world. This is also important for your older dog, too, if they haven't been hiking before.

Start with a daily 20- to 30-minute walk, but mix it up by taking your dog to different locations. This will acclimate them to a variety of experiences, and whenever you go someplace new, they won't be surprised. They'll be ready to explore.

This is a good time to crate train your dog if your plan is to crate them when traveling and to get them used to riding in the car. You should also start to desensitize them to hiking gear. Bring out your gear a little at a time—packs, boots, hiking sticks, and so on—and slowly introduce your pup to them.

Do not take young puppies out on long hikes until they are at least 6 months old; their bones are not developed enough to handle much stress. For older dogs, ease them into longer hikes as well, especially larger breeds that can experience hip and joint disorders. In either case, always check with your vet to make sure they are good to go.

From there, it is a gradual work-up until you're ready to take to the trail. David Mullally, the author of *Best Dog Hikes Northern California*, has an excellent regimen that you can use for both your puppy and older dog to prepare them for the trail.

SAMPLE 5-WEEK TRAINING REGIMEN BY DAVID MULLALLY

Weeks 1, 2, and 3: Morning and Evening
- Warm-Up: 15- to 20-minute sniff and stroll
- Cardio Workout: 10-minute brisk walk with no pit stops at the fire hydrant
- Cool Down: 5-minute sniff and stroll

Week 4: Morning and Evening
- Warm-Up: 15-minute sniff and stroll
- Cardio Workout: 30-minute brisk walk; start to incorporate some hill or stair climbing, but be sure to stop for rest and water breaks
- Cool Down: 10-minute sniff and stroll

Week 5: Morning and Evening
- Warm-Up: 15-minute sniff and stroll
- Cardio Workout: 30-minute brisk walk; start to incorporate some hill or stair climbing but be sure to stop for rest and water breaks
- Cool Down: 10-minute sniff and stroll
- Add an additional longer walk at the end of the week of about 1.5 hours. Include some uphill work. This additional walk is about distance, not speed.

PACING

The pace of your hike is determined by a lot of factors: your stride, the stride of your dog, the weather, the terrain, how many stops you make, and, of course, how many stops Fido needs to make to explore and mark that tree.

All of this needs to be taken into account when planning your hike with your dog. This will determine the number of miles and how long you can walk. Remember, what goes out on a trail has to come back. It's (literally) a two-way street—or trail.

You may want to climb Mount Everest with them, but look at the trek you're planning honestly and objectively, and then make plans to do something they can hike comfortably. Long hikes are great but not if you have to walk 4.0 miles per hour to finish before the park closes, which your dog will never be able to keep up with. This is not the Bataan Death March. It's a time for exploring and enjoying the time you have with the best hiking partner you'll ever have.

The average hiker walks 2.5 to 3.0 miles per hour on a relatively level trail, 2.0 miles per hour on hilly terrain. Add in the other factors mentioned before and you will have a good base to start looking for trails that will be guaranteed fun for all.

BODY LANGUAGE

It's very important to be able to read your dog through their body language. That is the only way you will know how they are feeling, if they are enjoying the hike, if they are hungry or thirsty, or if they are uncomfortable and whether problems could arise.

You may see one or several of these indicators with your dog while on the trail: If their tail is up or horizontal and not stiff and if they are walking smoothly with alertness in their step, they are feeling pretty good. If the tail droops down or is between their legs, if their movement becomes stiff or staggered, if they lower their body, or if they start to look lethargic, they could have an injury, or feel ill or fatigued. Stop immediately, try to relax them, provide water, and determine what the situation might be.

Sometimes a dog will dig a hole in the dirt and lie down in it. This indicates that they are hot, and it is their way of cooling off.

Other common cues that you can pick up from your dog include the following:

- Yawning: not necessarily tired; could be trying to relieve stress
- Lip or nose licking, averting the eyes: possible signs of stress
- Head tilt: curious
- Tail up, ears forward: alert or suspicious
- Hunched back, ears back, tail between the legs: anxious

PREPARATION AND SAFETY

Some people are fortunate. They rescue a dog from the shelter, thinking that it will be the perfect hiking companion, and take to the trail straight away. And that does happen occasionally. For the rest of us, Fido needs a little more attention to get them to that point, both healthwise and behaviorally.

The key to raising well-behaved puppies is spending time with them. Keeping them in the backyard with little to no contact isn't going to cut it. You need to regularly interact with your dog. Play with them, train them, just sit and watch TV with them. They live to be with their owners and want to make us happy. If they show disruptive behavior, many times it's either because they are bored or are trying to get your attention.

Just remember, dogs looks to us for guidance and caring. Be patient with them. It will go a long way.

THE IMPORTANCE OF SPAYING AND NEUTERING

There are many good reasons to have your pet spayed or neutered. Needless to say, it reduces the number of homeless pets, but it is also important for the health and safety of your dog, too.

Studies show that pets that have been spayed or neutered are healthier and may live longer. On average, male dogs live 18 percent longer, while females live 23 percent longer. It may also alleviate or reduce many behavioral issues like roaming, aggressiveness, and barking.

BASIC TRAINING AND SOCIAL ACCLIMATION

Basic obedience training—sit, stay, come, heel—is a must. If you Google "dog trainers" in your area, you will see pages and pages of listings, but don't just randomly pick one to train your dog. Ask your friends and neighbors who are dog owners for their recommendations.

When you find one you think you like, ask about their training methods (some use harsh spiked collars and other cruel tactics to make a dog obey) and the compatibility of their training philosophy with yours and your goals, and check their certifications thoroughly.

A good place to start your search is with the American Kennel Club (AKC). Their website (akc.org) has a list of certified trainers across the country.

Whether you're training your pup or just playing, remember that any behavior rewarded with a treat or a positive reaction will likely be repeated. So if they do something you don't want them to do, don't pet them and cheerfully say, "That's okay," which

reinforces that behavior. And remember, you need to correct your family and friends, too, if they reward your dog's bad behavior. If the dog jumps on them when they walk into a room and say that it's okay, nicely tell them that no, it's not okay and explain why.

Socialization is just as important as obedience training. If you have a new puppy, you need to begin the process of familiarizing them with people and other dogs as early as possible. Your dog needs to be calm and respectful. That's not to say you can't teach an old dog new tricks, but you will need a greater supply of patience to make it happen.

A VISIT TO THE VET

I know many people who get a new dog and think that it's only a dog. You should be able to simply leash them up and off you go. Not so fast.

It's important before you begin hiking, especially on more difficult treks, that you visit your vet to make sure Fido is physically ready to go. If your dog is very young, make sure their bones are developed enough to hike. Also have the vet check them for any spinal or joint issues, especially in older dogs.

I'll give you a "for example": my rescue Lab, Archer. Archer is a happy puppy. He loves to regularly visit a local nature preserve for walks. As I was getting ready to write this book, I took him to his vet to make sure he was ready for this big adventure. You would think that with all of the local walks we did, he would get the green light and we would be ready to go. Turns out that he had issues with the cartilage in not one but both knees and had to have major surgery. Just goes to show you.

Be sure to have all of immunizations up to date and carry a record of them with you on your hike. And don't forget to ask about any recommendations on preventative medications, as well, for heartworm, flea, and tick prevention.

GEARING UP

You're going to hear me say this over and over, but it's worth repeating: Your best defense against injury to Fido and keeping them safe on the trail is to leash them. Use a solid, short leash and not a retractable one. It is recommended that you use a harness on them as well. The force of a pull on a standard neck collar can do severe damage to your dog's throat. A harness puts little to no pressure on the neck, and you'll have better control over your dog. It also tends to quiet them down a bit.

Before you set one foot out of the door, be sure you have your pup's shot record with you, an ID tag with—at minimum—their name plus your contact information, and a rabies tag. It is a good idea to have your dog microchipped in case they do get lost. The best place to have this done is at your vet.

One way to help keep your pup on their best behavior is to give them a job to do on the trail. They love to work. That's why outfitting them with a doggie backpack is a good idea. It keeps them focused and gives them purpose.

Before buying a pack, take your dog's measurements. Measure the circumference of their chest; most brands list a chest size on the label. Then bring Fido along to the store and pick out a couple of packs. Try them on to see what fits best. To do this, loosen all the straps. Place the pack on their back, toward their front legs, at the widest part of their body. It should rest squarely on the middle of the back so the weight will be distributed evenly on each side of their body. Tighten the girth straps (the ones that go under their body) and fasten the snaps to hold it in place. Next, tighten the chest strap and snap it closed. When you're fastening the snaps, be careful not to pinch your dog's skin or pull the fur.

Make sure the straps are not too tight, which could impede your dog's breathing. You should be able to slide two fingers under the straps.

Once you've selected the correct pack, remember to check it a few times while you're on the trail to make sure it doesn't loosen up and slip out of position.

No matter whether you're on a short day hike or an overnighter, don't forget to pack the dog bowls. What you choose—collapsible plastic or nylon bag that folds up—is a purely personal preference; just make sure your dog will eat and drink from them before you leave the house.

And don't forget to pack the first aid kit (see Appendix B: Trail Emergencies and First Aid). You can pack your own or buy a preloaded kit. Either way is fine; just remember to learn how to use it before you leave your house! You'd be surprised just how many hikers don't know a thing about what's in their kit, let alone how to use it. Read those instructions!

FOOD AND WATER

There are no hard and fast rules when it comes to feeding your dog or giving them water on the trail. Every dog is different. Every trail is different. Dogs have different weights, different dietary needs, different energy levels, and so on. Add to that the different trail conditions and difficulties you may encounter.

The general rule is if you are thirsty, hungry, or tired, then so is your dog.

When feeding, give them the same food they eat at home. The trail is not the place to experiment. A good measure is to feed them their normal ration plus 1 cup extra for every 20 pounds of dog weight. Of course, this is assuming a long, hard day hike or overnighter. If you're doing an easy 2-mile hike, some energy snacks may be all that are needed.

You should feed them a small amount at least an hour before you hike to boost their energy and then again 30 minutes after the hike. See *Training and Trail Acclimation* (above) for more on feeding when in trail training.

No matter how long or difficult the hike, a dog's water requirements will be much different on the trail than at home. Generally speaking, large dogs over 20 pounds drink 0.5 to 1.0 ounce of water per pound, per day. That means that a 30-pound dog could drink up to 30 ounces of water a day, even more when on a hike or in warmer weather. Dogs under 20 pounds usually drink 1.5 ounces of water per pound a day. Always play it safe and pack extra. Offer your pup water every 15 to 30 minutes.

For extra energy, there is nothing wrong with giving them an over-the-counter vitamin or supplement, but many dog owners find that dog food with a higher protein and fat content does the trick.

Naturally, we all want to spoil our pups a little. There are many great recipes online for homemade and healthy energy treats.

PUPPY PAWS AND GOLDEN YEARS
Homemade Puppy Power Bars
Ingredients
- 1 cup mashed cooked sweet potato, cooled
- 3 cups garbanzo bean flour (also called chickpea flour, found in Asian or specialty health food stores)
- ½ cup mashed banana
- ¼ cup raw honey (locally produced is best)
- 1 egg
- Extra-virgin olive oil

Place the cool mashed sweet potatoes in a large bowl and mix in the flour, mashed banana, honey, and egg. Mix thoroughly. Grease a cookie sheet with the olive oil and pour the batter onto it, spreading it evenly across the pan. Bake at 350 degrees for 30 minutes. Let cool, then cut into small squares.

SAFETY

Besides all of the above, there are some common hazards on the trail that you need to be aware of to keep your puppy safe.

As I've mentioned, the summer heat can be brutal in the South. Keep a close eye on Fido for signs of fatigue. If you see they are getting tired, stop and rest in the shade or in a cool creek. Watch for signs of heat stroke: excessive panting, dehydration, drooling, reddened gums, either small amounts of urine or none at all, and a body temperature over 103 degrees.

If you plan on using streams, ponds, or lakes for your drinking water, play it safe and treat the water before drinking. That goes for your dog's water, too. Dogs can suffer from the same waterborne illnesses as humans.

Dogs like to eat grass, normally to cure indigestion but sometimes just because, like my dog Archer. Who needs a lawnmower? Out on the trail, do not let them eat any plants! Poison ivy can affect them just as it does humans, but imagine getting it in your mouth. They may ingest burrs and thorns that can get caught in their nose and eyes, not to mention causing serious discomfort in their mouth and stomach issues. And, of course, there is the possibility that the plant they are gnawing on is toxic.

WHAT TO EXPECT ON THE TRAIL

Not only will you and your dog encounter unbelievable landscapes and wildflowers along the trails of Alabama, but you'll also face other hikers, trail runners, mountain bikes, and horses. Knowing how to handle those situations with Fido is as important as knowing how to get from point A to point B.

Before you set foot on a hiking trail with your dog, make sure they are trail ready. If your dog is aggressive in any way to other people or overly protective of you, they are not ready and need more training. Imagine if you are hiking down a trail and you see a dog bounding your way down the path. Not all, but most people are naturally afraid and rightfully cautious when they see a dog approach. It's up to you to make it a happy encounter by following these suggestions.

A NEW LEASH ON LIFE

First and foremost: Obey the leash laws. There will be many of you reading this saying, "I am in perfect control of my dog off leash. There won't be any issues." And you may be right, but landowners and managers established these rules for a reason.

You will notice that on the hikes in this book, there are very few times that your dog can run off leash. This is becoming the norm. But please, don't take it wrong and think that "the man" is setting down harsh rules to keep you from having fun with Fido in the wilderness. They're doing it for the safety of your dog and the safety of others.

In reality, having your dog on leash is an educational experience for both of you. Each of you will be more alert, exploring and discovering more than you normally would if they weren't with you or if they were off leash. It becomes more of a bonding experience between you and your pup if you can control them on a leash. And, of course, you will keep them out of unknown safety hazards you could encounter when they're this close at hand. Plus, other trail users will appreciate it, too.

Taking your dog on a leashed hike sounds easy enough—just hook 'em up and go—but Fido still needs to be what experts call "trail worthy" on a leash. This means your dog should:

- Not yank on the leash at all when walking

- Walk easily on a loose lead

- Hike at a heel, or slightly behind your knee, when asked

And speaking of leashing, some of you will not be happy when I say this, but a dog on a retractable leash is out of control. They are still able to roam at will, sometimes too far ahead for you to handle a situation that may arise, like an oncoming mountain bike. On the trail use a standard nonretractable leash.

TRAIL ETIQUETTE

It is a wonderful experience to bring your dog with you on the trail, both of you exploring the unknown, discovering new natural wonders that you might not normally see on your own. And as with us human hikers, dogs need to have manners and practice trail etiquette as well:

- Make sure you hike on dog-friendly trails. Yes, all of the trails listed in this guide are pet-friendly, but once you get the bug, you'll want to head out on your own and explore more trails. Just make sure that dogs are permitted before heading out.

- If you are hiking off leash and a hiker, runner, cyclist, or equestrian approaches, leash your dog immediately.

- When other hikers, other dogs, horses, or bikers approach, yield the right of way. Move off the trail as far as you can and have your dog sit and wait patiently for others to pass.
- If other hikers have a dog of their own, ask for permission before allowing the two to get acquainted.
- And just like all of us, we need to practice Leave No Trace (LNT) with our dogs: Be sure to clean up after them and pack it out. Leave only paw prints.

MOUNTAIN BIKES

You will find that more and more hiking trails are being shared with mountain bikers. We all have the same desire for outdoor recreation and adventure, so it's only natural, since the trails are already there. But hikers, with or without a dog, and cyclists have certain responsibilities to each other on the trail.

- Don't wear headphones and tune the world out. First of all, you miss half the fun of being in the outdoors, but more importantly, you may miss safety signals.
- Mountain bikers are asked to yield to hikers and horses.
- It is the responsibility of the cyclist early on to alert you that they are approaching with a friendly greeting, something like "Let me know when it's safe to pass."
- Move your dog off to the side of the trail and make them sit and wait patiently.
- When ready, give the cyclist the all clear to let them know it's safe to pass.
- When the cyclist is passing, they should announce which side they are passing on so that you both get it right, something like "Passing left!" or "Passing right!"
- Don't forget to thank the cyclist as they pass.

HORSES

Unless they were raised around horses, dogs will be freaked out by this huge creature. Hikers should yield to horses, giving them plenty of passing room. You should stay on the downhill side of the trail from the horse because spooked rides tend to run uphill.

Equestrians and hikers should talk to each other as they pass. A horse can be easily frightened not only by your dog but your pack as well, perceiving it to be a predator. Your voice will "humanize" the experience and help keep them calm.

SEASONAL NUISANCES

Ah, the joys of hiking. There are many, but—as the song says—you take the good, you take the bad, and there are those pesky nuisances that all hikers face. Trouble is, when you're hiking with your dog, those nuisances are amplified. These are the most common seasonal nuisances you will encounter and some of the ways to help you and your dog combat them.

DON'T GET BUGGED

One of the most dangerous bugs that can bite your dog is the mosquito, which can lead to heartworms. This is probably the most important reason to take your pup to the vet

for regular checkups and to keep up with their shots and medications, which should include heartworm preventatives.

Mosquitoes and gnats congregate around moist environments, usually stagnant water but also in places like dewy grass fields. Do not use human insect repellent on your dog! Most products humans use or slather on are made with DEET, which can cause vomiting, skin irritations, and seizures in dogs.

Several brands of canine insect repellent are available over the counter at most pet stores. Brands include *Honeydew* and *Vet's Best*. Also effective are natural alternatives like lemon eucalyptus oil, which has a pungent aroma.

YELLOW FLIES

If you or your dog haven't been attacked by a yellow fly, you're in for a real treat (that's sarcasm, friends). These large flies bite (and bite hard) with ferocity normally around your head, neck, and shoulders. The "season" generally runs from May through July as they congregate in shaded, humid areas along the edges of forests, rivers, and creeks.

For people, an insect repellent with pyrethrum seems to work, but many hikers also wear long-sleeve shirts, long pants, and hats to help avoid yellow flies.

For your dog, permethrin-based insect repellents are also effective; however, if applied incorrectly or ingested, it could be toxic to your pet. My advice is to play it safe before spraying down your dog: Visit with your vet to find the right preventative.

TICKS

What would a hike be without ticks? It's true that an extremely long, cold, harsh winter can deter the tick population, but let's face it, they never go away. They are most prevalent in warm months.

All ticks need to be removed from you and your dog as soon as possible. The one species you especially need to look out for is the deer tick. With its black body and red or orange back, this species can carry Lyme disease, which can cause fatigue, joint pain, and even neurological problems in both humans and their pets.

The good news is that a tick has to be attached to you or your dog's skin for 24 hours or more before the disease is transmitted. But do remove it as soon as possible.

The best way to control ticks on your pet is by using a preventative. Your vet is the best source of information for what is right for your dog. Medications range from liquid spot treatments that you drop on the back of their neck (like Frontline and K9 Advantix), to flea and tick collars (such as Seresto), to a chewable oral preventative (like *NexGard*).

If you do find a tick on your dog, the most common removal method is to use tweezers to pull it off. Household tweezers, however, have blunt tips, so pack a set that has fine points. Spread your dog's fur and grasp the tick as close as you can to the dog's skin. Pull straight upward with a slow and steady motion. The idea is to pull it out without leaving its pincers attached. When done, rinse the tweezers in rubbing alcohol.

Using your fingers to do this is not recommended. You could leave a portion of those pincers in your pet, which can cause infection.

In any event, keep an eye on the location where the tick was located for any signs of infection, like the infamous red bull's-eye rash, or changes in your dog's behavior. If you spot any, contact your vet.

WEATHER

For the most part, the weather for hiking in Alabama is great year-round with some notable exceptions. The first is the heat.

Alabama has a subtropical climate, which means mild winters and extremely hot summers. Across the state during the summer months, the combination of high temperatures and humidity creates a dangerous heat index. You should either plan to hike early in the morning or consider rescheduling for another time.

That sultry mix can also produce severe summertime pop-up thunderstorms that produce torrential flooding rains, hail, high winds, possible tornadoes, and dangerous lightning.

Whether it's the heat or those thunderstorms, monitor the weather through the National Weather Service and local media before heading out. If there is a forecast for heavy rain, avoid areas prone to flash flooding. If the forecast is for severe storms, it's best not to venture out at all.

Even though Alabama has a small footprint on the Gulf Coast, it still sees its share of tropical storms and full-blown hurricanes during the season, which generally runs from June through November. Fortunately, you'll usually have plenty of time to prepare for these and know when not to hike or when to get off the trail. Again, keep a close eye on the tropics via the local news media and the National Hurricane Center and plan accordingly.

See the *Preparation and Safety* section for details on how to stay safe when you face the weather in Alabama.

HUNTING

Really, I'm not calling hunters a "seasonal nuisance," but they are something you need to consider when hiking in the fall.

Hunters share the trails with the hikers and mountain bikers of Alabama in its wildlife management areas, state forests, and national forests. You need to outfit yourself and your dog with hunter safety orange gear, such as packs and jackets, so that you will be seen in the forest.

In general, the best time for hunting is during the early morning or late evening, but that's not a hard-and-fast rule. Many states, including Alabama, allow hunting to begin 30 minutes before sunrise and continue until 30 minutes after sunset. Remember, if you hike during those times when the light conditions are low, you are at risk because hunters will have a harder time differentiating you from prey.

When hiking during hunting season, be sure to talk as you walk to let hunters in the area know you're passing through. Simply walking heavy won't cut it since they could think it's game approaching. Be sure to keep your dog leashed so they aren't mistaken for game, either.

Sometimes it's just best not to go to that trail during hunting season. Reschedule it for another time or pick another trail. For each hike described in this guide, I have indicated if hunting is allowed and the phone number and website where you can get information on restrictions during hunting season. You should also visit the Alabama Department of Conservation and Natural Resources website for season dates at www.outdooralabama .com/hunting/seasons-and-bag-limits.

HOW TO USE THIS GUIDE

Use the overview map to decide on a hike in the part of the state you would like to visit, then read the appropriate entry to begin more detailed planning for your trip. Each entry contains the following information:

Start: This is where the hikes begins; the trailhead.

Distance: The total distance in miles that the hike travels is listed here.

Approximate hiking time: This is an estimate of how long it will take to hike the trail. Note that this is just an estimate and can vary widely according to hiking pace and stops along the way.

Difficulty: A subjective opinion made by the author of the difficulty of the hike. Hikes are classified as easy, moderate, or difficult.

Trailhead elevation: This gives the height above sea level of the trailhead.

Highest point: The highest point above sea level along the trail is provided here.

Best season: This offers a suggested best time of year in which to hike the trail and hours of operation.

Trail surface: This indicates what type of surface you will be hiking on, such as dirt trail, boardwalk, paved path, and so on.

Other trail users: This section lists other trail users you might expect to see during your hike, such as hunters, mountain bikers, horseback riders, and the like.

Canine compatibility: This tells you if it is legal to bring your dog on the trail and if there are any restrictions.

Land status: This indicates who owns or manages the land through which the trail passes, for example, whether it's a national forest or private resort.

Fees and permits: This self-explanatory entry will ensure that you have enough cash or that you have obtained proper paperwork, if required.

Trail contact: The address and phone number for acquiring up-to-date local information is included here.

Nearest town: The closest city or town with basic amenities is listed here.

Trail tips: This included practical advice for enhancing your hiking experience.

Maps: The National Geographic TOPO! / United States Geological Survey map that is applicable to this hike.

Other maps: Any supplemental maps that might be available are listed here.

Finding the trailhead: Directions to the trailhead are provided. Often, two or more sets of directions are listed to get you to different trailheads or to guide you from different starting points. This information should be used in conjunction with the maps in this guide, USGS maps, and state road maps.

Trailhead GPS: This provides the global positioning coordinates for the trailhead.

The hike: Generally, the hike described is the most interesting or most scenic hike in the park or area. Alternate routes or suggestions for other nearby hikes may also be included here.

Creature comforts: Information on local lodging, campsites, and food

Miles and Directions: Turn-by-turn directions to navigate the hiking trail

Puppy Paws and Golden Years: Sidebar and supplemental information so you and your dog can enjoy the outdoors even more!

NORTH REGION

Taking it from the top, literally, we begin our journey in Alabama's North Region, or what is known geologically as the Cumberland Plateau. This is a mountainous region where sandstone and limestone bedrock has been carved away by the elements, creating spectacular canyons, caves, and channels for breathtaking waterfalls.

One of the highlights of this region, encompassing a little of everything it has to offer, is the Cane Creek Canyon Preserve in Tuscumbia. This 400-acre preserve has a myriad of trails that wind from a beautiful mountain vista called the Point down into a canyon that has been carved by the elements and the preserve's namesake creek.

The preserve has an intricate maze of hiking trails, 15-plus miles in all, that take you to towering rock bluffs, deep stone shelters, enumerable species of wildflowers, and tall, tumbling waterfalls. So even though I describe one route through the preserve, you will surely come back time and time again to explore your own routes and discover more of the canyon.

Rushing streams and breathtaking waterfalls are the focus of many of the hikes I have included in this section. Hikes through Shoal Creek Preserve (Hike 1), Falls Loop (Hike 7), and Fall Creek Falls (Hike 9) showcase the region's waterfalls and fast-flowing creeks. Your dog will appreciate splashing at Shoal Creek, while both of you will have a chance to cool off in a great little swimming hole at Hurricane Creek Park (Hike 8).

Then there is the Bankhead National Forest and what is arguably its star, Caney Creek Falls (Hike 10). This is an utterly amazing curtain waterfall in a roundish grotto. It tumbles over a rock shelter, and you can walk behind the falls that are framed by colorful mountain laurel. Both you and your dog will want to jump into the beautiful blue-green pool of the falls during the summer.

The weather for hiking in the North Region is pleasant most of the year, with temperatures averaging 50 degrees during the day and 36 at night in winter, and 90-degree days and 73-degree nights in the summer. This area does get high heat and humidity in the summer, so prepare accordingly with plenty of water and sunscreen for both you and your dog. Throughout the winter, you will see days with significant accumulation of snow of around 5 inches and icy conditions in the region.

1 SHOAL CREEK PRESERVE

No matter what season you chose to explore the Shoal Creek Preserve, you and your pup are in for a treat, from the lush green canopy of spring and summer, to the brilliant fiery colors of fall, to the frosty views of Indian Camp Creek in the winter. The highlight of this hike is its water features: the Jones and Lawson Branches, two beautiful glistening streams that your dog will love to frolic in, and cascades for you to relax by.

THE RUNDOWN

Start: From the trailhead kiosk on the north side of the parking lot
Distance: 4.3-mile double loop
Approximate hiking time: 3.5–4 hours
Difficulty: Easy over rolling hills with only a couple of short climbs
Trailhead elevation: 715 feet
Highest point: 729 feet
Best season: Year-round; open sunrise to sunset
Trail surface: Hard-packed dirt footpath
Other trail users: Hunters
Canine compatibility: Leash required
Land status: State nature preserve
Fees and permits: None
Trail contact: Alabama State Lands ADCNR, 64 N. Union St., Montgomery, AL 36130; (334) 242-3484; www.alabamaforeverwild.com/shoal-creek-preserve

Nearest town: Florence
Trail tips: The parking lot at the trailhead is large with room for 20–30 vehicles. Bring a camera to capture the wonderful cascades. Allow time for Fido to enjoy them, too. There is plenty of canopy to help you beat the heat of summer, and it displays beautiful colors in the fall. Be sure to watch for equestrians as you cross the horse trails.
Maps: USGS: Pruitton, AL
Other maps: Available online at conservationgis.alabama.gov/Documents/Brochures/ShoalCreekPreserve.pdf
Other: Hunting is allowed on the tract. Visit https://www.outdooralabama.com/hunting/seasons-and-bag-limits for dates and restrictions.

FINDING THE TRAILHEAD

From Florence at the intersection of US 72 (Florence Boulevard) and Darby Drive, head north on Darby Drive / Old Jackson Highway S 4.4 miles. Turn left onto CR 61 (Butler Creek Road) and travel 2.6 miles. A small sign is at the turn into the preserve on the right. Turn right and head down the gravel road 0.5 mile to the trailhead. Trailhead GPS: N34 54.437' / W87 37.233'

THE HIKE

We begin our journey at the very top of the state in the extreme northwestern corner, just a little north of the town of Florence. Here you'll find a really fun double-loop hike with plenty of water features that both you and your pup will love, all in the confines of a 298-acre nature preserve: Shoal Creek Preserve.

The preserve almost never came to be. The property was on the verge of being sold to developers who would eventually cut down the forest and build rows of houses and lanes of highways.

A soothing picture, and sound, along a tiered cascade on Jones Branch.

Fortunately for us, the state has a program that, whenever possible, heads off such sales and purchases the property on behalf of the citizens of Alabama. A division of the Alabama Department of Conservation and Natural Resources, that program is called Forever Wild. The agency purchases properties of historic and ecological significance and, whenever possible, reopens them for public recreation, such as paddling, biking, hunting, fishing, and, of course, hiking. And that's what happened here at Shoal Creek.

What makes this preserve special is the environment you will be walking through: beautiful mature upland hardwoods that blaze fiery colors in the fall and provide a respite from a blazing sun in the summer, tranquil and soothing scenic creek bottoms, and fertile fallow fields that are brimming with wildflowers in the spring and summer.

The standout features of this trek, however, are the water features. First, you will have splendid views of Shoal Creek and Indian Camp Creek as they meander their way southward for a date with the Tennessee River and Wilson Lake.

And then there are the two creeks, Lawson and Jones Branches. Both creeks are wide, clear, rock-strewn waterways that glow green in the spring and summer, reflecting the thick foliage of the trees that line their banks.

In several locations each stream tumbles over rocky bottoms, creating beautiful cascades and small waterfalls. You'll find the sounds soothing while your dog will love to frolic in the cool, clear water.

The trail itself is a double loop. The south loop is the 2.5-mile Jones Branch Loop. The north loop is the 1.8-mile Lawson Branch Loop. The hike begins by heading up the west side of the Jones Branch Loop for 0.7 mile until you reach a wooden bridge that takes you across Lawson Branch. This is where you'll get your first glimpse of one of the two creeks that make this hike special.

As you hike your way around to the northeast side of the property, you'll have views of Shoal and Indian Camp Creek before the trail once again joins up with Lawson Branch, where you'll see even more shoals and cascades.

Crossing back over the creek on the same bridge as before, you'll continue to the east on the Jones Branch Loop. Once again there are many beautiful cascades, including a horseshoe-shaped one. While you're walking, be on the lookout for whitetail deer, wild turkey, and wood ducks.

The trails are blazed with either red or double red paint blazes or yellow diamond markers with the trail name and a red blaze on it. You will cross the preserve's horse trail several times, but the intersections are well marked so there is no confusion about where to pick up the hiking trail on the other side. You can make this a shorter 2.5-mile hike by just walking the southern Jones Branch Loop.

Remember, hunting is permitted at the Shoal Creek Preserve. Please visit the Forever Wild website (see Trail Contact, above) for additional information about hunting season and restrictions. And if you do go out on a hike during hunting season, please remember to wear safety orange at all times.

CREATURE COMFORTS

RESTING UP

Quality Inn, 150 Etta Gray Dr., Florence; (877) 411-3436; www.choicehotels.com

Make your reservations by phone or online but make sure to ask for a pet-friendly room. The hotel allows two pets up to 75 pounds total weight. There is a $20 per pet, per night fee.

CAMPING

Joe Wheeler State Park, 4401 McClean Dr., Rogersville; (256) 247-1184; www.ala park.com/joe-wheeler-state-park-campground

Another great Alabama state park campground, Joe Wheeler features 116 improved campsites with water, electricity, picnic tables, and fire rings with grill. There are three clean restrooms. The park also has many primitive campsites plus excellent dining in the lodge. Make reservations by phone or online at guestrez.megahotel.com/Campground/Home/Index/P3R23.

FUELING UP

Wildwood Tavern, 108 E. Mobile St., Florence; (256) 349-2139; www.keepflorence funky.com

An amazing assortment of flatbread pizzas, baked pasta, sandwiches, and hot dogs fill the menu at the Wildwood Tavern. There is outdoor patio seating so your pup can dine with you.

MILES AND DIRECTIONS

0.0 Start at information kiosk to the north; the trail begins on the left side of the kiosk. Immediately it splits into 2 trails. The right is clearly marked for horses; the left is the western side of the Jones Branch Loop that provides access

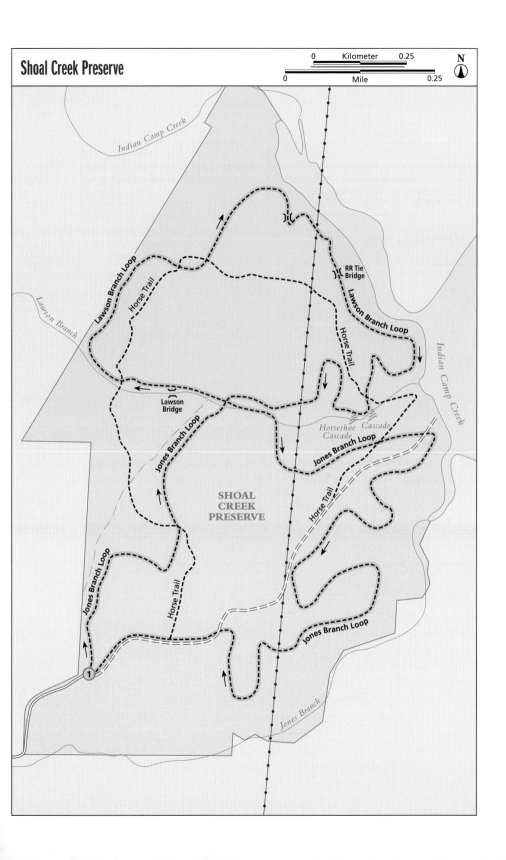

Shoal Creek Preserve

Indian Camp Creek

Lawson Branch Loop

Horse Trail

Lawson Branch

RR Tie Bridge

Lawson Branch Loop

Horse Trail

Indian Camp Creek

Lawson Bridge

Jones Branch Loop

Horseshoe Cascade

Cascade

Jones Branch Loop

Horse Trail

SHOAL CREEK PRESERVE

Jones Branch Loop

Horse Trail

Jones Branch Loop

1

Jones Branch

0   Kilometer   0.25

0   Mile   0.25

N

to the Lawson Branch Loop. Take the left trail. The trail starts as a wide dirt road and is marked with red paint blazes.

0.2   The trail narrows to a 2-foot-wide dirt path.

0.4   Cross the horse trail to the north (there is a bench here).

0.5   Walk next to a nice creek on the left.

0.7   Arrive at Lawson's Branch. There are some pretty cascades to the left. This is the intersection with the Lawson Branch Loop. The Jones Branch Loop continues straight to the east; we'll take that path on the return trip. Right now, continue straight to the north, crossing the branch over a bridge. On the other side you'll come to a T intersection. Turn left onto the Lawson Branch Loop (to the right is the return trail). There are excellent views and access to the branch throughout this section. Blazes are now double red. *OPTION:* To make this a shorter 2.5-mile hike, do not cross the bridge over Lawson Branch. Instead continue straight to the east and continue following the Jones Branch Loop. Pick up the mileage cues at mile 2.4 below.

0.8   Cross the horse trail to the southwest. There is a yellow LAWSON BRANCH sign here with double red stripes.

1.2   Cross the horse trail to the east. In less than 0.1 mile, cross the horse trail to the north.

1.4   Views of Indian Camp Creek are visible on the left (northeast). The best views are in winter/early spring.

1.5   Cross a runoff over a short footbridge.

1.6   Cross a railroad-tie footbridge over a runoff channel.

2.0   Come to a T intersection with the horse trail. Turn left onto the horse trail. In a few feet turn right (south) off the horse trail and continue on the double red-blazed Lawson Branch Trail. In 150 feet there will be a cascade to left with short side trail to its banks.

2.1   Come to a pretty horseshoe cascade in the creek.

2.3   Cross a power line with lots of wildflowers in the grass during spring. You will be walking alongside the creek once again.

2.4   Come to a Y intersection. The left fork takes you to the creek; take the right fork to the west. In less than 0.1 mile, arrive back at the bridge over Lawson Branch. Cross Lawson Branch again to the south. On the other side turn left (east) onto the double red-blazed Jones Branch Loop. In less than 0.1 mile, turn left (south) onto an old dirt road. In 20 feet turn right (south) and continue on the Jones Branch Loop.

2.7   Cross the horse trail to the east.

2.8   Cross a dirt road to the east. On the other side turn right (south) to continue the loop; there is a short game trail to the left that leads nowhere. In winter there are good views of Shoal Creek here.

3.3   The trail skirts the eastern edge of the power line as it heads to the south. It can be overgrown with grass, but the path is discernible.

3.4   As you approach a wall of trees along the power line, the trail turns left (northeast) back into the woods (you will see the blaze).

3.7   The trail skirts the edge of the power line again on its east side. There are wildflowers here spring through late summer.

3.8   Cross under the power line to the west and head back into the woods.

4.1   Pass a dirt road on the right. This last section of the trail is hard-packed clay.

4.3   Arrive back at the trailhead.

2 CANE CREEK CANYON PRESERVE

You and Fido will have plenty to explore on this fascinating hike through Cane Creek Canyon Preserve. The hike described here is only 7 miles of the over 18 miles of trails at the preserve, and you and your pup will find yourselves walking through some of the most beautiful canyon scenery in the state, with spectacular ancient rock shelters, tumbling waterfalls, pristine creeks and springs, and a rainbow of rare wildflowers. With each change of season, there is more to see, so you'll be coming back here time and time again.

THE RUNDOWN

Start: From the parking lot just south of the Lacefields' house. Be sure to sign in before heading out.
Distance: 7.0-mile out-and-back with loops
Approximate hiking time: 4 hours
Difficulty: Moderate generally but difficult if you do some of the steep side trails
Trailhead elevation: 802 feet
Highest point: 901 feet
Best season: Year-round; open 7 a.m.–5 p.m.
Trail surface: Dirt, rock, some gravel
Other trail users: None
Canine compatibility: Leash required
Land status: Privately owned, Nature Conservancy managed
Fees and permits: None
Trail contact: Friends of Cane Creek, 251 Loop Rd., Tuscumbia; (256) 381-6301; www.facebook.com/Friends-of-Cane-Creek-Canyon-Nature-Preserve-126802417335447/
Nearest town: Tuscumbia
Trail tips: Get your camera ready for some incredible shots of wildflowers, rock shelters, bluffs, and waterfalls! Cane Creek Canyon Preserve is very dog-friendly. Your pup is more than welcome to splash and frolic in the creek, just clean up after them and don't allow wildlife encounters. Vault toilets are scattered about the trails. In case you need a refill, jugs filled with water are also available at several locations along the route.
Maps: USGS: Frankfort, AL / Pride, AL
Other maps: Available at trailhead

FINDING THE TRAILHEAD

From Tuscumbia at the intersection of US 72 and Veterans Boulevard, take US 72 west 0.7 mile and turn left onto CR 65 / Frankfort Road. Travel 7.6 miles and turn right onto Loop Road. In 0.2 mile, as Loop Road bends to the right, continue straight on a gravel road (a sign points the direction to the preserve). Travel 0.3 mile, passing a poultry farm on the left, and drive through a gate with a sign indicating the entrance to the preserve. Keep going until you come to a Spanish-influenced house. This is the Lacefields' home. You will see signs plainly indicating where to park. You must sign the registry before hitting the trail. Trailhead GPS: N34 37.332' / W87 47.668'

THE HIKE

Alabama is recognized as one of the most ecologically diverse areas in the South, and in many cases, the country. For this reason, scientists at the University of Georgia call the state the "Fort Knox of the country's biodiversity."

I don't think there is any other hike in the state that encapsulates that diversity as well as a journey down the trails of the Cane Creek Canyon Preserve in Tuscumbia. The labyrinth of trails, almost 18 miles in all, crisscross the tract, taking you and your dog to fascinating rock bluffs, enormous rock shelters, breathtaking rainbows of wildflowers, tiered waterfalls, and the crystal-clear waters of Cane Creek itself.

The tract was a project of Jim and Faye Lacefield. The couple began purchasing this property in 1976 and, little by little, acquired what you see today. In turn they have opened it to the public so you can experience the beauty yourself. The preserve is managed in conjunction with the Nature Conservancy to maintain its pristine environment.

On your first visit to the preserve, you will quickly realize that the route described here is only one of many possible trips you can take, and you will surely want to come back to do more exploring.

The hike begins near the Lacefields' home, where you will park. When you arrive you are required to sign in before heading out. And don't forget to sign out before leaving, too. This way they can keep track of who is still on the trail at closing time.

From here, it's an easy walk to your first stop, the Point, where you will have an expansive view of the tree-covered canyon below and the mountains some 6 miles in the distance, with no trace of civilization between you and those mountains.

The canyon that you will now be descending into was part of an ancient barrier island millions of years ago. The towering sandstone cliffs are evidence of this. Look closely for the fossil record of that ancient ocean embedded in the rock.

That ocean helped create not only the canyon but also a prominent feature of this hike: tall and deep rock shelters. Rock shelters are deep depressions, almost cave-like, that have been carved into the rock walls over millions of years by nature. You will encounter the first one as you begin your trip downhill from the Point.

Some of the most impressive rock shelters and overhangs come at the far end of this hike on the Under Bluff Trail in an area known as Devil's Hollow.

Many of the shelters, like the first one you come to, are adorned with glistening waterfalls that tumble down and flow into the creek below. You will pass several waterfalls along the trip, including Yellow Wood, Karen's, and Johnson that are located at the turnaround for this hike.

From spring through summer you will see a dazzling array of wildflowers, including— to name only a few—yellow lady's slippers, trout lily, mountain laurel, and the rare giant American columbo. A favorite and unusual stop along the hike is the Boulder Garden, where a multitude of wildflowers grow on top of the rocks. You will also pass a beautiful and fragrant wildflower garden near the pond on your return trip near the end of the hike.

Finally, there is Cane Creek itself, a beautiful, crystal-clear creek that continues to shape and maintain the health of the preserve. Your pup is more than welcome to romp and splash through the creek.

A great place along the creek for both of you to stop and take a break is at Linden Meadows, where you can sit at picnic tables near the creek. Take a look into the creek while you're there, and you will see hundreds of periwinkles (small creek snails), a sign of the water's purity.

A spectacular view from the Point before heading down into the canyon.

Speaking of water, the Lacefields keep jugs of drinking water here and at other locations around the preserve so you can refill.

While Cane Creek Canyon is very dog-friendly, let's keep it that way. Please clean up after them, keep them on leash, don't let them be a nuisance to others, and—most importantly—don't let them have any contact or encounters with wildlife.

CREATURE COMFORTS

RESTING UP

Microtel Inns and Suites, 1852 US 72 E, Tuscumbia; (877) 411-3436.

Pets up to 20 pounds each are allowed. There is an additional $20 per pet, per night fee. Pet-friendly rooms can only be guaranteed by making your reservations through the BringFido.com phone number listed above.

CAMPING

Cedar Ridge Campground, 140 Campground Rd., Russellville; (256) 668-3438; www.cedarridgecampgroundal.com/

Cedar Ridge is located 11 miles south of Cane Creek Canyon Preserve. The campground is family operated with a camp store and is adjacent to Cedar Creek Lake, which means great swimming. Make reservations online or by phoning the campground.

Cane Creek Canyon Preserve, Friends of Cane Creek, 251 Loop Rd., Tuscumbia; (256) 381-6301; www.facebook.com/Friends-of-Cane-Creek-Canyon-Nature-Preserve -126802417335447/

There are five primitive backcountry campsites available on a first come, first served basis at the preserve. You must reserve a campsite at least 2 weeks in advance. Visit the preserve's Facebook page, listed above, to download a registration form.

FUELING UP

Wildwood Tavern, 108 E. Mobile St., Florence; (256) 349-2139

You and your pup are invited to chow down at one of Wildwood's outdoor tables. You'll find an eclectic menu of hot dogs, flatbread pizzas, and baked pastas. Dive into one of the Tavern's "Fancy Dogs," like the Sweet Heat with sriracha mayonnaise and home-made sweet banana peppers, or the Korean with bulgogi barbecue sauce or homemade kimchi. A local favorite is the Wildwood Wildcard Pasta with Caribbean jerk sauce, Cajun chicken, jalapeño, and grilled pineapple.

MILES AND DIRECTIONS

0.0 Start at parking lot at the Lacefields' house. Take the dirt road a few hundred feet. A trail forks to the right (west); turn right here onto that trail. In a few feet you will pass a portable toilet on the left.

0.2 Arrive at Small Point. Pass three portable toilets and a campsite. A sign here indicates the direction of the Waterfall Trail. A series of stairs leads down the hill a short distance.

0.3 Come to a waterfall and rock shelter. Keep your dog close, and be very careful along the rim of the gorge! Follow the advice of the sign here that reads, BEST VIEW OF FALLS IS ON ROCK LEDGE ACROSS FOOTBRIDGE. Cross the narrow footbridge to the south and come to a Y. A sign here points to the left fork and the way to the Point and the Canyon Rim Trail. Take the left fork uphill to the west. In less than 0.1 mile, pass a bench on right; there are good views of the falls here in late fall and winter.

0.4 Come to a T intersection at a wide dirt road. Take the right fork; a sign here reads CANYON RIM TRAIL and points the direction.

0.7 Come to a portable toilet and campsite. Turn to the right (northwest.)

0.8 Arrive at the Point, with its panoramic view. There are benches here and, in late spring, walls of mountain laurel. To the left (west) there is a Y. The right fork is the Steep Trail. Take the left fork to the south on the Canyon Rim Trail. At this point the trail turns into a narrow dirt and rock path. There are nice views of the valley below to your right.

0.9 Pass an overlook from an outcropping hanging over the canyon. Be careful if you walk out! In less than 0.1 mile, pass another overlook.

1.1 Come to a T intersection. Turn right (southeast) onto the wide path, which is a dirt road covered with large gravel to protect it from washout. In less than 0.1 mile, come to a Y. The left fork takes you back to the house. Take the right fork (southwest). In less than 0.1 mile, pass an old dirt road on the left. In a few feet you will pass a bench and go through a metal gate; this is part of South Boundary Road. In a few yards, arrive at the Tree Fern Cave Rock Shelter on the right, and just after that, come to another Y. Take the right fork. A sign points the way to the main Cane Creek Trail.

1.2 Pass a bench and get your first look at Cane Creek.

1.3 Come to a Y. The West Cane Creek Trail is down the left fork to the west. Take the right fork. You are now on the East Cane Creek Trail. In less than 0.1 mile, pass Azalea Footbridge on the left.

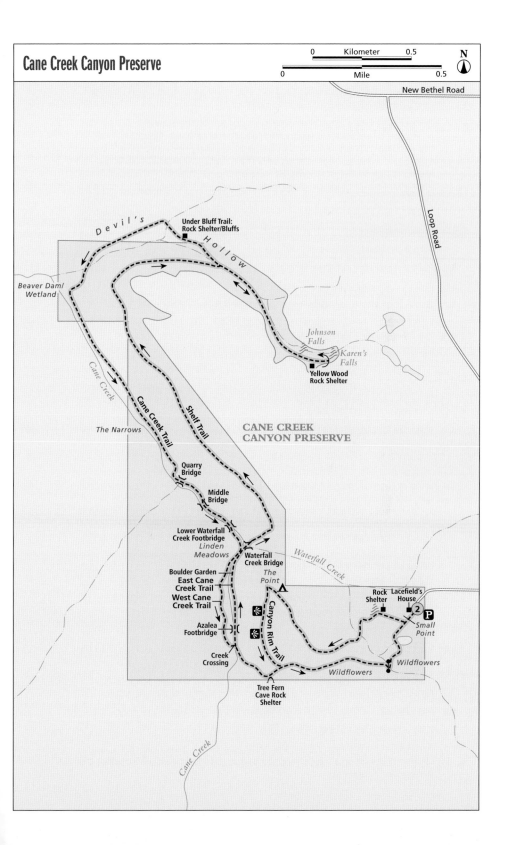

Cane Creek Canyon Preserve

0   Kilometer   0.5

0   Mile   0.5

N

New Bethel Road

Loop Road

Devil's *Hollow*

Under Bluff Trail:
Rock Shelter/Bluffs

Beaver Dam/
Wetland

Cane Creek

Johnson
Falls

Karen's
Falls

Yellow Wood
Rock Shelter

The Narrows

Cane Creek Trail

Shelf Trail

CANE CREEK
CANYON PRESERVE

Quarry
Bridge

Middle
Bridge

Lower Waterfall
Creek Footbridge

Linden
Meadows

Waterfall
Creek Bridge

Waterfall Creek

Boulder Garden
East Cane
Creek Trail
West Cane
Creek Trail

The
Point

Rock
Shelter

Lacefield's
House

2

P

Small
Point

Azalea
Footbridge

Canyon Rim Trail

Creek
Crossing

Wildflowers

Wildflowers

Tree Fern
Cave Rock
Shelter

1.5 A short 30-foot trail to the left leads to the Cascades of Cane Creek.

1.6 A small trail leads off to the right (east.) A sign indicates that this is the Boulder Garden. Turn right here and loop around the 2 big boulders and wildflowers until you come to a short side trail to the right (west) that will take you back to the East Cane Creek Trail.

1.7 Back on the East Cane Creek Trail, turn right onto the trail. In less than 0.1 mile, pass a footbridge and Linden Meadows on the left. Continue straight to the northeast. There is a stand of bamboo growing here. Soon you'll come to a Y. To the left is the East Cane Creek Trail; right, Waterfall Creek Bridge. Take the right fork to the northeast. You are on the south end of the Shelf Trail. Pass an informational sign that reads WATERFALL CREEK BRIDGE 30 YARDS, THE GAP 6/10THS OF A MILE. In a few yards, cross the footbridge over a nice rocky stream.

2.2 Pass the middle trail on the left. Continue northwest on the Shelf Trail.

2.4 Turn right (east) into Devil's Hollow.

3.1 Pass a small spring on the right.

3.5 Pass the towering Johnson Falls on the right.

3.7 Come to the Yellow Wood Rock Shelter and Karen's Falls. This is your turnaround.

4.0 Take the Under Bluff Trail that splits off to the right (northwest).

4.8 Pass an old beaver pond and a tranquil wetland where you may spot some rare butterflies. Head south on the main Cane Creek Trail.

5.2 Come to a section along the creek called the Narrows, where the creek—no surprise here—narrows, causing a rushing flow through the boulders. There is a nice swimming hole here.

5.5 Pass the Quarry Bridge over Cane Creek.

5.6 Pass Middle Bridge.

5.7 Cross the creek over the Lower Waterfall Creek Footbridge.

5.8 Back at the Y at mile 1.7. Continue straight to the southwest. In a few yards turn left and cross Cane Creek over a stone-and-cement footbridge. Look for periwinkle in the stream. After crossing, you are at the Linden Meadows picnic area again. Turn right (southwest) onto the West Cane Creek Trail. The trail is more enclosed and is a narrower dirt road on this side of the creek.

6.1 Cross Cane Creek again to the north over a footbridge. In less than 0.1 mile, come to a Y. The left fork takes you to the East Cane Creek Trail; take the right fork onto the Southern Boundary Road.

6.4 Back at the intersection of the Boundary Road and Canyon Rim Trail, continue straight on the South Boundary Road.

6.5 Pass a wildflower patch.

6.6 Pass a trail that leads back to the Point on the left. Continue straight to the east.

6.7 Come to a Y. The left fork is a shortcut back to the parking lot, which is rather steep. Take the right fork across a short footbridge over a creek

6.8 Pass through a gate. Wildflowers bloom in a large field to the right.

6.9 Pass a pretty little pond on the right.

7.0 Arrive back at the first Y from the beginning of the hike. Continue straight to the northeast and the parking lot. In less than 0.1 mile, arrive back at the parking lot / trailhead.

PUPPY PAWS AND GOLDEN YEARS
Key Underwood Coon Dog Memorial Graveyard

On Labor Day 1937, Key Underwood bid a sad farewell to his beloved coon-hunting dog, Troop. Underwood buried his hunting companion in an old hunting camp that, for over fifteen years, the pair loved to visit in the town of Cherokee just 30 miles south of Florence. Other coon hunters who loved their dogs just as much followed suit, and today the graveyard has 185 dogs interned there. When asked by a reporter why only coon dogs were allowed in the cemetery, Underwood replied, "You must not know much about coon hunters and their dogs if you think we would contaminate this burial place with poodles and lap dogs."

Bring your dog's favorite toy on the hike.

3 PLATEAU LOOP

A little bit of history and a whole lot of beautiful landscapes await you as you take a walk around the summit of Monte Sano Mountain in Huntsville on this double-loop trail. Your pup will love the relatively flat South Loop, where there is a lot to explore and engage them while you take in amazing views from O'Shaughnessy Point. On the North Loop you'll cross several seasonal creeks, visit a beautiful 70-foot waterfall off a side trail, and see the handiwork of the Civilian Conservation Corps from 1935.

THE RUNDOWN

Start: From the south side of the Hiker's Parking Lot at the kiosk
Distance: 5.4-mile double loop
Approximate hiking time: 3.5 hours
Difficulty: Moderate due to distance if the entire double loop is hiked over slightly hilly terrain
Trailhead elevation: 1,623 feet
Highest Elevation: 1,707 feet
Best season: Year-round; open 8 a.m. until 30 minutes before sunset
Trail surface: Dirt and rock, a very small section is on gravel road
Other trail users: Cyclists
Canine compatibility: Leash required
Land status: Alabama state park
Fees and permits: Day-use fee: adults $5; children 4–11, seniors 62-plus $2; children under 3 free
Trail contact: Monte Sano State Park, 5105 Nolen Ave., Huntsville; (256) 534-3757; www.alapark.com/monte-sano-state-park
Nearest town: Huntsville
Trail tips: There are several panoramic views of Huntsville's mountains and valleys, so don't forget the camera. If you don't want to do the entire hike, you can just walk the 3.5-mile South Plateau Loop or for an even shorter trek, the 1.9-mile North Plateau Loop. Both trails start at the same trailhead. Be sure to check out the stargazing show at the Wernher von Braun Planetarium every Saturday. The Von Braun Astronomical Society hosts the event, which usually begins with a presentation inside the planetarium; however, pets are not allowed. After the presentation the Society opens their outdoor telescopes for public viewing of the stars, and dogs are allowed then.
Maps: USGS: Huntsville, AL
Other maps: Available at the park entrance gate, park office, or online at www.alapark.com/sites/alapark.com/files/Main%20Park%20Trails%20-%204-21-2016.pdf

FINDING THE TRAILHEAD

From the intersection of I-565 and Governors Drive SW in Huntsville, travel east on Governors Drive SW 5.1 miles. Turn left onto Monte Sano Boulevard SE. Travel 2.4 miles and turn right onto Nolen Avenue SE. Travel 0.8 mile to the entrance gate. After paying your day-use fee, continue straight on Nolen Avenue SE. Travel 0.4 mile and come to a Y intersection. Take the right fork and, in just a few hundred feet, the Hiker's Parking Lot / Trailhead will be on the right. Trailhead GPS N34 44.619' / W86 30.670'

One of several trail shelters you'll pass on the South Plateau Loop section of this hike, the perfect place for you and your pup to get out of the sun and relax with a view.

THE HIKE

Monte Sano Mountain, "mountain of health" in Spanish, is the site for this double-loop hike around the mountain top in the state park that bears its name.

Out of all the trails at Monte Sano State Park, this is one of Archer T. Dog's and my favorites. It packs in so much in the 5.4-mile circuit: geology, views, a waterfall just off a side trail, and lots of history. We especially love arriving early in the morning when the park first opens and a light fog shrouds the trail, giving it a very intimate feel. This is probably one of the reasons that the mountain earned its name and reputation back in the early 1800s, when it was thought that the cool, crisp mountain air would help cure yellow fever. A sanitarium was built here in 1827 for just that purpose.

For a quick hike you can do either the 3.5-mile south loop or the 1.9-mile north loop, but we prefer to do the entire 5.4-mile double-loop around the top of the 1,400-foot limestone mountain. The park's Hiker Parking Lot joins the two trails together, and this is where you'll begin the trek on the South Plateau Loop.

The south loop is highlighted by the mountain's geology. The limestone bluffs and outcroppings of Monte Sano offer spectacular views from several vantage points, where you can take in the beauty of Huntsville's mountains and valleys. The best view is of Big Cove from O'Shaughnessy Point, named for Colonel James O'Shaughnessy, who supervised the construction of a railroad line from Georgia to Missouri that would pass through Huntsville. He also helped supervise the building of the Monte Sano Hotel following the Civil War.

It's easy to follow the blue blazes of the North Plateau Loop trail.

Keep in mind that the bluffs are 30 to 50 feet tall and straight down. Heed the warning signs and use caution.

The white-blazed trail is dotted with Civilian Conservation Corps (CCC) stone shelters where you can sit and relax in shade, and if you're quiet you may catch a glimpse of a bobcat, whitetail deer, or woodchuck.

Speaking of the CCC, their stone handiwork from the 1930s is on full display on the North Plateau Loop trail. Along the blue-blazed path you will see stone picnic pavilions, an amphitheater, and the beautiful remodeled lodge, all made from carefully layered stones hand laid by the young men of the Corps.

As you make your way to the picnic area, you will pass the McKay Hollow Trail. It's worth your while to head down the steep trail a few yards to take a look at the 70-foot seasonal waterfall. Remember, it is a steep climb.

You will also be treated to two more amazing panoramic views, one at the lodge, the other from the overlook that looks down into McKay Hollow itself.

Both trails are relatively flat, easy walks; the north loop is a bit hillier. The hike is given a moderate difficulty rating mainly due to its length.

There is also a little bit more modern history on the North Plateau Loop as it passes the Von Braun Planetarium. The facility was built and opened in 1956 by Dr. Wernher von Braun, the famed rocket scientist who helped the United States make the first lunar landing.

The planetarium, operated by the Von Braun Astronomical Society, opens its doors to the public every Saturday night where they host an astronomy-related show. Many times those shows also feature a presentation by astronauts, astronomers, and scientists.

Now, of course, you can't bring your dog into the planetarium, but on clear nights the Society brings out their telescopes so the public can get an amazing view of the night sky.

CREATURE COMFORTS

RESTING UP

La Quinta Huntsville Research Park, 4870 University Dr. NW, Huntsville; (256) 830-2070; www.lq.com

Make your reservations online. Two pets of any size are welcome with no additional fees. Remember, pets must be crated if left unattended.

CAMPING

Monte Sano State Park, 5105 Nolen Ave., Huntsville; (256) 534-3757; www.alapark .com/monte-sano-state-park

Make reservations online. The park has fifty-nine improved campsites with water and electricity for only $26 a night. One of the twenty-one primitive sites with no amenities is $13.39 per night. A one-night deposit is required when reserving in advance, which is recommended.

FUELING UP

Shaggy's Burgers and Tacos, 1267 Enterprise Way, Huntsville; (256) 270-9999; www .shaggysburgersandtacos.com/

Burgers, chili dogs, tacos, chips with white queso sauce—just some of the unbelievable Tex-Mex fare found at Shaggy's Burgers and Tacos. Like they say, the food is "shagg-a-licious." The restaurant has outdoor seating so your pup can dine with you.

MILES AND DIRECTIONS

0.0 Start from the south side of the Hiker's Parking Lot at the kiosk. This is where the North and South Plateau Loops join together, along with the red-blazed Fire Tower Trail. Start with the white-blazed South Plateau Loop. Head to the southwest and in a few feet come to an intersection with the Bucca Family Trail. Continue straight to the south to stay on the South Plateau Loop.

0.2 Come to a Y. The left fork is the Fire Tower Trail. Continue straight to the south to stay on the South Plateau Loop, a 5-foot-wide dirt path.

0.5 Cross a stream over a 20-foot bridge. After a rain there is a nice little cascade here.

0.6 Cross another stream on a 10-foot bridge.

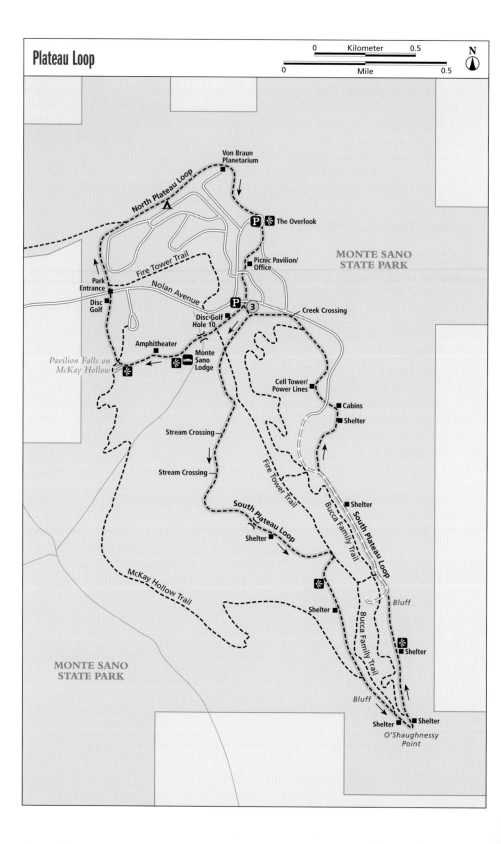

Plateau Loop

0   Kilometer   0.5

0   Mile   0.5

N

Von Braun
Planetarium

North Plateau Loop

The Overlook

MONTE SANO
STATE PARK

Fire Tower Trail

Picnic Pavilion/
Office

Park
Entrance

Nolan Avenue

Disc
Golf

3

Disc Golf
Hole 10

Creek Crossing

Amphitheater

Monte
Sano
Lodge

Pavilion Falls on
McKay Hollow

Cell Tower/
Power Lines

Cabins

Shelter

Stream Crossing

Stream Crossing

Fire Tower Trail

Shelter

South Plateau Loop

Shelter

Bucca Family Trail

South Plateau Loop

McKay Hollow Trail

Shelter

Bluff

Shelter

MONTE SANO
STATE PARK

Bucca Family Trail

Shelter

Bluff

Shelter

Shelter

O'Shaughnessy
Point

0.9 Cross an intermittent stream and boggy area over a bridge. Just past the crossing some views of the valley and farms below can be seen through the trees.

1.0 Pass the first of several covered trail shelters you can relax in. Just after the shelter pass some rock outcroppings on the right.

1.1 The Bog Trail comes in from the left. There are 2 benches here. Continue straight to the southeast.

1.2 Come to a Y. The Fire Tower Trail comes in from the left. Take the right fork to the south and continue following the white blazes.

1.3 Take in some nice views on your right.

1.4 Pass another trail shelter.

1.6 The McKay Hollow Trail comes in from the right at another trail shelter. Continue straight to the south.

1.7 A short 100-foot trail on the right takes you to a bluff.

1.8 The Bucca Family Trail joins the South Plateau Loop from the left. Continue straight to the southeast. You'll have more views just after the intersection.

1.9 Arrive at O'Shaughnessy Point, with a wonderful open view from the bluff. When you're done taking in the view, continue on the South Plateau Loop to the north. In a few feet the Warpath Ridge Bike Trail splits off to the south. Turn left (north) to continue the loop. In less than 0.1 mile, the Mountain Mist Trail splits off to the right, the Bucca Family Trail to the left. Continue straight to the north.

2.1 Pass a trail shelter.

2.3 Pass a bluff with a view on the right. In less than 0.1 mile, the dirt path merges with a gravel road that comes in from the left. Continue to follow the white blazes to the north.

2.4 The Fire Tower Trail splits off to the left. Continue following the white blazes to the north. In less than 0.1 mile, the Mountain Mist Trail rejoins the loop from the right.

2.6 Pass a trail shelter.

2.7 The gravel road turns to the left. Continue to follow the white blazes to the north. The trail is once again a wide dirt footpath.

2.9 Pass a trail shelter.

3.0 Pass the park's cabins on the right. The trail crosses a paved road to the northeast.

3.1 Pass a cell-phone tower then cross under a set of power lines and cross a gravel road to the north.

3.3 The Bucca Family Trail rejoins the loop from the left. In less than 0.1 mile, come to a Y. The Sinks Trail enters from the right. Continue to follow the white blazes to the west. In 100 feet, cross a short bridge over an intermittent creek.

3.5 Arrive back at the trailhead. You can end the hike here and leave the North Plateau Loop for another day, but for this hike we'll continue on the North Plateau Loop. Immediately after passing the kiosk, turn right (southwest) onto the blue-blazed trail. In less than 0.1 mile, pass the park's disc golf course on the right.

3.6 Cross the Fire Tower Trail.

3.7 Cross a runoff with a small cascade over a 30-foot bridge.

3.8 Arriving at the Monte Sano Lodge, take a short walk off the trail behind the building for a spectacular view.

3.9 Just after passing the amphitheater on the right, walk through the picnic area. In less than 0.1 mile, pass an overlook.

4.0 Pass another overlook on the left. In a few yards you'll pass the CCC picnic pavilion on the left. The north end of the McKay Hollow Trail can be found on the right side of the pavilion. Continue to follow the loop's blue blazes to the northeast. The trail will leave the picnic area and return to the woods. *OPTION:* You may want to hike a few yards down the McKay Hollow Trail to view a beautiful—but seasonal—waterfall. Remember, it's a steep and slippery climb.

4.2 Cross the disc golf course. Just past this you'll cross the main park road at the entrance station.

4.3 Pass the Fire Tower Trail on the right. Just after, you'll be passing the primitive campground also on the right.

4.4 The trail meanders just below the park's campground that's perched up on a ridge. Watch your pup through here; there is a sharp drop-off on the left.

4.5 Pass the Cold Springs Trail on the left.

4.6 Make your closest approach to the campground to your right.

4.8 Pass the Von Braun Planetarium on the right.

5.0 Arrive at what looks like a T intersection. The left turn is merely a game trail; turn right (southeast) to continue on the North Plateau Loop. In a few yards you'll cross a road to reach the Overlook parking lot and the Overlook for a sweeping view down into McKay Hollow and the surrounding mountains. Continue to the south through the parking lot and pick up the trail as it heads back into the woods.

5.2 Cross a paved road to the south.

5.3 Pass a picnic pavilion on the right. Continue to the south.

5.4 Cross another paved road and arrive back at the Hiker's Parking Lot.

PUPPY PAWS AND GOLDEN YEARS
Tasty (and Healthy) Homemade Peanut Butter Dog Biscuits
What you'll need:
- Vegetable oil cooking spray (optional)
- ½ cup oats
- 2 cups whole wheat flour
- 1 tablespoon baking powder
- 1 cup low-sodium chicken broth
- 1 cup creamy peanut butter
- ¼ cup grated Parmesan cheese
- Bone-shaped cookie cutter (optional)

Preheat your oven to 345 degrees. Spray a cookie sheet with vegetable oil spray or line it with parchment paper or a silicone baking mat. In a large bowl combine the dry ingredients. Add the broth and peanut butter and mix until the dough is crumbly.

Form the dough into a ball and knead for 30 seconds on a floured surface. Roll the dough into a 10-inch, ½-inch-thick circle and cut it into shapes using a cookie cutter, if desired. Sprinkle the biscuits with Parmesan, place them on the prepared cookie sheet, and bake until light golden brown, about 20 minutes. Let cool on a wire rack.

4 HONEYCOMB TRAIL

A surprising little hike around a rocky knob on the banks of Lake Guntersville, the Honeycomb Trail presents a lot of exploring opportunities for Fido while giving you some beautiful views of the lake from its northern bank. The path along a section that follows a power line is lined with wildflowers, like flaming star plus honeysuckle and blackberry bushes.

THE RUNDOWN

Start: From the southwest side of the parking lot at the kiosk
Distance: 3.1-mile lollipop loop
Approximate hiking time: 2 hours
Difficulty: Easy over a rocky or packed clay footpath
Trailhead elevation: 622 feet
Highest point: 710 feet
Best season: Year-round; summer can be tough walking the first 0.5 mile with no canopy along a powerline; open sunrise to sunset
Trail surface: Packed clay along the power line for 0.5-mile; remainder is dirt and rock
Other trail users: None
Canine compatibility: Voice control; however, you may want to leash them along the banks of the lake where there are a couple of drop-offs.
Land status: Tennessee Valley Authority (TVA) Small Wild Area
Fees and permits: None
Trail contact: Tennessee Valley Authority, 400 W. Summit Hill Dr., Knoxville, TN 37902; (865) 632-2101; www.tva.gov/Environment/Recreation/Copy-of-TVA-Trails

Nearest town: Guntersville
Trail tips: You would think that walking a section of open power line would be boring, but on this hike beautiful wildflowers grace the path from spring through summer, making it a pleasurable walk. But remember, in the summer there is no shade on this section, so wear sunscreen (you and your dog) and carry plenty of water for both of you. Bring the camera to capture gorgeous sunrises and sunsets. There are a couple of access points where your dog might get a drink and cool down, but be careful: Most of the banks on the loop have drop-offs, and the lake is deep in some sections. Restrooms are available at the campground just a few yards past the trailhead; ask the attendant to use them.
Maps: USGS: Mount Carmel, AL
Other maps: Available online at www.tva.com/file_source/TVA/Site%20Content/Environment/Recreation/On%20the%20Lands/trail_maps/Honeycomb_8.pdf

FINDING THE TRAILHEAD

From the intersection of US 431 and AL 227 / Lusk Street in Guntersville, take US 431 north for 11.8 miles. Turn left onto Camp Ground Road. Parking and the trailhead will be on the right just before the entrance gate to the TVA campground. It is a very small parking lot, with room for maybe 10 cars. Trailhead GPS: N34 27.092' / W86 20.115'

THE HIKE

While at Lake Guntersville visiting the state park, I learned of a trail that Archer and I had never hiked before: the Tennessee Valley Authority (TVA) Honeycomb Trail. It is located on the northern banks of the lake on one of TVA's reservations and Small Wild Areas. So we decided to stop and check it out, and what a surprise! Turns out it was a

Wildflowers like these red cardinal flowers grace the path.

really nice little hike around a rocky knob that protrudes into the lake.

The Honeycomb Trail offers a lot of exploring opportunities for Fido through the understory and around the rocky loop. For you, there are some beautiful views of the lake with gorgeous sunrises and sunsets.

The TVA has set up several such trails across the region as part of their program to provide recreational opportunities to the public on their land. A couple of other TVA favorites I would recommend include the Nature Trail in Florence and the Cave Mountain Trail just down the road from this hike. You can learn more about these hikes in the fourth edition of my book *Hiking Alabama* or by visiting the Trail Contact website above.

The full trail is actually a 9.0-mile point-to-point or 18-mile out-and-back, but since we were hiking on one of "those" summer days (i.e., high humidity and temps), we opted for this shorter loop. If you decide you want to do the entire length of the trail that follows the banks of the lake for almost its entire length, visit the website provided in Trail Contact for more information.

The trail begins only a few feet away from the entrance to the TVA's Honeycomb Campground in a very small parking lot. If you need the restroom, the gate attendant is happy to let you use it.

From the parking lot and after a short walk in the woods from the trailhead, the path peeks out under a power line and follows it for about 0.5 mile. The path is hard-packed clay and gravel through this section, but it is made much more enjoyable because it is lined with wildflowers, like flaming star, plus fragrant honeysuckle and juicy blackberry bushes.

Remember that this 0.5 mile is out in the open sun, and in the summer it can be hot, so wear that sunscreen and take precautions for your pup, too (see Joe's Five Hiking Tips).

As you look ahead at the power line that stretches before you, you will see a very steep hill. Don't be afraid: You won't have to climb it. At the bottom of that hill, the trail veers off to the south and makes its way into the loop section of the hike through a thick, mixed hardwood forest. The canopy of beech, yellow poplar, and oak is thick and welcome on hot summer days. The trail is marked with white paint blazes.

The loop is a dirt and rock footpath that will lead you to the banks of the lake, where you will get some picturesque views, especially of the sunrise and sunset. There are several points along the walk where your pup may be able to grab a drink in the cool, clear water, but use caution: Some of the banks are steep and the water deep, one of the reasons you should keep them on a leash for this hike. Your best spot would be at mile 1.9, where there is a gradual gravel bank down into the water.

And be forewarned, great blue herons frequent the shoreline here, and you and your dog may be startled if, as from out of nowhere, a bird gets a little perturbed that you're visiting and sounds off.

CREATURE COMFORTS

RESTING UP

Wyndham Garden Hotel, 2140 Gunter Ave., Guntersville; (256) 582-2220; www .wyndhamhotels.com

Two pets up to 80 pounds total weight are welcome, and your well-behaved pet is allowed to stay unattended in your room. There is an additional $20 per pet, per night fee charged up to $100. Make your reservation by phone to guarantee a pet-friendly room; otherwise you can make your reservation online.

Lake Guntersville State Park, 1155 Lodge Dr., Guntersville; (256) 571-5455; www .alapark.com/dog-friendly

The state park has a limited number of lodging options for you and your pup. There are two lakeside cabins, three chalets, and two lodge rooms. An additional $16.50 per pet, per night fee is charged. Make your reservations by phone and be sure to ask if any of these pet-friendly accommodations are available.

CAMPING

Lake Guntersville State Park, 1155 Lodge Dr., Guntersville; (256) 571-5455; www .alapark.com/lake-guntersville-state-park

Lake Guntersville has not only great hiking but also great campgrounds: sixty-five improved sites and one hundred primitive sites are available. Improved sites are $26 per night, primitive sites $14 per night. A one-time $4.50 transaction fee is also charged. Make reservations by phone or online at guestrez.megahotel.com/Hotel/Reservation/ Index/P3R24.

Town Creek Fishing Center, 11868 AL 227, Guntersville; (256) 582-8358; www.ala park.com/lake-guntersville-state-park-town-creek-fishing-center

Additional primitive sites are located at the Town Creek Fishing Center along the banks of the beautiful, wide feeder of Lake Guntersville and only 6 miles east of the state park. Sites are $14 per night with a one-time $4.50 transaction fee. The fishing center does not make reservations. All sites are available on a first come, first served basis.

FUELING UP

Carlile's Restaurant, 23730 John T. Reid Pkwy., Scottsboro; (256) 574-5629

Friendly staff, great food, dog friendly. That about sums up Carlile's in Scottsboro. You'll love the Carlisle Burger loaded down with "the works" or the Grilled Cajun Pork Chop Sandwich. No regrets here!

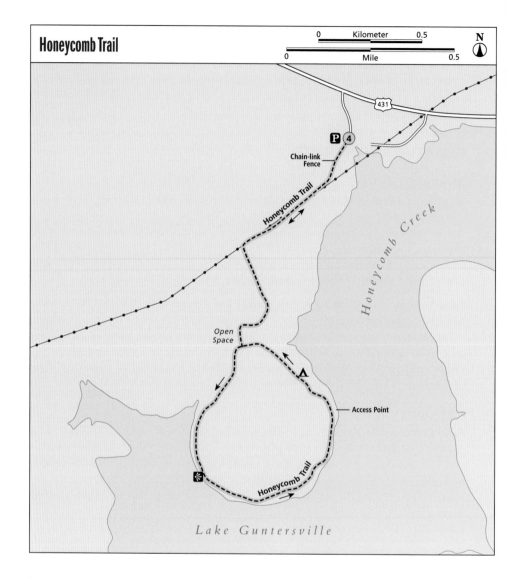

Honeycomb Trail

0   Kilometer   0.5

0   Mile   0.5

N

431

P 4

Chain-link
Fence

Honeycomb Trail

Honeycomb Creek

Open
Space

Access Point

Honeycomb Trail

Lake Guntersville

MILES AND DIRECTIONS

0.0   Start from the trailhead kiosk on the south side of the small gravel parking lot. In less than 0.1 mile, pass the campground's chain-link fence on the left.

0.1   Pass an old metal gate on the left. Continue straight to the southwest. You are now walking beneath a power line. Wildflowers grace the path spring through summer. The path is hard-packed clay and gravel through here.

0.5   Turn left (south) into the woods. You will start to see white paint blazes. This turn is just before the power line climbs a big, steep hill that begins with a short walk through fern-covered understory. The path is a 3-foot-wide, dirt and rock path littered with leaves. The canopy around the loop is very thick and provides great shade in the summer.

0.8   Come to a small open gravel space. Continue straight to the south.

0.9 Come to a T intersection. To the left is the return trail; turn right (southwest). For a short distance the path is a wide, abandoned dirt road. In less than 0.1 mile, come to a Y. Take the left fork to the southwest.

1.1 Arrive at the banks of Honeycomb Creek and Lake Guntersville. The trail narrows to a 2- to 3-foot dirt footpath with rocks to navigate through.

1.2 Pass a possible access point for your dog.

1.3 Start getting some really nice views of the lake.

1.9 Here is the best access point if your dog wants a drink or just to cool its paws. It is a gradual slope from the bank with a light gravel bottom.

2.0 You will see the campground on the right to the east.

2.1 Cross a runoff over a large, flat boulder. The runoff becomes a nice little cascade after a good rain.

2.1 Come to an intersection with a wide gravel road. Turn left (west) onto the road and head uphill. Soon the road narrows to 3 feet wide.

2.3 Back at mile 0.9, turn right (north) and retrace your steps to the trailhead.

3.1 Arrive back at the trailhead.

5 TOM BEVILL LOOP

A beautiful walk in the woods is in store for you on this loop nature trail around the top of Ellenburg Mountain, especially in the fall when the leaves are radiant with color. Fido will love exploring the rocks and understory. Wildlife like whitetail deer will surprise you as you round bends, wildflowers like spiderwort and mountain laurel grace your path spring through summer, and you'll have a couple of nice views of the lake and hollow.

THE RUNDOWN

Start: From the parking lot on AL 227 next to the park ranger office, head north across the highway to pick up the trail
Distance: 3.8-mile loop
Approximate hiking time: 2–2.5 hours
Difficulty: Easy walking on dirt footpaths except for a short (0.1-mile) moderate hike up to the ridge at the start of the hike
Trailhead elevation: 624 feet
Highest point: 892 feet
Best season: Year-round; open sunrise to sunset
Trail surface: Dirt and rock footpath
Other trail users: None
Canine compatibility: Leash required
Land status: Alabama state park
Fees and permits: None
Trail contact: Lake Guntersville State Park, 1155 Lodge Dr., Guntersville;
(256) 571-5440; www.alapark.com/lake-guntersville-state-park
Nearest town: Guntersville
Trail tips: This is just a really nice walk in the woods. From the trailhead it's a moderate 0.1-mile hike up to the main trail, but from there it's a fairly level walk. You will love walking through the rows of wildflowers that line the trail in season, including jack-in-the-pulpits and hepatica. Remember, there is no reliable water on this hike; you will cross a spring, but it is seasonal, so be sure to carry plenty for both you and your dog.
Maps: USGS: Columbus City, AL
Other maps: Available at the camp store 3 miles north of the trailhead on Aubrey Carr Scenic Drive or online: www.alapark.com/lake-guntersville-state-park-hiking-trails

FINDING THE TRAILHEAD

From the intersection of US 431 and AL 227 (Lusk Street) in Guntersville, take AL 227 southeast for 5.6 miles. The ranger station is just after the third long bridge you cross. The parking lot is on the northeast side of the ranger station (on its right side). The trail begins across AL 227 from the parking lot. Trailhead GPS: N34 22.203' / W86 12.936'

THE HIKE

Way back in 2000—or what seems like an eternity ago—when I was writing the first edition of *Hiking Alabama*, I described the Tom Bevill Loop, a beautiful interpretive trail built by the Young Adult Conservation Corps in the late 1970s. The loop was studded with numbered markers that, along with a brochure, told the history of the families that lived here on top of Ellenburg Mountain, the wildlife, and the wildflowers.

Well, that was then. Devastating tornadoes in 2011 took out much of the state park and its trails, and the Bevill Loop saw its share of destruction. But while the interpretive

The Tom Bevill Loop is lined with beautiful wildflowers.

markers are very nearly gone, the trail to me is still just as wonderful as before, a beautiful walk in the woods through a pine and hardwood forest with wildflowers like spiderwort, yellow poplar, and jack-in-the-pulpit lining the way. Some sections wind through tunnels of white and pink mountain laurel.

The path itself is a good intermediate trail for those hikers and their dogs who are just starting out. The 2- to 3-foot-wide dirt and rock path provides a good combination of rolling hills, with one moderate initial climb from the trailhead. The entire path has an excellent canopy, and for most of the trail, the summer sun isn't a problem. And don't be surprised if whitetail deer come bounding out of the brush before you across the trail or are walking down the trail in front of you as you round a bend.

The mountain is circled by AL 227 and Aubrey Carr Scenic Drive. The first section of the hike runs high above and parallel to the roadways, so if you can, the best time to hike this trail is in the early morning on weekends when there are fewer road traffic sounds.

The loop I'm describing here uses the main Tom Bevill Loop, but at mile 0.3, there is a Y intersection. The left fork is the continuation of the main Tom Bevill Loop and remains blazed with orange paint. The right fork is the Bevill Alternate Trail. The difference in the two is that the main trail here is a bit more rugged, with a steeper incline moving it higher up the mountain. The Alternate Trail is less rugged but is also 0.2 mile longer. It isn't blazed, but it's easy to follow. The Miles and Directions section takes the alternate route, but feel free to take the main trail. It will lead you back to the directions at mile 1.1.

You can also make this a longer 4.9-mile double-loop hike by combining the Tom Bevill Loop with the King's Chapel Loop (Hike 6).

For the double loop, begin the hike as you would for hike 6, the King's Chapel Loop. When you reach the cemetery, use the Graveyard Fire Road and head south 0.2 mile, crossing an old gravel road, then take the short connecting trail to mile 1.6 in the Miles and Directions section below. Walk the entire Tom Bevill Loop back to this point, then take the connector back to the cemetery. From there, complete the King's Chapel Loop by using the Terrell Trail.

As I mentioned earlier, in 2011 northern Alabama was hit by not one but twenty-eight devastating tornadoes. Along the north and northwestern ends of this hike, you will see some evidence of the damage: Uprooted trees and blowdowns that were cut away to reopen the trail are off to the side. They are now being covered by vines, new trees, and tall grass. As you will see, Mother Nature is resilient, and she is reclaiming her forest quite nicely.

CREATURE COMFORTS

RESTING UP

Wyndham Garden Hotel, 2140 Gunter Ave., Guntersville; (256) 582-2220; www .wyndhamhotels.com

Two pets up to 80 pounds total weight are welcome, and your well-behaved pet is allowed to stay unattended in your room. There is an additional $20 per pet, per night fee charged, up to $100. Make your reservation by phone to guarantee a pet-friendly room; otherwise you can make your reservation online.

Lake Guntersville State Park, 1155 Lodge Dr., Guntersville; (256) 571-5455; www .alapark.com/dog-friendly

The state park has a limited number of lodging options for you and your pup. There are two lakeside cabins, three chalets, and two lodge rooms. An additional $16.50 per pet, per night fee is charged. Make your reservations by phone and be sure to ask if any of these pet-friendly accommodations are available.

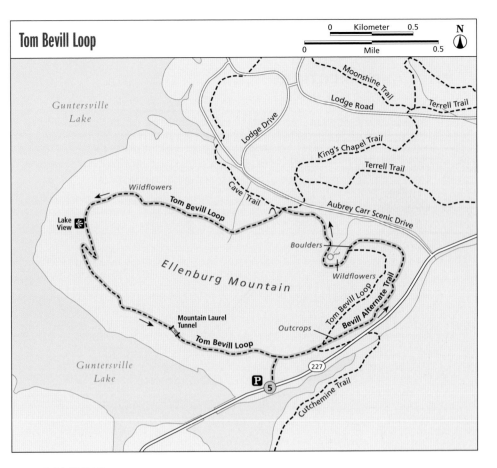

CAMPING

Lake Guntersville State Park, 1155 Lodge Dr., Guntersville; (256) 571-5455; www .alapark.com/lake-guntersville-state-park

Lake Guntersville has a great campground with sixty-five improved sites ($26 per night) and one hundred primitive sites ($14 per night). A one-time $4.50 transaction fee is also charged. Make reservations by phone or online at guestrez.megahotel.com/Hotel/ Reservation/Index/P3R24.

Town Creek Fishing Center, 11868 AL 227, Guntersville; (256) 582-8358; www.ala park.com/lake-guntersville-state-park-town-creek-fishing-center

Additional primitive sites are located at Town Creek, which is located right on the banks of the beautiful, wide feeder of Lake Guntersville and is only 6 miles east of the state park. Sites are $14 per night with a one-time $4.50 transaction fee. The fishing center does not make reservations. All sites are available on a first come, first served basis.

FUELING UP

Carlile's Restaurant, 23730 John T. Reid Pkwy, Scottsboro; (256) 574-5629

Barbecue, burgers, and wings are the fare at Carlile's. You've got to try the Carlisle Burger with "the works" or their chicken wings with a choice of nine different dipping sauces, everything from your basic BBQ sauce to their Great White Sauce and everything in between.

MILES AND DIRECTIONS

0.0 Start from the parking lot on the south side of AL 227. Carefully cross the highway, where you'll see a sign for the Tom Bevill Loop. The trail begins with a rather steep climb until it reaches the main trail. In less than 0.1 mile, you'll come to a Y intersection. An orange arrow painted on a rock points to the right. Take the right fork to the east.

0.1 Come to a Y. There is an orange blaze on a tree in the middle of the fork. Take the right fork to the east.

0.3 A side trail Ys to the right (southeast). A sign here reads To CUTCHENMINE; take the left fork to the northeast. In less than 0.1 mile, you'll come to another Y. The main Tom Bevill Loop heads to the left (north) while the Bevill Alternate Trail heads to the right (northeast). For this hike, I describe the Alternate Trail. This trail is not blazed but easy enough to follow. *FYI:* If you decide to walk the main Tom Bevill Loop, simply take the left fork to the north and follow the orange blazes. It will lead you to the intersection with the Alternate Trail at mile 1.1 of this description.

0.4 Begin to pass next to and around large rock outcroppings and boulders.

1.1 After passing among some boulders, the main Tom Bevill Loop rejoins from the left. Continue straight to the southwest. The orange paint blazes start again

1.2 The trail makes a short downhill between boulders. You will be surrounded by a variety of wildflowers in season.

1.4 Come to a Y. Take the left fork to the northwest. The brush makes the trail feel very enclosed through here.

1.5 Cross a spring that originates from under the rock bluff to your left.

1.6 Come to a major intersection. A sign points the directions: Cave Trail (to the north), Terrell Trail (right to the northeast), Tom Bevill Loop (back the way you came), Tom Bevill Loop (left to the southwest). Turn left here to the southwest to continue on the Tom Bevill Loop. *OPTION:* See the text for an option to extend the length of the hike.

2.4 Pass through a tunnel of mountain laurel; after, the trail is lined with wildflowers (red buckeye, yellow poplar, red cardinal, to name a few) and dogwoods. In less than 0.1 mile, you will begin to round the lake side of the mountain and may start feeling a lake breeze as the trail narrows.

2.6 In the fall and winter, you will get a view of the lake just before beginning a switchback downhill.

3.3 Pass through another tunnel of mountain laurel.

3.7 Arrive back at the intersection at mile 0.1. Turn right to the south to take the approach trail back to the trailhead.

3.8 Carefully cross AL 227 once again to the south and arrive back at the trailhead parking lot.

6 KING'S CHAPEL LOOP

Take in a little of Guntersville's history on this 2.3-mile loop trail to the King's Chapel Cemetery, which dates back to the late 1800s. The trail is named for one of the previous owners of the property, which is now part of Lake Guntersville State Park. This is a pleasant walk through the hardwood forest, especially in the fall when the hills are ablaze in color. There is plenty for your dog to explore around the rock outcroppings. You can combine this hike with the Tom Bevill Loop (Hike 5) to make a nice 4.9-mile double loop.

THE RUNDOWN

Start: From the parking lot on Aubrey Carr Scenic Drive, cross the road to the south to pick up the trail
Distance: 2.3-mile loop
Approximate hiking time: 1.5–2 hours
Difficulty: Moderate
Trailhead elevation: 798 feet
Highest point: 964 feet
Best season: Fall; open year-round sunrise to sunset
Trail surface: Dirt and rock footpath
Other trail users: Cyclists on the Terrell Trail Connector
Canine compatibility: Leash required
Land status: Alabama state park
Fees and permits: None but a donation box is set up at the trailhead where you can contribute to help maintain the trail

Trail contact: Lake Guntersville State Park, 1155 Lodge Dr., Guntersville; (256) 571-5455; www.alapark.com/lake-guntersville-state-park
Nearest town: Guntersville
Trail tips: The trailhead is across Aubrey Carr Scenic Drive from the parking lot, so use caution when crossing. At the cemetery, make sure you clean up after Fido, and keep it clean out of respect for the families who still visit.
Maps: USGS: Columbus City, AL
Other maps: Available at the camp store 3 miles north of the trailhead on Aubrey Carr Scenic Drive or online: www.alapark.com/lake-guntersville-state-park-hiking-trails

FINDING THE TRAILHEAD

From the intersection of AL 227 and AL 79 in Guntersville, take AL 227 south 6.6 miles. Turn left onto Aubrey Carr Scenic Drive. Travel 7.2 miles and make a left to continue on Aubrey Carr Scenic Drive (you will pass an entry station that is usually closed). Travel 0.5 mile to the parking lot on the right. The trail begins across the highway to the south and is well marked. Trailhead GPS: N34 23.099' / W86 12.388'

THE HIKE

The King's Chapel Loop at Lake Guntersville State Park gives you and Fido a chance to take in a quiet hardwood forest and a little of the area's history, too.

The names of the trails, King and Terrell, harken back to the early 1800s, when these families owned the land that is now the state park. This hike will take you to the King's Chapel Cemetery that was established in 1850 by Andrew King. You will notice on the tombstones not only the family names King and Terrell but also Rollins. King married Mary Ann Rawlings in 1836. Her family name was later changed to Rollins, which explains the difference.

Archer investigating the King's Chapel Loop.

The cemetery, however, has seen better days. Over the years, nature has reclaimed some of the graves, tombstones were removed or stolen, or they just broke down over the decades. Descendants of these families and the state park are attempting to re-mark all of the graves.

The nineteenth-century King and Terrell families wouldn't recognize the area today. First of all, the lake itself wasn't created until 1939, when the Tennessee Valley Authority dammed the Tennessee River to provide power to the region. And then there is the state park itself, with its campground, golf course, and the beautiful lodge situated on top of a hillside overlooking the lake.

For this loop we will be using three trails: the King's Chapel Loop, Terrell Trail, and the Terrell Trail Connector. The hike begins by crossing the Aubrey Carr Scenic Drive to the south. On the other side you will see the sign indicating the beginning of the red-blazed King's Chapel Loop.

The trail is a nice 2- to 3-foot wide dirt and rock footpath that is lined with colorful wildflowers like red cardinal and spiderwort. The entire hike travels under a thick canopy provided by the hardwood forest, a welcome relief from the heat if you are hiking the loop in the summer months. Your dog will love exploring the smells and unearthing surprises in the understory, like the small lizards darting in and out of the rocks and the whitetail deer grazing nearby.

In 0.7 mile, you will arrive at the cemetery, which is located at the intersection of the King's Chapel Loop and Terrell Trail. Quietly pay your respects and take in some of the inscriptions. When you're ready, return to the main trail and start back on the yellow-blazed Terrell Trail.

As you walk the trail, you will notice a lot of branches and blowdowns off to the side. These are remnants of the devastating tornadoes of 2011 and 2013, which made some of the hills in the park look like they had been clear-cut. But nature is resilient, as you will see from the new growth of beautiful foliage that has emerged.

You will cross Aubrey Carr Scenic Drive one more time as you near the end and pick up the white-blazed Terrell Trail Connector that will take you back to the trailhead.

As I mentioned in the hike specs section above, you will pass an entrance gate on the way into the park. As long as I have been going to Lake Guntersville, the station has not been open to pay a day-use fee, but that doesn't mean it never will be open. If so, pay your fee and continue on to the parking area, where you will note a metal tube on the backside of the lot. This is a donation box and the park asks that you donate $3 per car to help local hiking clubs maintain the trails. That's not too much to ask to help keep these great trails in shape.

CREATURE COMFORTS

RESTING UP

Lakeside Inn, 14040 US 431, Guntersville; (256) 582-3200; lakesideinn431.com/

Two pets of any size are allowed. There is a $10 per pet, per night fee charged. Phone the hotel to reserve a pet-friendly room.

Lake Guntersville State Park, 1155 Lodge Dr., Guntersville; (256) 571-5455; www .alapark.com/dog-friendly

The state park has a limited number of lodging options for you and your pup. There are two lakeside cabins, three chalets, and two lodge rooms. An additional $16.50 per pet, per night fee is charged. Make your reservations by phone and be sure to ask if any of these pet-friendly accommodations are available.

CAMPING:

Lake Guntersville State Park, 1155 Lodge Dr., Guntersville; (256) 571-5455; www .alapark.com/lake-guntersville-state-park

Lake Guntersville not only has great hiking but also wonderful campgrounds: sixty-five improved sites ($26 per night) and one hundred primitive sites ($14 per night) are available. A one-time $4.50 transaction fee is also charged. Make reservations by phone or online at guestrez.megahotel.com/Hotel/Reservation/Index/P3R24.

Town Creek Fishing Center, 11868 AL 227, Guntersville; (256) 582-8358; www.ala park.com/lake-guntersville-state-park-town-creek-fishing-center

Additional primitive sites are located at Town Creek Fishing Center, which is located right on the banks of Town Creek, the beautiful, wide feeder of Lake Guntersville and only 6 miles east of the state park. Sites are $14 per night with a one-time $4.50 transaction fee. The fishing center does not make reservations. All sites are available on a first come, first served basis.

FUELING UP

Aqua Restaurant, 2140 Gunter Ave., Guntersville; (256) 264-0141; www.aquarestaurant al.com/

Aqua has three pet-friendly outdoor seats waiting for you and your well-behaved pup. The menu has mouthwatering sandwiches, like Philly cheesesteaks and shrimp po' boys, as well as pasta dishes and seafood like the pan-seared wild salmon and seared ahi tuna.

MILES AND DIRECTIONS

0.0   Start on the north side of Aubrey Carr Scenic Drive at the trailhead parking lot. This is a large gravel lot with room for 10-plus cars. From the parking lot, cross the road to the south and pick up the red-blazed trail on the opposite side. A sign reading KING'S CHAPEL let's you know you're in the right place. Cross the runoff ditch over a short foot bridge, then hit the narrow 2-foot-wide dirt trail.

0.4   Pass a short rock outcropping on the right.

0.7   Arrive at the King's Chapel Cemetery. Feel free to explore the cemetery and pay your respects. When done, walk back to the trail and turn right (south).

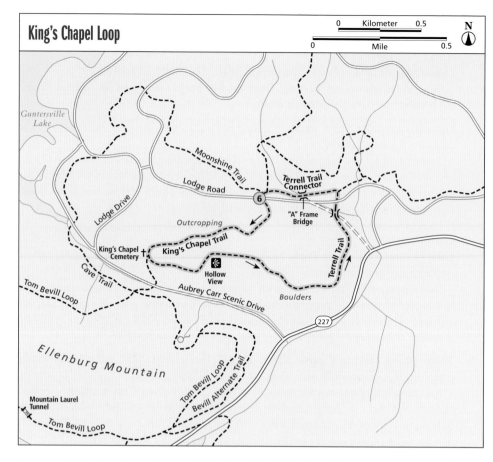

A sign here shows the way to the Terrell Trail (right) and the King's Chapel Loop back the way you came. Turn right (south) onto the yellow-blazed Terrell Trail. The canopy, which begins to thin a little through here, is very pretty in the fall. Numerous blowdowns have been cut and stacked on the sides of the trail, evidence of the big EF3 tornado of 2011.

1.1   View of the hollow to the right (southeast).

1.5   Pass a small boulder field and rock outcropping on the left.

1.9   Cross a 35-foot-long foot bridge over a runoff. You'll hear the road as you get closer.

       In less than 0.1 mile, cross a 30-foot-long foot bridge over a runoff ditch next to Aubrey Carr Scenic Drive.

2.0   Cross Aubrey Carr Scenic Drive to the north and pick up the Terrell Trail on the other side (still yellow blazed). In less than 0.1 mile, come to an intersection. A sign here points the way to Taylor Mountain (to the right) and Terrell Trail Connector to the left. There is also a trail map available here in a kiosk. Turn left onto the white-blazed Terrell Trail Connector. This trail is also used by mountain bikes, so keep your eyes open.

2.2   Cross a 30-foot-long wooden A-frame-type bridge.

2.3   Arrive back at the parking lot.

7 FALLS LOOP TRAIL

Not one, not two, but three waterfalls are found along the Falls Loop Trail at DeSoto State Park. You'll visit the beautiful Lost Falls, Laurel Falls, and Azalea Cascade as they tumble down their rocky ledges. Fido will love playing in several creeks you will cross. In the spring at the aptly named Azalea Cascade, you'll find yourself walking through tunnels of beautiful azalea, rhododendron, and mountain laurel.

THE RUNDOWN

Start: From the Lost Falls Trailhead on CR 618 (DeSoto Parkway)
Distance: 3.1-mile lollipop loop
Approximate hiking time: 2 hours
Difficulty: Moderate over the rocky terrain with scrambles to get a better look at the falls
Trailhead elevation: 1,740 feet
Highest point: 1,740 feet
Best season: Year-round, but falls are seasonal and may not be running in the summer; open sunrise to sunset
Trail surface: Dirt and rock
Other trail users: None
Canine compatibility: Leash required
Land status: Alabama state park
Fees and permits: None
Trail contact: DeSoto State Park, 7104 DeSoto Pkwy. NE, Fort Payne; (256) 845-5380; www.alapark.com/desoto-state-park

Nearest town: Fort Payne
Trail tips: This one is for the camera, so don't forget to bring it along to catch amazing snaps of the three waterfalls. Remember, falls are seasonal, so they may be dry or just a trickle in the summer. There is a nice, clean restroom at the trailhead. The parking area is big enough for about 20 cars, and there is a clean restroom. Even though there isn't an entrance gate and you can drive right to the trailhead without paying, please stop at the park office and pay the day-use fee. It helps keep the park and the trails in top shape.
Maps: USGS: Jamestown, AL
Other maps: Available at the park office for $1 (proceeds go to the Nature Center Fund) or online at www.alapark.com/hiking

FINDING THE TRAILHEAD

From Fort Payne on I-59, take exit 218 east on Glenn Boulevard SW / Pine Ridge Road SW 1.0 miles and turn left onto Gault Avenue S. Travel 1.1 miles and turn right onto 5th Street. Travel 0.4 mile and turn left onto Wallace Avenue NE. Follow Wallace Avenue NE 2.0 miles and turn left onto CR 89 / DeSoto Parkway NE. Travel 5.7 miles and turn left onto DeSoto Parkway. In 1.2 miles the clearly marked parking area is on the right. The trailhead is across the road to the south. Trailhead GPS N34 30.069' / W85 38.057

THE HIKE

What makes DeSoto State Park so special is the number of water features packed into this compact park. Within its boundaries you will find the frothing-white turquoise water of the West Fork of Little River as it races over its boulder-strewn channel. You can visit the river along the park's DeSoto Scout Trail.

Then there are the waterfalls: not just one but five within the park itself, including Indian and Lodge Falls, slender ribbons cascading down the rocks into the river that can be viewed from the Cabin and DeSoto Scout Trails.

A curtain of water flows over the rocky face of Laurel Falls.

This hike, which I call the Falls Loop, takes you on a 3.1-mile journey to the other three falls: Lost and Laurel Falls and Azalea Cascade. But it's not only the waterfalls that make this hike special; there are fascinating rock outcroppings, small rock shelters, and in the spring you will be rewarded with brilliant wildflowers lining the path. On the aptly named Azalea Cascade Trail, you will be walking through tunnels of fragrant blooming mountain laurel, azaleas, and rhododendron in the spring.

Three separate trails interconnect to create the circuit: the orange-blazed Lost Falls Trail, the blue-blazed Laurel Falls Trail, and the red Azalea Cascade Trail. The trails are well marked, with the paint blazes easily found at just the right locations on trees and rocks; you would have a hard time getting lost. The loop is a moderate trek due to its rocky footing that involves some climbing on the Azalea Cascade and Laurel Falls Trails.

You and your pup will find that there are short side trails that access the bottom of the falls and the streams, but remember, the paths are slippery on the rocks and there are some steep bluffs, so you need to exercise caution and common sense when venturing down. Your dog will also love the creek crossings along the route.

We begin our trek at the large gravel parking lot just off of DeSoto Parkway. This is a major hub for bike and hiking trails in the park. Two bike trails converge here: the Family Bike Trail and Never-Never Land Loop, as well as the Campground (hiking) Trail and Laurel Falls Trail, which is where we will begin our hike to the waterfalls.

The parking lot is big enough for twenty-plus cars. The park has also installed a very nice and clean restroom here.

Start this hike by picking up the orange-blazed Laurel Falls Trail on the south side of the parking lot. The trail, which has been named a National Recreational Trail, is a nice dirt and rock footpath through stands of pines and hardwoods. The first waterfall, Lost Falls, is only about 0.5 mile from the trailhead, so if you don't want to make the entire loop or if you have a young pup with you or small children who can't make the full 3.1 miles, you can still visit one of the falls by doing a simple 1.0-mile out-and-back (see Miles and Directions for details.)

Lost Falls is an impressive 50-foot (or so) cascade tumbling down two tiers of rock. At 0.5 mile into the hike, you will see a small carved rock on the ground with the inscription Lost Falls. A side trail takes you down to the falls. Once you have finished visiting the falls, you can either retrace your steps to where you were or you can turn right (east) and continue following the side trail, which will link back with the main trail in about 50 feet.

Following the waterfall, the trail meanders just behind the campground before it begins to get a bit rockier, and you find yourself hiking through some stone cuts before intersecting with the red-blazed Azalea Cascade Trail. The trail leads you directly to the stream and the cascade.

After passing the cascade, you will pick up the Laurel Falls Trail. There is a rugged little climb up to a bluff with several small rock shelters carved into it. Eventually you will arrive at Laurel Falls. Be on the lookout for another short side trail on your right that will take you to the falls and stream.

Before returning to the trailhead you will have one more chance to see Lost Falls, this time from the opposite side of the stream.

CREATURE COMFORTS

RESTING UP
Econo Lodge, 1412 Glenn Blvd. SW, Fort Payne; (256) 845-4013; www.choicehotels .com/alabama/fort-payne/hotels

Make your reservations online. There is a two-pet maximum allowed per room, with an additional pet fee of $10 per pet, per night. Be sure to ask about the availability of pet rooms when making your reservation.

CAMPING
DeSoto State Park, 7104 DeSoto Pkwy. NE, Fort Payne; 1-800-760-4089; www.ala park.com/improved-campsites

The park has ninety-four beautiful and secluded improved campsites with electricity and water, and twenty-one primitive sites all tucked away among the trees. Improved sites are $36 per night, primitive $15 per night. There is also a $4.50 convenience fee plus tax. A deposit of one night's rent plus the convenience fee and tax is required. Primitive campsites are available on a first come, first served basis; improved sites may be reserved online, and a two-night minimum stay is required.

FUELING UP
Sonic Drive-In, 511 Gault Ave. S, Fort Payne; (256) 845-4578; locations.sonicdrivein .com/al/fort-payne/511-gault-avenue-southeast.html

You know it, you love it. Sonic is a good old-fashioned drive-in diner with everything you would expect: hamburgers, hot dogs, shakes, the works—and many times carhops on roller skates even bring your order to your car. You and Fido can eat in the car or at the outside tables. "Burn one, take it through the garden, and pin a rose on it." (That's old-time drive-in slang for a hamburger with lettuce and tomato.)

MILES AND DIRECTIONS

0.0 Start from the parking lot on CR 618. Cross the road to the south and you will see the Lost Falls trailhead clearly marked. As you enter the woods, there is a sign that points to the Never-Never Land Bike Trail to the right (west) and the Laurel Falls Trail to the south; follow the orange blazes of the Laurel Falls Trail. The path throughout is a combination of dirt and rock bed. It is wide here, about 4 feet, with plenty of pine trees.

0.1 Cross a wide stream. The canopy opens with some grassy edging along the sides of the trail.

0.4 The trail is a large flat rock bed. Come to a Y intersection. The right fork (south) is the blue-blazed Lost Falls Trail, which will be used for the return trip. Take the left fork (southeast) and continue on the orange-blazed Laurel Falls Trail.

0.5 Come to a Y. A small carved sign on the ground marks the short trail that leads to Lost Falls. The Laurel Falls Trail splits here to the left (east) and right (south.) Take a right and hike down to Lost Falls. Be careful on the bluffs around the falls—they are slippery and can be dangerous! When done, turn around and head back to the Y, then turn right (east) to continue on the main orange-blazed trail.

Cross a wide stream. There's a nice cascade here.

0.9 The orange-/silver-blazed Campground Trail comes in from the left (north.) Continue straight, following the orange blazes. The trail bed starts turning rocky.

1.2 Another carved stone on the ground marks the short side trail to Laurel Falls. Turn right here onto the unmarked trail to visit the falls in less than 50 feet. Again, be careful on the slippery rocks. When done, turn around and head back to the Laurel Falls Trail. Turn right (northeast) and continue on the orange-blazed trail.

The Campground Trail comes in from the left (north.) Continue following the orange blazes to the right (east.)

1.5 Pass rock outcroppings on the right. Follow the trail around them past the campground on the left. Walking behind the campground, the trail climbs through cuts in outcroppings. In less than 0.1 mile come to a Y. The orange trail heads to the left, the red-blazed Azalea Cascade Trail heads to the south. Turn right onto the Azalea Cascade Trail.

1.6 Come to a T intersection. The trail heads left and right (east and west, respectively). Turn right and continue following the red blazes. This area is thick with azalea and rhododendron. In less than 0.1 mile, arrive at Azalea Cascade. Cross the stream and falls over a bridge. Come to a T intersection on the other side. The Lost Falls Trail heads left and right. Turn right (south) onto the blue-blazed trail. The trail heads uphill past rock outcroppings and rock shelters on the left (east). The path is a rock bed at this point.

1.8 The outcroppings end. The trail levels out and is a dirt footpath again.

Falls Loop Trail

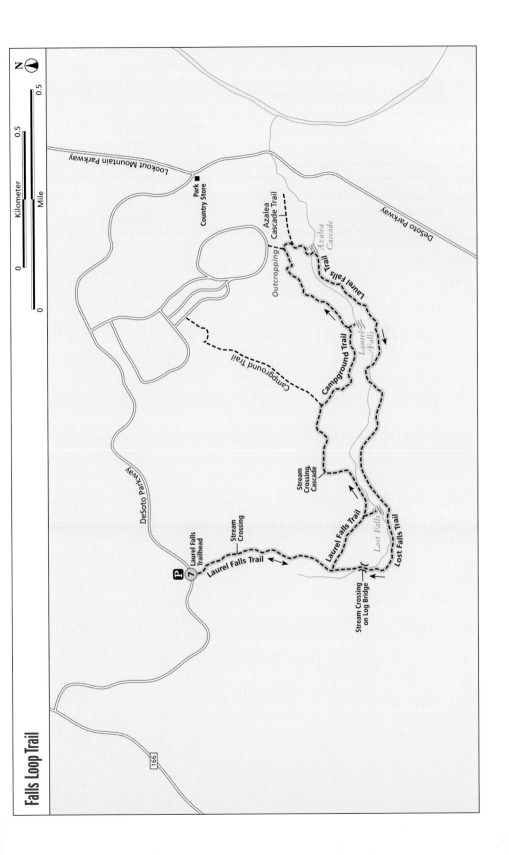

N

Kilometer
0   0.5   0.5

0   0.5
Mile

Lookout Mountain Parkway

Park
Country Store

Azalea
Cascade Trail

Outcropping

Azalea
Cascade

Laurel Falls
Trail

Laurel
Falls

Campground Trail

Campground Trail

DeSoto Parkway

DeSoto Parkway

Stream
Crossing,
Cascade

Laurel Falls Trail

Lost Falls

Lost Falls Trail

Stream Crossing
on Log Bridge

P

7

Laurel Falls
Trailhead

Stream Crossing

Laurel Falls Trail

166

2.4 A short 30-foot side trail to the right (north) leads to the opposite side of Lost Falls. Continue to the south following the blue blazes.

2.6 The trail walks alongside the stream that forms the falls on the right. Cross the stream on a unique log bridge.

2.7 The trail follows a long, wide flat rock. In a few yards the trail intersects the orange-blazed Lost Falls Trail. Turn left (north) and retrace your steps to the trailhead.

3.1 Arrive back at the trailhead.

PUPPY PAWS AND GOLDEN YEARS

A lot of people think dog booties are silly, but actually they can be very beneficial to Fido when hiking for a number of reasons. Even though you think your dog's pads are tough, they can still be injured on sharp rocks or gravel paths, and booties help prevent this. In the cold of winter, they help keep their paws warm and prevent snow and ice from packing between their toes and pads. And if you do any beach hiking, it helps protect their paws from getting burned on the hot sand.

8 HURRICANE CREEK PARK

You and your dog are guaranteed a good time along the trails at Hurricane Creek Park just north of Cullman. The trail begins atop a ridge and winds its way down to the park's namesake creek, passing beneath tall rock bluffs, rock shelters that invite exploring, and waterfalls you can walk behind. If that's not enough, at the bottom, between the two ridges, there is the perfect swimming hole and a walk along the Creek Trail with tumbling shoals and more water fun for the pup.

THE RUNDOWN

Start: From the patio at the old building to the east
Distance: 2.2-mile double loop with extension
Approximate hiking time: 2 hours, but leave time to linger at the falls and creeks
Difficulty: Hurricane Trail is difficult, Creek Trail is easy, and the North Highland Trail is moderate
Trailhead elevation: 870 feet
Highest point: 870 feet
Best season: Year-round; open sunrise to sunset
Trail surface: Packed dirt studded with rocks and roots; some natural stone stairs
Other trail users: None
Canine compatibility: Leash required
Land status: City preserve
Fees and permits: None
Trail contact: Hurricane Creek Park, 22550 2nd Ave. NW, Falkville; (256) 735-9157; cullmanrecreation.org/facilities-parks/hurricane-creek-park/
Nearest town: Cullman
Trail tips: Seems like I've said this for every hike, but bring the camera for spectacular waterfalls and geology. The trail described here starts by using the Hurricane Trail, a very steep and difficult climb down if you and your dog are not experienced or in shape; see the hike description for an alternate route. You'll want to spend some time at the picnic area, where there are picnic tables, garbage cans, and a great swimming hole. Gnats and mosquitoes could be a bother around the wet cliffs and boggy areas, so bring the insect repellent.
Maps: USGS: Falkville, AL
Other: Online at cullmanrecreation.org/facilties-parks/hurricane-creek-park/

FINDING THE TRAILHEAD

From the intersection of I-65 at exit 308 and US 278 / 4th Street SW in Cullman, head east on US 278 / 4th Street SW for 1.4 miles. Stay to the left at the fork onto Main Avenue SW. Travel 0.6 mile and turn left onto US 31 N / 2nd Avenue NW. Travel 7.9 miles; the parking lot will be on the right. You will see a building to the southeast. Walk to the building and around its right side, crossing a patio. This is the trailhead. Trailhead GPS: N34 17.206' / W86 53.698'

THE HIKE

Located just north of Cullman in the little town of Falkville, there is a wonderland of geology and waterfalls that makes for an amazing day hike, Hurricane Creek Park.

The hike described here uses four trails—the Hurricane, South Ridge Trail, North Highland Ridge Trail, and Creek Trails—to form this 2.2-mile double loop with extension, the extension being the Creek Trail, which juts out like a tail from the main double loop.

The trail arrives at Twilight Tunnel, which may be too frightening for your dog. The Bypass Trail takes you around the tunnel.

The Hurricane Trail is rated as difficult, a 500-foot drop into the gorge, and could be very hard for your dog—and you—to navigate, depending on both your experience and conditioning. I'll cover that more fully in just a moment.

Overall, this is a beautiful hike over extremely rocky dirt paths. The geology is remarkable. You'll hike below tall sandstone bluffs, weathered away over the centuries by nature. Several seasonal creeks cascade down these rock walls, many of which have carved out the bluff and formed deep rock shelters where you can walk behind the waterfalls. One of the most impressive falls is on the return trip, where you cross all three tiers of the cascade over wooden bridges.

That geology also holds a couple of surprises, like the Twilight Tunnel. This is a long—and very dark—tunnel or cave through a rock jumble. While the tunnel looks fun for you, it might not be for your pup, who can be frightened by the darkness and the echo. No worries. There is a Bypass Trail that takes you around the tunnel to the other side.

There is also the Bottleneck, a very narrow cut in a boulder you could shimmy through, but a sign there tells you to go around it. Heed that sign.

Then there is the centerpiece of the park, Hurricane Creek itself. A wide, rushing creek, its waters tumble over a rocky bed. The creek feeds into the park's picnic area, where an old dam has created a wonderful swimming hole both of you will love. Get there early in the morning, though. This is a local favorite.

Finally, from the picnic area we'll take a short walk along the Creek Trail that parallels Hurricane Creek. There are several places your dog can jump in and splash around. From spring through summer, the trail is lined with wildflowers like dwarf iris, buttonbush, and red cardinal, which brighten the path as it meanders through a forest with oakleaf hydrangea and tulip poplars.

The hike begins at the old park entrance. Walk around to the right side of the building and cross the patio. This will be the intersection of the North Highland Ridge Trail, which will be our return leg, and the Hurricane Trail. The hike described here begins by taking a right onto the Hurricane Trail, but be warned, the path is rated as difficult by the Cullman City Parks and Recreation, and they aren't kidding. It's a very steep and rocky downhill climb to the creek. Use your best judgment, and keep your dog's safety and conditioning in mind before attempting this part of the double loop.

An option would be to avoid the Hurricane Trail altogether and instead start by going straight on the North Highland Ridge Trail to the picnic area described at mile 1.1. This trail is rated as moderate and uses a series of switchbacks to help you down, making the walk much easier. Once at the picnic area you can continue as described in Miles and Directions (below).

If you decide to try the Hurricane Trail to the creek, you will pass an interesting artifact from the area's past: an abandoned cable car that was installed by the park's former owner, Buddy Rogers, back in 1961 to haul visitors to the bottom and the fun of Hurricane Creek. The park was donated to the state in 2003 when Buddy turned eighty-one, and it is now managed by the City of Cullman.

CREATURE COMFORTS

RESTING UP
Best Western Fairwinds Inn, 1917 Commerce Ave., Cullman; (256) 737-5009; www .bestwestern.com

The Best Western in Cullman allows two dogs per room with a maximum weight of 80 pounds total. A $20 total per night pet fee is charged. While you can make your reservations online, Best Western recommends you call the hotel directly to confirm there are available pet-friendly rooms and verify any restrictions.

FUELING UP
Sweet Pepper's Deli, 303 2nd Ave. NW #A, Cullman; (256) 736-2600

With pet-friendly outdoor seating, Sweet Pepper's features an amazing selection of mouthwatering sandwiches, flatbreads, soups, and salads. Try the Sweet Pepper Sub that's loaded to the rafters with your choice of turkey, hickory smoked ham, roast beef, or salami. Or something you rarely see in Alabama, an incredible Waldorf salad with baby greens, seedless grapes, candied pecans, celery, and a few twists—Gorgonzola cheese, oven-roasted chicken breast, and a balsamic vinaigrette. The owners remind you that your pup can't come inside the deli, so they will have to be tied up outside or wait in the car while you order.

MILES AND DIRECTIONS

0.0 Start just behind the building in the parking lot on the right side of the patio. Walk across the wooden patio. In less than 0.1 mile, the trail forks. Straight ahead to the northeast is the return trail. A sign reads To TWILIGHT TUNNEL and points to the right. Turn right (east) onto the Hurricane Trail. *FYI:* This is a very difficult trail with a steep, rock-strewn climb down to Hurricane Creek. Please read the text for details about what to expect and an option to avoid this section. In less than 0.1 mile, pass an abandoned cable-car rail on the right. The steep switchback continues, heading downhill. There is a good canopy here and some small wildflowers.

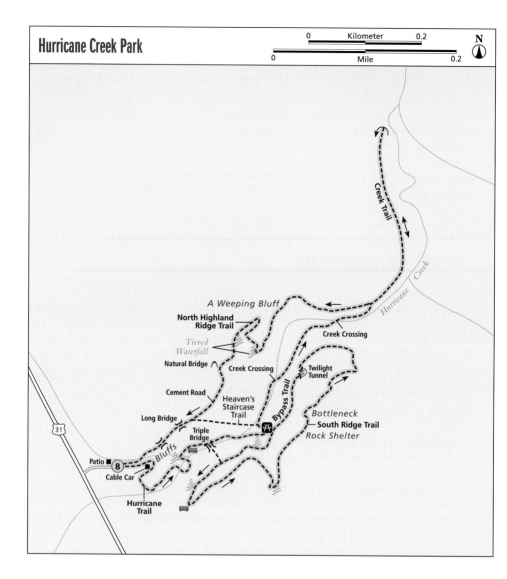

0   Kilometer   0.2

0   Mile   0.2

0.2   You will hear and see Hurricane Creek below on your right. To your left, impressive rock bluffs begin, and soon you will be walking through a rock shelter behind a 2-tier waterfall. In less than 0.1 mile, pass a bench next to the bluff on the left. You'll have a good view of the creek on the right. In less than 0.1 mile, a trail splits off to right with a sign reading To TWILIGHT TUNNEL / SOUTH RIDGE TRAIL. Turn right (southeast) here.

0.3   Cross the creek on a triple wooden bridge over the rushing waters of Hurricane Creek. On the other side there is a bench and a T intersection with the South Ridge Trail. Turn right (southeast) onto the South Ridge Trail, which heads uphill next to more bluffs. In less than 0.1 mile, pass a bench on the right. The bluffs drip, making the trails wet. In less than 0.1 mile, pass another waterfall on the right, crossing its runoff over a short 20-foot bridge. There is a bench here as well and, after crossing, a sign that reads SIDE TRAIL TO TWILIGHT TUNNEL. Keep heading to the northeast.

0.4 Arrive at the Twilight Tunnel. A sign here reminds you to stop for a moment when you go in to allow your eyes to adjust. Most dogs don't want to venture in. To be safe, take the Bypass Trail to the left (a sign leads the way).

0.5 The Twilight Tunnel rejoins the Bypass Trail. The signs here can be confusing, with several arrows pointing in different directions and a couple showing the way to the picnic area. Keep walking to your right along the base of the bluff and head uphill to the south. You will see a sign for the Hidden Valley. Make the steep climb up to the top of the ridge.

0.6 Arrive at the Bottleneck.

0.7 Pass a deep rock shelter on the left. In less than 0.1 mile, you have another chance to walk behind a waterfall as the trail follows the U shape of the bluff canyon.

0.9 Pass a bench on the left; a series of railings begin here. These are steel cables running through PVC pipe. The cables are supported by T-posts and attached to nearby trees. There are some very sharp drop-offs along this section—use caution. In less than 0.1 mile, pass another multitiered waterfall. A yellow sign with an arrow points to the right (northeast). Another set of switchbacks begin as you head down a set of stairs made of 6x6 railroad ties. There are more cable railings here with sharp drop-offs on the side of the narrow trail, which is just over a foot wide.

1.0 Return to the intersection at mile 0.3. Cross the creek to the northwest. On the other side of the creek, turn right (northeast).

1.1 Arrive at the picnic area with the beautiful low cascading falls of a dam and a deep, cold swimming hole. From here take a right (northwest) onto the High Trail. A sign reads LONG WAY BACK. The trail is 4 to 5 feet wide here as it rambles next to the creek. In less than 0.1 mile, cross the creek on a bridge, and on the other side turn left (northeast) onto the Creek Trail. There are nice shoals in the creek with a few access points for your pup. The trail is very level.

1.2 Come to a bridge and a good water access point for your pup to splash around a bit. Cross the creek on the bridge to the northeast. On the other side, turn right (northeast) and continue along the creek. In the spring and summer, the path is lined with brightly colored wildflowers.

1.5 Pass another bridge on the right. This is the turnaround for the Creek Trail. Retrace your steps back to the bridge at mile 1.2.

1.8 Back at the same bridge from mile 1.2, turn right to the north and you will see the sign that reads HIGH TRAIL LONG WAY BACK TO PARK. Continue north. Shortly the trail swings to the left (northwest).

1.9 Pass another weeping bluff on right. In less than 0.1 mile, pass a waterfall on the right. From here there is another set of sharp switchbacks uphill with another handrail. At the end of the first switchback cross a long bridge over a tier of the waterfall.

2.0 Come to the end of the switchbacks and walk past the top of the waterfall. In less than 0.1 mile, at the top of the ridge, the trail turns sandy with some rocks but levels out. Arrive at a sandstone natural bridge on right.

2.1 Pass a sign that reads HIGH TRAIL BACK TO PARK ENTRANCE. In less than 0.1 mile, come to the upper end of a cement road. Turn right onto the road, following it only about 100 feet before the trail veers off the road to the left (southwest). Stay on the trail. In less than 0.1 mile, cross a narrow 60-foot-long bridge over a drop-off.

2.2 Pass a side trail on the left that goes straight down to the picnic area. In less than 0.1 mile, cross a 150-foot bridge over a fast-moving stream. In less than 0.1 mile, arrive back at the trailhead.

9 FALL CREEK FALLS

Once again, the Sipsey Wilderness does not disappoint on this amazing 5.6-mile out-and-back that will lead you through a short cave (don't worry, it's optional) and past remarkable rock bluffs and shelters, and a 90-foot ribbon waterfall. For your dog—and you— here's a chance to romp in the beautiful, clear, cool waters of the Sipsey and Borden Creek.

THE RUNDOWN

Start: At the Trail 200 (Borden Creek Trail) trailhead
Distance: 5.6-mile out-and-back
Approximate hiking time: 3.5 hours, but leave time to enjoy the falls and the creek crossing
Difficulty: Easy along Trail 200; more moderate with hilly, rocky climbs on Trail 209
Trailhead elevation: 612 feet
Highest point: 713 feet
Best season: Year-round; open sunrise to sunset
Trail surface: Dirt with rocks and roots; stretches of sandy path near the creeks
Other trail users: None
Canine compatibility: Leash required
Land status: National wilderness area
Fees and permits: None
Trail contact: Bankhead National Forest, Bankhead Ranger District, 1070 AL 33, Double Springs; (205) 489-5111; www.fs.usda.gov/ detail/alabama/about-forest/ districts/?cid=fsbdev3_002553
Nearest town: Moulton
Trail tips: Bring the camera! The bluffs, rock shelters, 2 crystal-clear creeks, and Fall Creek Falls are simply beautiful. The National Forest Service asks that you keep your pet on leash, but you will undoubtedly want to let them frolic in the confluence of the 2 creeks. Use your best judgment, and don't let them annoy others. The creek bottoms are sandy or light gravel. The trail gets narrow at times on the Trail 209 (Sipsey Trail) section with drop-offs to the river, so use caution with Fido.
Maps: USGS: Bee Branch, AL
Other maps: Available at the Warrior Mountain Trading Post, 11312 AL 33, Moulton, or online at https:// www.fs.usda.gov/Internet/FSE_ DOCUMENTS/fseprd493196.pdf

FINDING THE TRAILHEAD

From the intersection of AL 33 / S. Market Street and AL 24 in Moulton, take AL 33 south 13.9 miles. Turn right onto Cranal Road and travel 0.7 mile. Turn right onto CR 5 / Bunyon Hill Road. Travel 2.7 miles; the trailhead and parking will be on the left. Trailhead GPS: N34 18.567' / W87 23.658'

THE HIKE

I don't know of any time when I have visited the Sipsey Wilderness that I left disappointed. The geology, wildflowers, and water features are unbelievable.

The wilderness is known as the "Land of a Thousand Waterfalls" and for good reason. It seems that around every bend there is a cascade flowing down the sandstone canyon walls. Now keep in mind that most of these waterfalls, like many throughout the state, are seasonal and, depending on the weather, may or may not be there, but after some rain, they are beautiful.

One of the more famous waterfalls in the Sipsey is Fall Creek Falls, our destination for this hike. We'll be using two trails to get there: Trail 200 (aka the Borden Creek Trail) and Trail 209 (aka the Sipsey Trail).

Trail 200 is a plain and simple fun trail. The rock outcroppings, towering bluffs, and deep shelters are spectacular and invite exploring, which you and your dog will love.

About 0.5 mile into the hike comes a little surprise: a short walk through a cave called Fat Man's Squeeze. It's an L-shaped walk through a tunnel, nothing too difficult and long, but it can be a bit slippery when the small ribbon falls at one end are flowing.

The Squeeze adds a little excitement to the hike. If you have kids, they'll love it—your dog, maybe not so much. Even though the tunnel is short, it does get dark inside, and there's a bit of an echo that could frighten them. The option would be to carefully hike down off the trail to Borden Creek and wade through the creek to the opposite side of the tunnel—as if your dog would be upset with that! But, having said that, keep in mind that the creeks and rivers in the Sipsey are prone to flash flooding. If the creek is up and flowing, do not attempt to wade across!

Trail 200 meets up with Trail 209 at mile 2.2 and the confluence of the Sipsey River and Borden Creek. Time to get wet! Turn to the right (northwest) and cross Borden Creek. While the forest service asks that dogs are kept on leash, many people let their well-behaved pups frolic free. Use your best judgment and, please, don't be a nuisance to others.

Trail 209 is dotted with beautiful white and pink mountain laurel during the spring and summer months, with good views of the shoals in the Sipsey as the trail rambles high above the creek.

Neither trail is blazed. They have signs marking only where they start and at intersections, but they are pretty easy to follow since they have regular traffic. The paths have dirt and rock footing with some fine sand along the creeks.

If you would like to see the falls but don't want to hike the 5.6-mile trail described here or go through Fat Man's Squeeze, you have a shorter option. Instead of starting at the Trail 200 trailhead, do not turn down Bunyon Hill Road. Instead, continue down Cranal Road an additional 3.3 miles and park at the Sipsey Wilderness Recreation Area. There is a $3 per car day-use fee charged to park here. It is a large lot with room for at least thirty cars. There is also a restroom here and a great place where you can picnic and swim in the river.

From the rec area, head to the north and pick up Trail 209 and Trail 200 under the bridge. Follow the two trails about 0.5 mile to where they separate (the junction is well marked). At this point pick up at mile 2.2 in the Miles and Directions (below), turning left to cross the creek instead of right. Just remember that on the return trip after crossing Borden Creek again, do not turn left onto Trail 200. Instead turn right (south) to continue on Trail 209 back to your vehicle.

You will notice several areas along the trail where people have spent the night. You are welcome to pack in and pitch camp for an overnight along the trails of the Sipsey Wilderness, but there are rules and regulations in place to keep the wilderness as pristine as possible. Please call or visit the website provided in Trail Contact (above) for rules and regulations.

CREATURE COMFORTS

RESTING UP

Best Western River City Hotel, 1305 Front Ave. SW, Decatur; (256) 301-1388; www .bestwestern.com

The Best Western in Decatur is about 20 miles north of the Sipsey Wilderness and allows two dogs weighing up to 80 pounds total. There is a $20 per day pet fee. A $50 refundable damage deposit may be required at check-in. If you leave your dog in the room while you're gone, they must be crated.

CAMPING

Corinth Recreation Area, 2540 CR 57, Double Springs; (205) 489-3165; www .recreation.gov/camping/corinth-recreation-area/r/campgroundDetails.do?contract Code=NRSO&parkId=70833

Corinth is one of the more popular campgrounds in the Bankhead National Forest area, and for good reason. Located on the banks of Lake Lewis Smith, the campground is exceptional with nice, clean bathhouses, ice machines, swimming, and fifty-two improved campsites. The campground is open from the first weekend of March to the end of October. Make your reservations online. Fees range from $17 per night to $28 per night for a lakeside site.

FUELING UP

Moe's Original BBQ, 202 Moulton St. E #C, Decatur; (256) 686-4112; www .moesoriginalbbq.com/lo/decatur/#decatur-menu-section

What's not to love at Moe's? Delicious pulled pork, smoked turkey and chicken sandwiches, and platters with either sweet-and-tangy traditional or Moe's famous Alabama white BBQ sauce, not to mention their nachos and wings. Moe's has eight outside dog-friendly tables where you and Fido can enjoy a meal together.

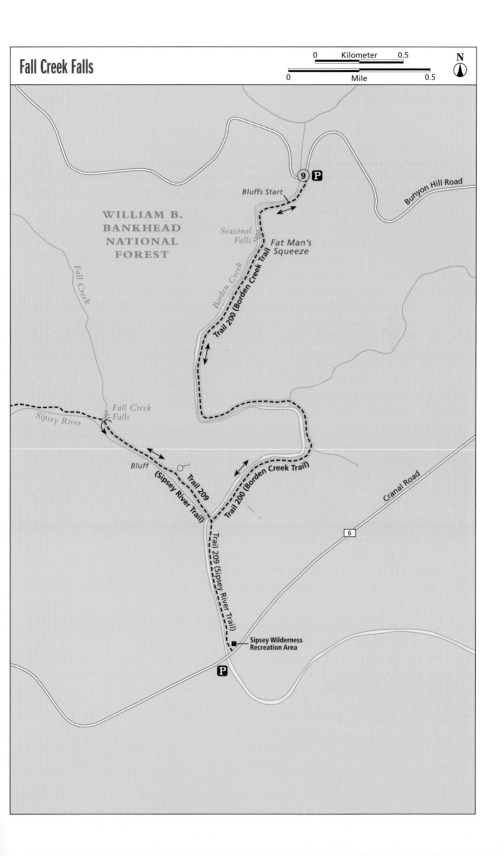

Fall Creek Falls

0   Kilometer   0.5

0   Mile   0.5

N

Bunyon Hill Road

Bluffs Start

9   P

Seasonal Falls

Fat Man's Squeeze

WILLIAM B. BANKHEAD NATIONAL FOREST

Fall Creek

Borden Creek

Trail 200 (Borden Creek Trail)

Fall Creek Falls

Sipsey River

Bluff

Trail 209 (Sipsey River Trail)

Trail 200 (Borden Creek Trail)

Cranal Road

6

Trail 209 (Sipsey River Trail)

Sipsey Wilderness Recreation Area

P

MILES AND DIRECTIONS

0.0 Start from the Trail 200 (Borden Creek Trail) trailhead to the south on Bunyon Hill Road.

0.2 Pass a side trail to a campsite with the creek on your right and a big rock bluff to the left.

0.5 Pass a very big rock bluff on the left with seasonal falls.

0.6 Arrive at Fat Man's Squeeze. The cave is about 200 feet long with a slight bend to it. Walk through the cave, and on the other side there is a small waterfall. In less than 0.1 mile, pass a rock shelter on the left.

0.8 Cross a seasonal stream (there may be a small fall here during times of rain).

1.1 Pass a large bluff.

1.4 The trail moves away from the bluffs, and the forest opens up for a short distance.

1.5 The trail comes to another nice creek. Hike straight across it and pick up the trail on the other side, where you will cross an unmarked trail that heads left and right (north and south, respectively). Continue straight to the west.

1.7 Come to a Y intersection. Take the left fork. There is a campsite here and a creek. Cross the creek to the northwest and in a few yards cross a second creek.

1.8 Pass a shoal in Borden Creek. In a few yards, another nice rock bluff with shelters will be on the left.

1.9 Cross a rocky creek.

2.1 Cross a seasonal creek.

2.2 Come to the intersection of Trails 200 (Borden Creek Trail) and 209 (Sipsey River Trail). Turn right (northwest) and head downhill to the banks of the creek. At the bottom of the hill, it's time to get wet. Cross Borden Creek to the north and climb up a steep set of 6x6 railroad ties used to control erosion (but also as stairs). At the top turn left (northwest) onto Trail 209.

2.4 You will have nice views of the Sipsey River and several shoals on the left, and big weathered rock outcroppings on the right.

2.5 Cross a spring coming from the bluffs on the right.

2.7 Pass a large rock shelter on the right and shoals in the Sipsey on the left.

2.8 Arrive at Fall Creek Falls. Feel free to explore, but use caution on slippery rocks. When done retrace your steps to the trailhead.

5.6 Arrive back at the trailhead.

OPTION: As mentioned in the hike description, there is a shorter route you can take to the falls. Park at the Sipsey Wilderness Recreation Area on Cranal Road. Trail 209 starts here under the Cranal Road bridge to the north. In 0.5 mile, you will arrive at the intersection of Trails 200 and 209. Follow the directions in the Miles and Directions section above from mile 2.2 to the falls, except turn left (northwest) to cross the creek instead of right. On the return, at the intersection of the 2 trails, turn right (south) onto Trail 209 and follow it back to the parking lot. Remember, there is a $3 day-use fee to park at the Sipsey Wilderness Recreation Area.

Caney Creek Falls is the most photographed waterfall in Alabama, and when you get there you will understand why. It's a beautiful cascade tumbling over a rock shelter, and you can (carefully) walk behind the curtain. The falls are outlined in brilliant blooming mountain laurel and azalea spring through summer, and the cool, green waters of the pool invite you and Fido to take a swim.

THE RUNDOWN

Start: From the north side of the parking lot at the metal gate
Distance: 2.0-mile out-and-back
Approximate hiking time: 1 hour, but leave a lot of time for the falls!
Difficulty: Easy over an old abandoned dirt road and dirt footpath. There is a climb down and up to the falls that could be considered moderate for some.
Trailhead elevation: 889 feet
Highest point: 890 feet
Best season: Year-round; the falls rarely disappoint; open sunrise to sunset
Trail surface: Rutted gravel road, dirt footpath, rocks heading down to the falls
Other trail users: None
Canine compatibility: Leash required, but you'll want to let your dog romp in the cool, clear pool.
Land status: National forest
Fees and permits: None
Trail contact: Bankhead National Forest, Bankhead Ranger District, 1070 AL 33, Double Springs; (205) 489-5111; www.fs.usda.gov/detail/alabama/about-forest/districts/?cid=fsbdev3_002553
Nearest town: Double Springs
Trail tips: Do not forget your camera for this one! The falls and pool are simply amazing! It is asked that you keep your dog leashed to be considerate of others while hiking the trail, and it does get rather steep over slippery rocks as you near the falls. When you get to the falls, you will undoubtedly want to take a dip in the pool with your pooch. Again, just be considerate of other visitors and make sure you clean up after your dog.
Maps: USGS: Double Springs, AL
Other maps: Available online at www.fs.usda.gov/Internet/FSE_DOCUMENTS/fseprd490240.pdf
Other: Hunting is allowed in national forests. Information is available through the Trail Contact (above), or visit www.fs.usda.gov/activity/alabama/recreation/hunting for dates and restrictions.

FINDING THE TRAILHEAD

From the intersection of Court Street and AL 33 S / Market Street in Moulton, take AL 33 S / Market Street south for 21.8 miles. Turn right onto CR 2. The trailhead will be on the right in 3.7 miles. It is in a very small dirt and gravel lot, a bit rutted, with room for fewer than 10 cars. The perimeter of the lot is taped off because private property surrounds it. Be considerate and don't block any one in or disturb private property. Trailhead GPS: N34 14.113' / W87 26.041'

THE HIKE

Anyone will tell you if you want to see magnificent waterfalls in Alabama, then you need to head to the Bankhead National Forest and the Sipsey Wilderness. The Sipsey is known as the "Land of a Thousand Waterfalls," but to be honest, the Bankhead, in which

It's no wonder that Caney Creek Falls is the most photographed waterfall in Alabama especially with mountain laurel in bloom.

the Sipsey is located, is dotted with its own majestic falls. One in particular stands out. It is arguably the most photographed waterfall in the state: Caney Creek Falls.

There is good reason for that. I have visited the falls on numerous occasions and have met several families and individuals who were seeing the falls for the first time, and they all used the same word to describe it: spectacular!

The waterfall is a curtain-type falls that tumbles over a rocky ledge to an incredible, almost glowing green pool. That ledge is a good-size rock shelter that spans the grotto and gives you the chance to walk behind the curtain and along its edges, where a mist from the spray shrouds you. When the creek is really flowing, a second falls forms to the right of the main show.

The falls rarely disappoints. There is usually a good flow any time of year, and each season brings with it a new face: Spring through summer delicate mountain laurel, azalea, and dogwood bloom around the falls, framing it in color; the fall leaves replace the laurel with a fiery frame; and in winter the falls continue, but the walls around it are draped in beautiful icy sheets.

The hike itself is relatively easy, starting out on an old, rutted gravel road before narrowing to a dirt footpath and making its way down the ridge to the creek—a nice walk in the woods. There are a few red cardinal plants and spiderwort dotting the trail. Your dog will love tracking the smells and investigating the understory for whatever might turn up.

But then as you start heading down, you will hear it—the roar of the cascade. The trail saunters downhill, using a couple of switchbacks, but please stay on the trail. Cutting across and heading straight down causes erosion to the trail that volunteers will have to repair—backbreaking work.

Nearing the bottom of the narrow path, use caution on the slippery rocks. When you arrive and the cascade is really flowing, the sound is tremendous. Feel free to explore, cross the creek, and in the summer, take a dip with your dog in that wonderful clear pool.

The trail itself is not blazed, but it's hard to get lost. Parking at the trailhead is a bit of an issue. It is a very small dirt lot that can hold five or six cars comfortably, but it has deep ruts, so be careful pulling in. Some people park on the side of the road, but remember that the property next to the lot is private, so be considerate.

The path starts only a few feet from where you park on the north side of the lot. A steel pipe gate blocks the dirt road from traffic, and a sign announces that you're in the right place. Simply walk around the gate to begin your trek.

CREATURE COMFORTS

RESTING UP

Best Western River City Hotel, 1305 Front Ave. SW, Decatur; (256) 301-1388; www .bestwestern.com

The Best Western in Decatur is about 20 miles north of the Sipsey Wilderness and allows two dogs weighing up to 80 pounds total. There is a $20 total per day pet fee. A $50 refundable damage deposit may be required at check-in. Dogs in the room while you're gone must be crated.

CAMPING

Corinth Recreation Area, 2540 CR 57, Double Springs; (205) 489-3165; www.recreation.gov/camping/corinth-recreation-area/r/campgroundDetails.do?contractCode= NRSO&parkId=70833

Corinth is a beautiful campground located in the Bankhead National Forest, arguably one of the most popular in the area. Located on the banks of Lake Lewis Smith, the campground is exceptional, with nice, clean bathhouses, ice machines, swimming, and fifty-two improved campsites. The campground is open from the first weekend of March to the end of October. Make your reservations online. Fees range from $17 to $28 per night for a lakeside site.

FUELING UP

Moe's Original BBQ, 202 Moulton St. E #C, Decatur; (256) 686-4112; www .moesoriginalbbq.com/lo/decatur/#decatur-menu-section

Moe's knows barbecue, believe me. They serve up delicious pulled pork, smoked turkey, and chicken sandwiches and platters with either sweet and tangy traditional sauce

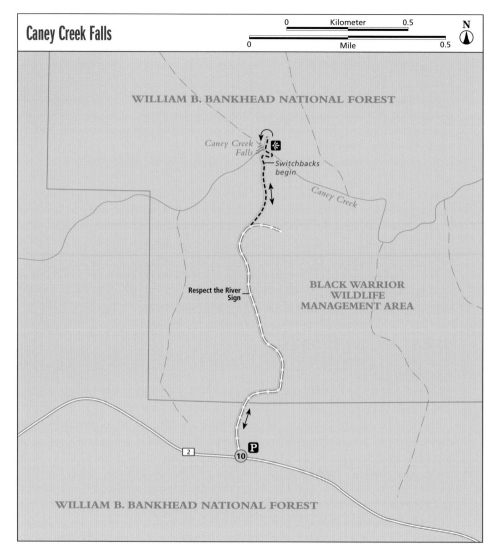

WILLIAM B. BANKHEAD NATIONAL FOREST

Caney Creek Falls

Switchbacks begin

Caney Creek

Respect the River Sign

BLACK WARRIOR WILDLIFE MANAGEMENT AREA

2   10   P

WILLIAM B. BANKHEAD NATIONAL FOREST

or Moe's famous Alabama white BBQ sauce. And don't forget their nachos and wings. Moe's has eight dog-friendly tables outside where you and Fido can enjoy a meal together.

MILES AND DIRECTIONS

0.0 Start from the dirt and gravel parking lot to the north. Walk behind the steel gate to the right. The path is a wide gravel and dirt road, heavily rutted due to erosion.

0.5 The trail briefly narrows to a 2-foot-wide pine-needle-covered dirt and gravel path with short pines lining the route. It's also a bit brushier through here. In less than 0.1 mile, you'll pass a sign reminding you to RESPECT THE RIVER.

0.7 The downhill walk to the falls begins. Shortly you will hear the falls in the distance.

0.8 Come to a Y. The right fork is a cutoff careless people have made to get to the falls quicker. Please don't use this (see the Hike description); take the left fork to the northwest. The trail uses a series of switchbacks to meander downhill.

0.9 Come to a small rock overlook of the falls on the left. From here the switch-backs become narrow and very close to the edge. Use caution; the path is rock and root strewn.

1.0 Arrive at the falls. Feel free to explore and take a swim but use caution on the slick rocks behind and surrounding the falls. When done, retrace your steps to the trailhead.

2.0 Arrive back at the trailhead.

PUPPY PAWS AND GOLDEN YEARS

Whether we are at home or on the trail, we all need to practice Leave No Trace. That applies to your dog, too. Remember these guidelines when you're on the trail:

- Keep your dog from digging.
- Keep your dog leashed around people.
- Keep them away from public swimming areas.
- Do not leave your dog unattended at a campsite.
- Give your pet plenty of food and water.
- Bring your own poop bags to clean up after your dog and dispose of it properly.
- Keep your dog at a safe distance from wildlife.
- Keep barking to a minimum.

CENTRAL REGION

Geologically speaking, the Central Region of Alabama is known as the Piedmont Plateau, an area that runs from just north of Montgomery to just north of Birmingham. The Piedmont is where the Appalachian Mountain range terminates—or begins, depending on your perspective.

In this region you will find the state's highest mountain, Cheaha, which stands 2,407 feet above sea level, and the mountain that is recognized as the southernmost in the chain, Flagg. You'll visit Flagg Mountain by trekking down the Flagg Mountain Loop (Hike 19), where you'll view the magnificent handiwork of the Civilian Conservation Corps (CCC) from the 1930s as you pass the old log cabins and the stonework of the fire tower that graces the summit.

This region is known for its more challenging and arguably most scenic treks. Most of the hikes I have selected for this section are moderate in difficulty, giving both novice and experienced hikers some options. One of my favorites is Hike 12, the Chinnabee Silent Trail / Lake Shore Loop. This combination of two trails encompasses everything that makes the Talladega National Forest spectacular: a beautiful, shimmering lake, a rushing mountain stream that your pup will have a blast splashing around in, and a couple of impressive waterfalls, Cheaha Falls and the breathtaking Devil's Den Falls.

For you history buffs, take a walk back in time on Hike 16, the Tannehill Ironworks Historical State Park loop. The trail leads to the beautiful and wide Roupes Creek and the completely rebuilt stone Tannehill Furnace.

Weather-wise, hiking this region is pleasant from fall through spring. You will be treated to the brilliant color changes over the landscape in the fall, light blankets of snow in winter, and mountains dotted with blooming and fragrant dogwood, mountain laurel, and native azalea in the spring.

The hottest temperatures arrive around July, when daytime highs average 91 degrees and nighttime lows are 71. And yes, you do get the humidity here, although it just doesn't seem as bad when you're on a mountain or cooling off in a stream. But don't let that fool you! Heat indexes can still skyrocket, so pack plenty of water for you and your pup during the summer months, and as always, keep your eyes on Fido for any signs of fatigue and heat issues.

As for winter, you are more likely to see snow and ice here than in the areas below Montgomery. Temperatures range from 55 degrees in the day to 33 at night, but you can also expect days below 30 degrees.

11 TURKEY CREEK NATURE PRESERVE

A beautiful little walk in the woods, that's what's in store for you and your pet as you hike the trails at the Turkey Creek Nature Preserve. From a rocky bluff atop a ridge, you'll get some views of the surrounding valley, and after your hike, the cool water of Turkey Creek is the perfect swimming hole for both you and your pup. To top it off, there is the soothing sound of a rushing cascade.

THE RUNDOWN

Start: From the north side of the gravel parking lot
Distance: 2.3-mile loop
Approximate hiking time: 1 hour
Difficulty: Moderate due to slight hill climbs
Trailhead elevation: 592 feet
Highest point: 791 feet
Best season: Year-round; open Wed–Sun, 9 a.m.–5:30 p.m., with special pedestrian/hiker-only hours Fri–Sun, 7 a.m.–9 a.m. Closed Mon and Tues.
Trail surface: Packed dirt with some rocks
Other trail users: None
Canine compatibility: Leash required
Land status: City preserve

Fees and permits: None
Trail contact: Turkey Creek Nature Preserve, 3906 Turkey Creek Rd., Pinson, AL 35126; (205) 680-35126; www.turkeycreeknp.com
Nearest town: Pinson
Trail tips: Restrooms, changing rooms, and picnic tables are available at the trailhead. Swimming is allowed in Turkey Creek (use caution—the rocks are slippery and there are no lifeguards), and it can be crowded in the summer months.
Maps: USGS: Pinson, AL
Other maps: Available online at turkeycreeknp.com/trail-map/

FINDING THE TRAILHEAD

From exit 128 on I-20/I-I59 in Birmingham, take AL 79 north 12.1 miles. Turn left onto Old Bradford Road / Turkey Creek Road. Travel 0.4 mile to the preserve's entrance. Continue straight on Turkey Creek Road 0.6 mile. The trailhead and parking are on the left. Trailhead GPS: N33 42.173' / W86 41.782'

THE HIKE

Turkey Creek Nature Preserve in the town of Pinson may be small in size, but it will be a blast for you, your pup, and the entire family.

The Alabama Forever Wild program, which protects tracts of land that have historic or ecological significance, saved this 462-acre preserve from development and opened it to the public; it has beautiful hiking and mountain-biking trails and one of the best swimming holes around. More on that in a moment.

The reason for preserving this property is because it is the prime habitat for several rare and endangered species of darter fish that call the cool, clear, and fast-flowing creek their home, including the watercress, rush, and vermilion darters. The latter, the vermilion darter, is found only here in Turkey Creek and nowhere else in the world. Fearing development in the upper Turkey Creek watershed that would severely impact or kill

The perfect place to cool off after you hike the trails of Turkey Creek.

off the darter, the US Fish & Wildlife Service placed the fish on the endangered species list. Thanks to the state preserving this land and waterway, the vermilion stands a fighting chance.

The centerpiece of a visit to Turkey Creek Preserve is the same creek that the darters call home. The creek is a tributary of Locust Fork and is a swift-flowing stream over impressive boulders and rocky bottoms, and it includes a spectacular drop cascade.

The creek has long been a favorite swimming hole of locals. It is an exhilarating swim after a hot summer day hiking the park's trails. While the river is just plain fun to swim around in, be cautious. The rocks are very slippery, and there are a couple of deep spots near the water chutes.

There are three main trails in the preserve. The Narrows Trail is primarily a mountain-bike trail but can be shared with hikers. The hike described here uses two other trails, the Thompson Trace and Hanby Hollow Trails, to form a 2.3-mile loop through a hardwood and pine forest with a thick canopy that offers plenty of shade on a hot summer day.

The path climbs a ridge on a dirt and rock footpath for a nice little view of the surrounding hills and valley and crosses several natural springs that feed the creek. Be on the lookout for remarkable mushrooms along the path.

Both trails are well marked using yellow diamond markers with the hiker emblem on them. There are also blue paint blazes along the Thompson Trace and yellow on the Hanby Hollow. Hard turns in the trail are identified by what are called "dit-dot" blazes— two paint blazes, one on top of the other, with the top blaze offset to either side. If it's to the left, the trail turns left; if it's to the right, it turns right. Intersections are clearly marked with signage pointing the direction to go.

There are a couple of things you should keep in mind when visiting Turkey Creek. First, while the parking lot can easily hold ten cars, people park two or three rows deep, so it is very easy to get blocked in. Look for a spot near the road so you can leave when you want.

Also, along the Hanby Hollow trail, there are a few swales that fill with water after a rain, and you know what that means: mosquitoes in the summer. Bring bug spray.

The trails cross the Thompson Trace bike trail several times. Be on the lookout for mountain bikes when crossing.

While you're at the preserve, you should also check out the Boy Scout Trail. The trail is only a 0.7 mile long out-and-back, but it follows directly along the banks of the beautiful creek.

CREATURE COMFORTS

RESTING UP

Days Inn, 616 Decatur Hwy., Fultondale; (205) 849-0111; www.wyndhamhotels.com

Make your reservations by phone or online. One pet up to 50 pounds is allowed per room with a $25 per pet, per night fee. Be sure to call in advance to make sure that a pet-friendly room is available.

FUELING UP

Salem's Diner, 2913 18th St. S, Homewood; (205) 877-8797; www.salemsdiner.com

A little bit out of the way from Turkey Creek but well worth the trip, Salem's Diner has two outside tables so you and your dog can enjoy a meal. It's a good old-fashioned diner, serving up menu items like the Trashcan with hash browns, onions, peppers, tomatoes, cheese, and spicy sausage, or everyone's favorite, hotcakes. Get either the stack or short stack. They open at 6:30 a.m. but close early, so check with the diner before heading out.

MILES AND DIRECTIONS

0.0 Start from the north side of the parking lot. Take a short set of dirt and wooden stairs up a small hill. At the top there is a small kiosk and trail sign showing you the route of the red-blazed Narrows Ridge trail and the blue-blazed Thompson Trace trail. Take the blue Thompson Trace trail to the northeast. The trail is marked with yellow diamond directional signs and blue paint blazes.

0.1 The trail will be lined with vibrant green moss as it crosses the red Narrows Ridge trail to the northeast. As the path heads up the ridge, you leave the hardwoods and enter a pine forest. The trail levels off at the top of the ridge.

0.4 Topping out on the ridge, the trail levels off. The sound of Turkey Creek Falls can be heard to your right (northwest) and the traffic from the park road to your left (southeast).

0.7 To the left (southeast) pass a 10-foot side trail that leads to a short overlook of a valley and the highway below. In less than 0.1 mile, cross through a swale that will have water in it after a rain or will be muddy and slick until it dries.

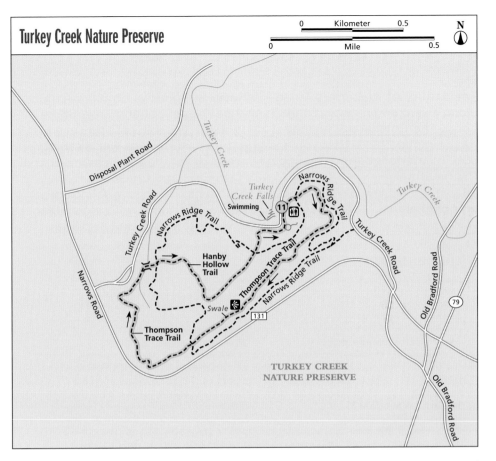

Turkey Creek Nature Preserve

0   Kilometer   0.5

0   Mile   0.5

N

0.8   Come to an intersection with the red Narrows Ridge trail. Continue straight to the southwest. You'll start heading down the first ridge out of the pines and back into the hardwoods as the trail nears the highway.

1.3   Come to a wooden directional sign. The Thompson Trace trail continues straight to the north, the yellow-blazed Hanby Hollow trail turns right to the northeast. Turn right onto the Hanby Hollow trail.

1.4   Cross a short 10-foot bridge over a spring. The path will follow the banks of the spring for some distance.

1.5   Cross the red Narrows Ridge trail to the northeast.

1.9   Cross the red Narrows Ridge trail to the north. Once again you'll hear the sound of the falls.

2.1   The path is rocky and can be slippery. The trail parallels the preserve road. As you approach the road do not get onto it. Turn right (north) to continue on the trail.

2.3   Come to a double blaze. Turn left (west). Cross a spring and arrive at the preserve road. Turn right (north) onto the road and in a few feet you're back at the trailhead.

12 CHINNABEE SILENT TRAIL / LAKE SHORE LOOP

The beauty of Alabama's Talladega National Forest is on full display along this combination of the Chinnabee Silent Trail and Lake Shore Loop. The Chinnabee meanders along its namesake, passing several fun swimming holes that you and your pup can enjoy as well as some scenic waterfalls before heading up the hillside for the Kodak moments: the breathtaking waterfalls at Devil's Den Falls and Cheaha Falls plus an expansive view of the Talladega Mountains. This hike also includes an optional fun 2.0-mile loop around Lake Chinnabee with incredible wildflowers and a man-made waterfall, the lake's dam, and a spillway.

THE RUNDOWN

Start: From the south side of the Lake Chinnabee Recreation Area parking lot

Distance: 7.1-mile out-and-back with loop

Approximate hiking time: 5 hours, but allow extra time for the water show

Difficulty: Moderate due to climbs and length

Trailhead elevation: 810 feet

Highest point: 1,140 feet

Best season: The trail and recreation area is open from Mar 1 to Dec 1, sunrise to sunset. It is closed the remaining months due to winter weather that makes travel to the trailhead and hiking dangerous.

Trail surface: Dirt, rock, and root-strewn footpath with an elevated bridge above a gorge and several creek crossings on the Lake Shore Loop.

Other trail users: None

Canine compatibility: Leash required

Land status: National forest

Fees and permits: $3 per car day-use fee

Trail contact: Talladega Ranger District, US Forest Service, 1001 North St. (AL 21 N), Talladega; (256) 362-2909; www.fs.usda .gov/detail/alabama/about-forest/ districts/?cid=fsbdev3_002555

Nearest town: Talladega

Trail tips: Nice restrooms are available right at the trailhead. Be sure to bring the camera; there are plenty of "Kodak moments" along this hike at several cascades in the creek, Devil's Den Falls, and Cheaha Falls, not to mention the wildflowers on the Lake Shore Loop. You can split the hike and do only the 5.4-mile Chinnabee Silent Trail or the 2.0-mile Lake Shore Loop by itself. Be ready to get wet on the Lake Shore Loop; you will cross the creek and feeders to the creek 3 times.

Maps: USGS: Ironaton, AL; Cheaha Mountain, AL

Other maps: A large map is posted at the trailhead kiosk.

Other: Hunting is allowed in the fall in Talladega National Forest. Please call the Trail Contact (above) or visit them online for dates and restrictions.

FINDING THE TRAILHEAD

From Lineville at the intersection of AL 9 and AL 49, take AL 49 north 14.2 miles. Turn left onto AL 281 S. Travel 4.9 miles (passing Cheaha State Park on the way), and turn right onto Cheaha Road. Travel 3.6 miles and turn left onto Lake Chinnabee Road. In 1.3 miles, arrive at the Lake Chinnabee Recreation Area. The trailhead and parking is on your left. Trailhead GPS: N33 27.594' / W85 52.433'

THE HIKE

Whether an avid hiker in Alabama or a novice, when asked about the best hiking trails they have walked in the state, most people will answer with the name of the same three trails: the Walls of Jericho, the Pinhoti Trail, and this trail—the Chinnabee Silent Trail / Lake Shore Loop. And for good reason. The Chinnabee/Lakeshore trails encompass all that makes the Talladega National Forest so special: massive quartzite rock outcroppings, a panoramic view, rainbows of wildflowers, raging streams, and impressive waterfalls.

Next to the Walls of Jericho north of Huntsville, this hike is one of the most popular in the state, but don't worry about it being overcrowded. I'll explain in a moment.

I always have to mention the history of this trail, because it's truly remarkable. The Chinnabee Silent Trail was named for Creek Indian chief Chinnabee, who was an ally of Andrew Jackson during the Creek Indian War. The "Silent Trail" moniker is to recognize the boys who assisted the USDA Forest Service with building it, Boy Scout Troop 29 from the Alabama Institute for the Deaf and Blind.

The troop worked for three years, from 1973 to 1976, to build what is, in my opinion, a spectacular trail. The path begins at the Lake Chinnabee Recreation Area. Don't forget to pay your $3 (per car) day-use fee. That money goes to help maintain the rec area and the trail. There are a couple of nice restrooms here at the trailhead.

From here the trail meanders along the banks of Chinnabee Creek. This wide creek is swift flowing and has several beautiful cascades that can be roaring at times over the rocky stream bed.

I said not to worry about the trail being overcrowded. Well, up to this point it can be. There are many swimming holes along this section of the trail that your dog—and you—will love, but you will be sharing with the locals.

After the swimming holes and initial cascades, the crowds thin out as you begin to walk up the side of a rock face using stone stairs and eventually a wooden catwalk high above what is known as the Devil's Den, a multitiered waterfall cascading far below. The view is spectacular! In the fall the water show is framed by brilliant foliage, and later by the bright greens of spring and summer.

The trail now starts moving up and down a couple of ridges away from the creek, where wildflowers like spring beauty and downy rattlesnake plantain brighten the path, until you come up on the Cheaha Falls Shelter. This shelter is used by backpackers doing overnight, weekend, or longer hikes through the wilderness. A personal favorite weekend trek for me is to combine the Skyway Loop, Chinnabee Silent, and Pinhoti Trails to make a 17.8-mile circuit (see Appendix E: Bonus Hikes at a Glance).

Just past the shelter is one more surprise—the multitiered Cheaha Falls, a beautiful, tumbling flow that you'll want to linger at, getting lost in its journey, for some time.

But you have to head back sometime. From here, retrace your steps, and at mile 5.2, you will come to the Lake Shore Loop Trail, a nice loop around Lake Chinnabee that is lined with wildflowers in season and frog's songs near the wetland on the lake's northern end. There is also an impressive CCC built dam that formed the lake.

You will have to get a little wet to do this loop as you have to ford not only Chinnabee Creek here but also the spillway from the dam halfway through the hike and once again nearing a wetland.

The crossing here can be a bit difficult, especially if the water is up some. Just use caution on the slippery rocks as you step to the opposite side. To cross at the dam, follow the trail to the bottom of the dam and its spillway—do *not* cross on the dam! Stay off of

it! You will have to pick your way across the stream; there isn't really a discernable way. Just head straight across, where you can then turn right (northeast) and pick up the trail again on the other side.

One other note: This area is known for flash flooding. Several flood-stage measuring sticks have been added to the recreation area. If the water is registering even a little on those gauges, don't attempt the hike. Reschedule your trip for another day.

CREATURE COMFORTS

RESTING UP

Cheaha Lodge, 18644 AL 281, Delta; (256) 488-5111; www.alapark.com/cheaha-state -park-hotel

Located only 4.4 miles from the Lake Chinnabee Recreation Area, Cheaha Lodge offers pet-friendly rooms high atop the state's highest mountain, Cheaha. Two pets of any size are allowed with an additional $16.50 per pet, per night fee charged. Pet-friendly rooms are limited, so make your reservations early by calling and requesting one. If you bring a dog into a non-pet-friendly room, you will be charged a $100 cleaning fee. The hotel is usually booked full the week of the Talladega 500 NASCAR race, which is held the second weekend in October.

CAMPING

Cheaha State Park, 19644 AL 281, Delta; (256) 488-5111; www.alapark.com/cheaha -state-park

The perfect location for a base camp to explore the Talladega National Forest and the Cheaha Wilderness right on top of the highest mountain in the state, Cheaha has seventy-two improved campsites all with barbecue grills, picnic tables, water, and electricity in two campgrounds. The Upper Campground is open year-round, the Lower is open Apr through Dec. Rates are $27 per night, plus a $4.50 transaction fee and tax. A deposit of your first night's stay is required. A two-night minimum is required on weekends and holidays. There are also twenty-five semi-primitive sites right across from the lookout tower at the top of the mountain, with a communal water spigot for $18 per night. There is a two-night minimum stay required for these sites on weekends, three nights on holidays. Make your reservations online at guestrez.megahotel.com/Hotel/Reservation/Index/P3R16.

FUELING UP

Cheaha Brewing Company, 1208 Walnut Ave., Anniston; (256) 770-7300; www.cheahabrewingcompany.com/vittles-menu/

Well-behaved pups are welcome on the spacious back deck.

MILES AND DIRECTIONS

0.0   Start from the south end of the parking lot. Don't forget to pay your day-use fee. In a few yards you will pass men's and women's restrooms on the left. The pavement ends and the path is now dirt, rock, and root strewn.

0.1   Come to a sign that reads LAKE SHORE LOOP. Continue straight to the southeast. We'll come back to this spot later. OPTION: If you want to do just the Lake Shore Loop, then turn right (southwest) here and pick up the directions at mile 5.2.

0.3   Pass a sign showing that the Skyway Loop Trail turns to the right (south). Continue straight to the southeast on the Chinnabee Silent Trail.

0.5   Start climbing up a rock wall on a series of stone steps.

0.6   You'll find yourself walking on a wooden gangway along the side of the cliff. Keep looking back to your right.

0.7   Spectacular views of the Devil's Den Falls begin.

2.6   Topping a ridge, you arrive at the Cheaha Falls Shelter.

2.7   Arrive at Cheaha Falls. Enjoy exploring but be careful on the rocks. When you're ready, turn around and retrace your steps the way you came.

5.2   Back at the sign for the Lake Shore Loop, turn left (southwest), crossing the creek. You may have to pick your way across. Just be careful on the slick rocks and in the sometimes swift current. OPTION: If you want to do just the Chinnabee Silent Trail, do not cross the creek. Instead, continue straight to the northwest. In less than 0.1 mile, the trail rises above lake. The picnic area is directly across from you. The path is thick with mountain laurel during season.

5.3   Cross a runoff directly across from parking area on the other side. In less than 0.1 mile, the trail becomes very narrow, only 1 foot wide in spots, with a sharp drop-off on the right—be careful. It will widen soon.

5.7   Pass a bench on the left just downhill next to the lake. In less than 0.1 mile, get your first view of the dam. Keep off of it—it's dangerous!

Chinnabee Silent Trail / Lakeshore Loop

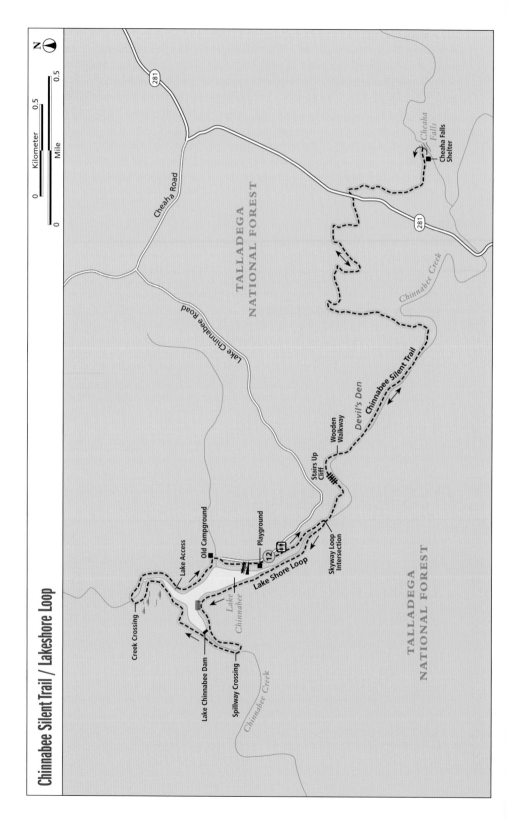

N

0   0.5
Kilometer
0   0.5
Mile

Cheaha Road

281

TALLADEGA
NATIONAL FOREST

Cheaha Falls

Cheaha Falls Shelter

281

Chinnabee Creek

Lake Chinnabee Road

Devil's Den

Chinnabee Silent Trail

Wooden Walkway

Stairs Up Cliff

Old Campground

Lake Access

Playground

12

Skyway Loop Intersection

Lake Shore Loop

Lake Chinnabee

Creek Crossing

Lake Chinnabee Dam

Spillway Crossing

Chinnabee Creek

TALLADEGA
NATIONAL FOREST

5.8 At the bottom of the dam, carefully cross the spillway. You may have to walk downstream just a bit to eventually cross, as I did, because of the flow.

5.9 After crossing, pick up the faded white blazes to your right (north). The trail may be still covered with blowdowns and debris from a serious flood several years ago. If that's the case, simply follow the rocky creek bank back to the dam.

6.0 You are now at the other side of the dam. Climb the hill next to the dam and you will see an informational sign about how the lake was formed. Again, stay off the dam! Continue on the trail to the north.

6.2 Pass an informational sign about the pileated woodpecker. In less than 0.1 mile, pass a side trail that goes straight downhill to a bench next to the lake on your right.

6.3 Pass an informational sign about largemouth bass. In less than 0.1 mile, begin your walk around a wetland on the right. There are a couple of small washouts along this section.

6.4 Cross the biggest washout.

6.5 Cross a stream to the northeast.

6.6 Pass an informational sign about wood ducks.

6.7 Pass an informational sign about moss and lichen on rocks. There are several excellent access points along here so your dog can enjoy the lake.

6.9 Cross a narrow creek at the site of the old campground. In just a few yards, arrive at Lake Chinnabee Road and follow it to the south.

7.0 Pass a boat ramp on the right.

7.1 Pass a playground on the right. In less than 0.1 mile, arrive back at the trailhead.

PUPPY PAWS AND GOLDEN YEARS
Puppy Trail Mix
You have your trail mix, now here's a simple and delicious mix for your pup. What You Need:
- Leftover cooked meat (whatever you have: chicken, roast, lunch meat)
- Leftover cooked vegetables (pick one or two: carrots, potato, sweet potato—but *no* onions!)
- Fruit (pick one or two: banana, apple, strawberry—*no* raisins or grapes!)

Dice all of the ingredients into ½-inch pieces and toss onto a greased or parchment-lined cookie sheet. Cook in a 200-degree oven until dry, stirring occasionally (make sure to check it every 15 minutes to prevent burning). Cool completely and store in the fridge until you're ready to use.

13 RUFFNER MOUNTAIN NATURE PRESERVE

Ruffner Mountain was once a major player in the iron and steel history of Birmingham. Today, the mountain is a beautiful nature preserve in the heart of the city with miles of trail to explore. This 4.6-mile hike will take you back in time to the old limestone quarry with its massive rock walls, a long since abandoned mine, a giant iron ore crusher, and spectacular views as you meander under the shade of a rich, dense forest canopy with plenty for Fido to explore around the rocks and understory.

THE RUNDOWN

Start: North side of Ruffner Mountain Nature Center parking lot under the wooden trailhead entrance
Distance: 4.6 miles out-and-back with loops
Approximate hiking time: 2.5 hours
Difficulty: Moderate with a few steep inclines
Trailhead elevation: 988 feet
Highest point: 1,132 feet
Best season: Winter to late spring; open year-round dawn to dusk. The Nature Center is closed on Mon.
Trail surface: Dirt and rock footpath
Other trail users: None
Canine compatibility: Leash required
Land status: Nonprofit nature center
Fees and permits: None
Trail contact: Ruffner Mountain Nature Center, 1214 81st St.,
Birmingham; (205) 833-8264; ruffnermountain.org
Nearest town: Birmingham
Trail tips: Restrooms are located in the Nature Center next to the trailhead, and while you're there, check out the fascinating exhibits (maybe the staff will be feeding their pet opossum; just have someone wait with your dog outside). And don't forget the camera to record the views you'll get from the Hawks View Overlook and of the area's amazing history here.
Maps: USGS: Irondale, AL
Other maps: Available at the Nature Center, online at ruffnermountain.org/visitruffner/#trailslink, or you can view one on the trail kiosk at the Gray Fox Gap intersection

FINDING THE TRAILHEAD

From Birmingham at the intersection of I-65 and I-59/I-20, take I-59/I-20 east 6.4 miles. Take exit 131 (Oporto Madrid Boulevard) and in 0.2 mile, turn right onto 77th Street North / Oporto Madrid Boulevard. In 0.6 mile, turn left onto Rugby Avenue and travel 0.7 mile. Turn right onto 81st Street South; in 0.4 mile, you will arrive at the Nature Center. Drive past the visitor center. The road will loop around past parking for special events, and you will come to another parking lot on the uphill side near the gift shop / visitor center. The trailhead is here on the north side of the parking lot. Trailhead GPS: N33 33.518' / W86 42.427'

THE HIKE

The Ruffner Mountain Nature Preserve is a literal oasis in the bustling metropolis of Birmingham. As you drive to the preserve, you will be traveling down the busy city streets until—poof! Suddenly there is a green space, and a quite an impressive one, too.

You'll find an amazing artifact of Ruffner Mountain's iron and steel history as you hike down to view this giant steel ore crusher.

This 1,000-plus-acre preserve was begun in 1977 when a grassroots group organized to prevent a developer from clear-cutting the mountain and putting up more subdivisions and commercial businesses. Today, the preserve is one of the largest private nonprofit nature preserves in the country.

At one time, Ruffner played an important role in the mining and steel history of the city, but today the mountain is a place of solitude and learning. The preserve has a wonderful exhibit hall and gift shop, where you can learn about the wildlife, the eco-system, and the history of the mountain. Its super-friendly and knowledgeable staff and volunteers can be found on any given weekend providing presentations on nature or history, holding demonstrations on a wide variety of topics, tending to gardens or the wildlife exhibit in the main center, or leading hikes on the preserve's 12 miles of trail.

This 4.6-mile out-and-back with loops hike will show you the geologic and mining history of the mountain and the city itself. With plenty of smells to investigate, this is a great trail for your dog, and they'll get a good workout on the side trails with a few moderate climbs. Just remember, there is no water available on this hike with the exception of one very small seasonal stream, so pack accordingly.

You will find that all of Ruffner's trails have excellent blazing, and getting lost is virtually impossible. All intersections have wooden signs that are reminiscent of the old "hometown signs" you saw in movies about World War II or Korea. You know the ones: large wooden signs with one end tapered and pointing the direction to "San Francisco 2,000 miles" or "New York 5,000 miles." Here they point the direction to each trail.

The hike begins on the preserve's "backbone" trail, the white-blazed Quarry Trail, which runs along the spine of the ridge. It's called the backbone because most of the preserve's other trails are spurs off this main path.

The trail is wide, relatively flat, and sports beautiful wildflowers like jack-in-the-pulpit and trillium in season. Along the route you'll have a nice view from the Jimmie Dell White Winter Overlook. It's aptly named, because with a canopy full of leaves from spring through fall, there isn't much of a view, but in the winter, it's a different story.

As I said, the Quarry Trail leads to several other spur trails. We'll be taking a few of those to complete this hike. The first is the Crusher Trail. This path is 0.7 mile long and heads down a ravine rather steeply and, of course, back up, crossing that seasonal stream I mentioned earlier, before it arrives at an amazing historical artifact—a giant steel iron-ore crusher. The steel crusher sits on top of a stone base and stands a good 30 to 40 feet tall. A set of wooden stairs on the right side allows you to walk to the top to look inside.

Miners would push heavy carts full of ore to the top of the crusher and dump it in. The crusher would pulverize it, then it was shipped off by train to local furnaces to make steel. You can see one of the mines if you walk behind the crusher up a short hill. The entrance is blocked off for safety reasons.

Continuing on down the Quarry Trail, we'll take a short jog around a ridge on the green-blazed Silent Journey Trail, and it's just that—a peaceful walk around the hillside on a narrow dirt and rock footpath with the sounds of songbirds all about you.

Arriving at a junction of several trails, which, by the way, is well marked with signage and has a kiosk with a trail map, we'll take the yellow-blazed Possum Trail around another hillside. From this trail you will get several good views of the limestone quarry, where the mineral was mined for Birmingham's steel industry. There are several side trails along the way that lead down into the quarry. You can go down into the quarry, but I must warn you that it is very steep and dangerous especially when the rocks are slippery.

The Possum Trail loops around the hillside with a few nice views along the way before it starts heading back to the trailhead, but not before you pay a visit to the Cambrian Overlook for the best view of the trek. The bluffs are steep, so again, use caution and keep your dog close at hand.

CREATURE COMFORTS

RESTING UP

Quality Inn, 3910 Kilgore Memorial Dr., Birmingham; (205) 956-4100; www.choice-hotels.com/alabama/birmingham/quality-inn-hotels

Make your reservations online. The hotel allows up to two dogs per room weighing up to 20 pounds each. You must use a credit card to reserve your room when you are traveling with pets. There is an additional pet fee of $20 per pet, per night. Well-behaved pets can be left unattended in rooms.

CAMPING

Oak Mountain State Park, 200 Terrace Dr., Pelham; (205) 620-2527; www.alapark.com/oak-mountain-state-park

There are lots of campsites and plenty of trails at Oak Mountain State Park in Pelham, just south of Birmingham. Make reservations by phone or online. The park has eighty-five improved sites with water and electricity and sixty primitive sites. Improved sites are $26.40 per night, primitive $17.60. There is also a $4.50 transaction fee plus tax. Weekends require a two-night minimum stay, holidays between Mar and Oct requires a three-night minimum. The campground is outfitted with seven nice, clean bathhouses. If you want to pack in to a campsite, Oak Mountain offers backcountry camping atop the twin mountains for $6 per person per night. Park rules say that dogs must be tethered with a 6-foot leash at campsites.

FUELING UP

East 59 Vintage and Café, 7619 1st Ave. N, Birmingham; (205) 838-0559; www.east59.net/

East 59 is an eclectic mix of vintage antiques and great sandwiches, like the Fifty-Niner with turkey, ham, Havarti cheese, fried onions, and delicious cranberry relish, or the chicken salad wrap with house-made chicken salad layered with grapes, pecans, and cheddar cheese in a whole wheat wrap. Then warm up with a hot cup of café au lait, or cool down with an iced coffee. Outdoor seating is available for you and your pup.

MILES AND DIRECTIONS

0.0 Start from the north side of the parking lot under the wooden trailhead archway at the right side of the Nature Center. In less than 0.1 mile, pass the Geology Trail on the left. Continue straight to the south on the white-blazed Quarry Trail.

0.1 Cross over a paved road to the south. On the opposite side of the road is an information kiosk and a donation box, where I hope you will drop a buck or two to help maintain the preserve. Continue straight on the Quarry Trail.

0.3 Come to Miner's Junction. A sign here shows the direction of the Quarry Trail and the Crusher Trail. Turn left here (south) onto the Crusher Trail.

0.4 Cross over the orange-blazed Ridge & Valley Trail to the east to continue on the Crusher Trail.

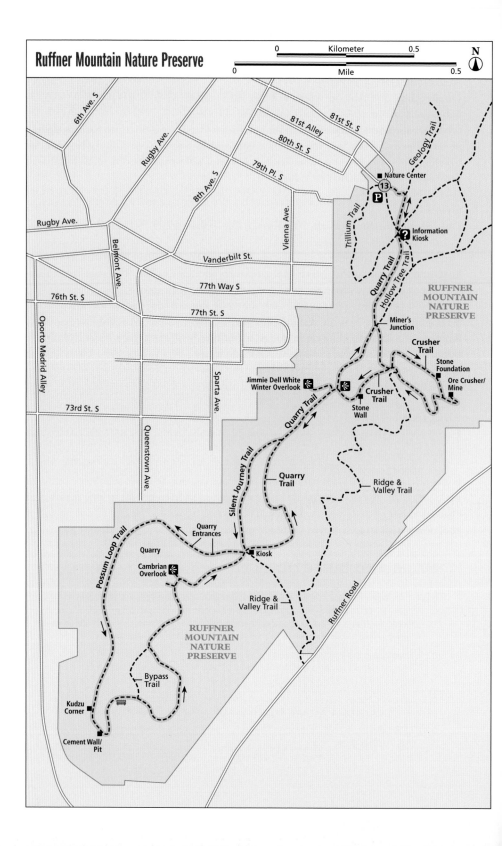

Ruffner Mountain Nature Preserve

Kilometer
0   0.5
Mile
0   0.5

N

6th Ave. S

Rugby Ave.

81st Alley

81st St. S

80th St. S

8th Ave. S

79th Pl. S

Rugby Ave.

Geology Trail

Nature Center

13

P

Vienna Ave.

Trillium Trail

Information
Kiosk

Vanderbilt St.

77th Way S

76th St. S

77th St. S

Belmont Ave.

Quarry Trail

Hollow Tree Trail

RUFFNER
MOUNTAIN
NATURE
PRESERVE

Miner's
Junction

Crusher
Trail

Stone
Foundation

Ore Crusher/
Mine

Oporto Madrid Alley

Sparta Ave.

73rd St. S

Jimmie Dell White
Winter Overlook

Crusher
Trail

Stone
Wall

Quarry Trail

Queenstown Ave.

Silent Journey Trail

Quarry
Trail

Ridge &
Valley Trail

Possum Loop Trail

Quarry
Entrances

Quarry

Kiosk

Cambrian
Overlook

Ridge &
Valley Trail

Ruffner Road

RUFFNER
MOUNTAIN
NATURE
PRESERVE

Bypass
Trail

Kudzu
Corner

Cement Wall/
Pit

0.7 Arrive at the impressive stone and steel iron-ore crusher. Feel free to explore; climb the steps to view the machine better. Behind the crusher you will see a small trail heading up the hillside. Climb that trail and, in a few yards, come to a dirt road where you can view one of the Ruffner iron mines on the other side. When done, retrace your steps to the crusher and continue on the Crusher Trail to the south. In less than 0.1 mile, you'll return to the start of the short loop that led you to the crusher. Turn right here to head back toward the Quarry Trail.

0.8 Pass an old, moss-covered stone foundation on your right.

1.0 Arrive back at the intersection with the Ridge & Valley Trail. Don't get confused and turn onto the orange trail; continue straight to the west.

1.1 Pass a stone wall on the right.

1.2 Arrive back at the Quarry Trail and turn left (southwest) onto the trail. In less than 0.1 mile, you'll arrive at the Jimmie Dell White Winter Overlook on the right. It's named the "winter" overlook because that's the best season to get a view there. When done viewing, return to the Quarry Trail and turn right (southwest) to continue.

1.5 Come to a Y. The Quarry Trail continues to the south using the left fork; we'll return on this section of the trail later. Right now, take the right fork to the southwest onto the green-blazed Silent Journey Trail.

1.8 Come to a major intersection with the Silent Journey, Quarry, and Possum Trails. There is a kiosk, a map, and a wooden directional sign here. Turn to the right (west) onto the yellow-blazed Possum Trail.

1.9 The Quarry Entrance Trail is to the left. This is a rugged, often slippery trail that takes you down into the quarry if you choose, but use extreme caution. Otherwise, continue straight on the Possum Trail. You will start getting some views to your right of the surrounding hills and in a little bit a view of Birmingham through the trees. In less than 0.1 mile, you will pass the second Quarry Entrance Trail. Keep going straight to the northwest on the Possum Trail.

2.0 Pass a No Burning sign on the left. Start getting a few better views on the right.

2.5 Arrive at Kudzu Corner. You'll recognize it even when it's dead for the winter, as its vines blanket the hillside.

2.6 Pass a very deep 10-by-10-foot stone and cement walled pit.

2.7 Pass a bench on your right. In less than 0.1 mile, come to an intersection with a sign showing directions for the Bypass Trail (to the left), another sign for the Quarry Entrance (back the way you came), and a third sign showing the Possum Trail is straight ahead. The Bypass Trail is a steep climb up a ridge that later rejoins the Possum Trail at mile 3.0. You can take the Bypass if you like. The directions here continue straight to the east on the Possum Trail.

2.8 Pass another cement foundation on the right.

3.0 Come to a Y. The northern end of the Bypass Trail comes in from the left fork. A sign here shows directions. Take the right fork to the north to continue on the Possum Trail.

3.2 Come to a very short little side trail on the left for a great view of the quarry from above. Be careful on the high bluffs and keep your kids and dog close at hand. When done viewing, retrace your steps and turn left (north) to continue on the Possum Trail.

3.3 Another side trail on the left with stone stairs going up a small hill takes you to the Cambrian Overlook for yet another great view of the quarry. When done, retrace your steps to the main trail. There is a Y here. Take the right fork to the southeast to stay on the Possum Trail.

3.5 Arrive back at the Y intersection where the Possum, Silent Journey, and Quarry Trails all meet at a kiosk you passed at mile 1.8. Instead of taking the Silent Journey Trail back to the trailhead, take the right fork to the east to follow the white-blazed Quarry Trail.

3.8 Arrive back at the intersection with the Silent Journey Trail from mile 1.5. Take the right fork to the northeast to continue on the Quarry Trail and follow it to the trailhead.

4.6 Arrive back at the trailhead.

14 RED MOUNTAIN PARK

One of the most popular parks for both dogs and their pet people in Birmingham is Red Mountain Park. Dogs love to explore the trails here, sniffing all of the nooks and crannies in the rocks, while their human friends love to discover the many mines and mining artifacts from the city's iron and steel past located along the iron-red-hued trails. Once done, turn your dog loose for a bit of fun with fellow pooches in Remy's Dog Park. This large fenced-in park within Red Mountain has three separate sections, one each for small dogs, large dogs, and a unique "special needs" section for shy dogs or those with disabilities.

THE RUNDOWN

Start: At the trailhead on Frankfurt Drive
Distance: 5.4-mile loop
Approximate hiking time: 2.5 hours
Difficulty: Difficult mainly along the Smythe and Ike Maston Trail sections, which are rated "most difficult" by the park
Trailhead elevation: 674 feet
Highest point: 951 feet
Best season: Year-round; open 7 a.m.–5 p.m. daily, closed Christmas Day; Remy's Dog Park is closed Wed from 8 a.m. to 10 a.m.
Trail surface: Dirt footpath, gravel road
Other trail users: Joggers, cyclists
Canine compatibility: Leash required
Land status: Red Mountain Park property
Fees and permits: None
Trail contact: Red Mountain Park, 277 Lyon Ln., Birmingham, AL 35211; (205) 202-6043; www.redmountainpark.org
Nearest town: Hoover
Trail tips: Restrooms are located at the trailhead welcome station, at the main information kiosk at mile 0.4, and on the BMRR South Trail at mile 4.2. The park features a spacious fenced-in dog park (Remy's Dog Park), so your pup can run free among the trees. Definitely bring a camera for shots of the mines, hoist houses, geology, and views. Water is not readily available, so be sure to pack extra for both you and your dog. You will pass many donation boxes along the way. While the park is free, please consider dropping in a buck or two to help with maintenance. If you need to leave the park in a hurry, look at the backside of the fiberglass trail signs located at intersections. They are marked with the letter P and an arrow, showing the way back to the parking lot.
Maps: USGS: Birmingham South, AL; Bessemer, AL
Other maps: Available online at redmountainpark.org/explore/trail-guide/ or at the park's welcome center located at the trailhead. Signs with trail maps are also scattered along the trails at key intersections.

FINDING THE TRAILHEAD

From I-65 in Birmingham, take exit 255 and head west on W. Lakeshore Parkway. Travel 3.2 miles and turn right onto Frankfurt Drive. The trailhead is at the bend as Frankfurt Drive becomes Lyon Lane. Park anywhere along Frankfurt Drive. GPS: N33 26.747' / W86 51.735'

THE HIKE

The first thing you'll notice when you hit the trails at Red Mountain Park is that they all have a red hue to them. That color harkens back to the 1800s, when the city of Birmingham appeared almost overnight as entrepreneurs realized the region sat on a goldmine. Not literally on gold, but something that would create Alabama's largest city.

It turns out that the area is one of the few places in the world that all three ingredients for making iron and steel—hematite (iron ore), limestone, and coke (coal)—can be found in one location. With that discovery, the "Magic City" was born, quickly making it a rival to the giant steel city, Pittsburgh.

Red Mountain Park provides a glimpse back in time to the mining heyday of the city as its over 15 miles of trail wind their way up and down slopes, visiting long since abandoned iron mines and hoist houses that once drove the monetary juggernaut.

Today, Red Mountain is much more than an historical preserve. It is a beautiful nature preserve as well with wildflowers, a frog pond, and wildlife like whitetail deer and fox roaming the paths. The park's trails weave their way around the mountainside, interconnecting with each other to form an intricate set of possible loop hikes that take more than a day to hike them all.

The trails are mainly dirt and rock footpaths that climb up and down the ridges. Some of the climbs are pretty steep, such as the Smythe and Ike Maston Trails, which bear diamond-shape trail markers warning you that they are considered "most difficult."

Some old mining roads are also used to connect trails. While your first thought is that they are just old, boring dirt roads, think again. The hardwood forests and rock bluffs make them cozy, inviting, and a pleasure to walk.

All of these trails lead you to two beautiful overlooks and, of course, the mining history we mentioned before. On the route you'll pass two abandoned mines, the remnants of an old mining bridge, and two hoist houses, the most impressive being the Redding Shaft Mine and Hoist House, a beautiful example of Mission-style architecture of the period. The mines themselves have been sealed off with cement "plugs" for safety reasons, but each has the name of the mine inscribed on it with the years it was in operation.

The many rocks and bluffs will engage your pup. There is plenty for them to explore, but having said that, be sure to keep on leash. Park employees explained to me that back in the day when the mountain was mined, the rubble was left behind in piles. Today, the trails wind their way through some of these piles, which leave gaps and holes that are covered by leaves and pine needles, and unsuspecting hikers or dogs could potentially injure themselves in the hole.

Also watch your dog along the northeast side of this hike on Sky High Ridge. The trail narrows here with some steep drop-offs along the sides.

After you hike the trails and explore the mountainside, it's time to cool down, and the best place for you and your dog to do that is in Remy's Dog Park, located only 0.2 mile from the trailhead.

Remy's is the largest dog park in Alabama. In fact, it consists of 6 acres of fenced-in joy for your dog under the shade of magnificent hardwoods. *Southern Living* magazine named it one of the ten great Southern dog parks.

The park is fenced off into three sections: the 1.7-acre large breed area, the 0.7-acre small dog area, and something extra special—the 0.3-acre Special Needs section, which was set up especially for dogs with mobility issues or otherwise physically challenged, elderly, injured, or shy canines. It's a fabulous idea that hopefully other dog parks will incorporate.

The beautiful Mission-style architecture of the Redding Hoist House.

The park is outfitted with plenty of water stations, waste disposal cans, and benches.

Remember, water is not readily available on the trails, so be sure to pack in extra for you and your pup. If you need to bug out of a hike early and want to know a quick way back to the parking lot, look at the back side of the fiberglass trail signs at intersections. They are marked with the letter P and an arrow showing the way out.

CREATURE COMFORTS

RESTING UP

Candlewood Suites, 400 Commons Dr., Birmingham; (205) 769-9777; www.ihg.com/candlewood/hotels/us/en/reservation

Make your reservations online, then contact the hotel in Birmingham itself. Give them your name and confirmation number and ask them to add your pet to the reservation. There is a $75 flat fee charged for anyone staying up to seven nights, $150 if you stay longer.

CAMPING

Oak Mountain State Park, 200 Terrace Dr., Pelham; (205) 620-2527; www.alapark .com/oak-mountain-state-park

Plenty of campsites and plenty of trails can be found at Oak Mountain State Park in Pelham just south of Birmingham. Make reservations by phone or online. The park has eighty-five improved sites with water and electricity and sixty primitive sites. Improved sites are $26.40 per night, primitive $17.60. There is also a $4.50 transaction fee plus tax. Weekends require a two-night minimum stay, holidays between Mar and Oct require a three-night minimum. The campground is outfitted with seven nice, clean bathhouses. If you want to pack in to a campsite, Oak Mountain offers backcountry camping atop the twin mountains for $6 per person per night. Park rules say that dogs must be tethered with a 6-foot leash at campsites.

FUELING UP

Purple Onion Deli & Grill, 479 Green Springs Hwy., Homewood; (205) 941-9979; www.thepurpleoniononline.com/splash.aspx

Fuel up before or after hitting the trail at the Purple Onion Deli & Grill. For breakfast try one of their amazing breakfast burritos, like the Mediterranean with two eggs, gyro meat, sautéed onions, and feta cheese, or the Hawaiian with pineapple, ham, two eggs, and cheddar cheese. Then for lunch or dinner, come back for a mouthwatering chili cheeseburger, rib-eye steak pita wrap, or chicken kabob. You can dine with your well-behaved pooch in their patio seating.

MILES AND DIRECTIONS

0.0 Start at the trailhead on Frankfurt Drive to the north on the gravel path. There is a new welcome center here where maps and information are available. In less than 0.1 mile, come to a Y. Take the right fork toward Remy's Dog Park.

0.2 Cross a 40-foot bridge and arrive at Remy's Dog Park.

0.3 Come to a T intersection with a wide gravel road. Turn left (west) onto the road.

0.4 Come to an intersection. At the junction there is a large set of glasses, a sculpture that represents the mission to look to the past and look to the future called the Schaeffer Spectacles. There is also a welcome kiosk and portable restrooms here. The BMRR South Trail goes straight to the west. Turn right (north) onto the #13 Mine Trail. In less than 0.1 mile, a side trail leads to a picnic area on the right; continue straight to the north.

0.5 The picnic area trail rejoins the main trail from the right. Continue straight to the north.

0.6 Pass a Boy Scout hammock area on the right. In less than 0.1 mile, come to an intersection with a gravel road. Turn right onto the gravel road to the northeast heading toward the Adventure Area. In a few yards arrive at the Adventure Area, walking around it on the right side. At the storage unit located here there is a Y. A sign here shows the Eureka Mines is to the left (northeast) and the BMRR South Trail to the right. Take the left fork and head to the Eureka Mines.

0.7 Pass under a rope skywalk.

Red Mountain Park

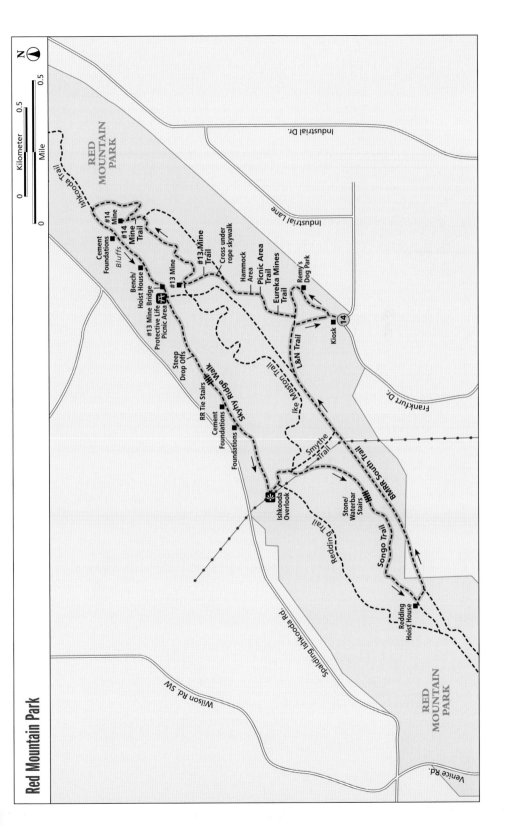

Red Mountain Park

0.9 Pass a bridge on the right (we'll come back to that in a moment) and continue straight to the northwest to visit the #13 Mine. When done retrace your steps back to the bridge and turn left, crossing the bridge to the east onto the Ike Maston Trail.

1.3 Come to an intersection. A sign shows the BMRR South Trail and the parking lot are to the right, the #14 Mine Spur and Ishkooda #14 mine to the left; turn left (north) onto the #14 Mine Spur Trail. The trail narrows to a 2-foot-wide rock and dirt path.

1.4 Arrive at the Ishkooda Mine #14. When done exploring, retrace your steps and, in less than 0.1 mile, turn left (southeast) onto the Redding/Ishkooda Trail.

1.7 Turn left (southwest) onto the rocky, wide Ishkooda Trail. *OPTION:* You can turn right here to the northeast on the Ishkooda Trail and add a 2.4-mile out-and-back to Grace's Overlook.

1.8 Pass old cement mining structures to the left. A tall rock bluff also begins on the left.

1.9 Pass a side trail on the left. Continue straight to the southwest.

2.0 Pass the foundation of a hoist house on the right. In less than 0.1 mile, pass a bench on the right and bluffs on the left.

2.1 Pass the Mine #13 Bridge on the left.

2.2 Arrive at the Protective Life Picnic Area and an intersection of several trails. Continue to the southwest on the TCI Connector. In less than 0.1 mile, a trail branches to the right at a sign that says STAY ON THE TRAIL. Take the left fork onto the Skyhy Ridge Walk.

2.3 Pass between two 6x6 posts.

2.4 The trail narrows again to a rocky 2- to 3-foot-wide path atop a narrow ridge with long and steep drops to either side.

2.5 Climb down a short set of railroad-tie stairs. You will start to see a bit of the city to your right through the trees.

2.6 Pass between 2 small cement foundations.

2.7 Pass a foundation and steel I-beams on the right. Climb down a short set of railroad-tie stairs.

3.0 Arrive at the Ishkooda Overlook, with its picnic table and a view of the Birmingham suburbs. Grab a snack, enjoy the view, then backtrack just a few yards and turn right (southeast) onto a short connector trail. In less than 0.1 mile, come to an intersection and turn left (northeast) onto the Redding Trail.

3.1 Come to the intersection with the Smythe Trail that bears off to the right and then straight. Continue straight to the southeast on the Smythe Trail. It's a steep, rocky downhill with many water bars to prevent erosion.

3.2 Turn right (west) onto the Ike Maston Trail.

3.3 Pass a view of the valley on your left.

3.5 Cross an intermittent run-off over a stone water bar that diverts water that would cause trail erosion . After crossing, climb a hill to the west on some old wooden stairs made from railroad ties.

3.8 The Songo Trail joins the Ike Maston Trail from the left (south). Continue straight to the northwest on the Ike Maston Trail. In a few hundred feet, cross a stream over a nice wooden bridge.

4.0 Pass an old 4-by-4-inch cement post on the right. In less than 0.1 mile, arrive at the Redding Hoist House. There are interesting signs here, telling the story of the hoist and the mine. Turn left (southeast) onto the Songo Trail, which is now a gravel and dirt road.

4.1 Turn left (northeast) onto the BMRR South Trail. A frog pond is here at the bend, and the frog song is marvelous.

4.7 Cross a clearing for a petroleum pipeline.

4.8 Pass the Smythe Trail on the left.

5.0 Pass the Ike Maston Trail on the left. In less than 0.1 mile, come to a Y. Take the right fork to the east onto the L&N Trail.

5.1 Pass a small outdoor classroom/amphitheater on the right.

5.2 Arrive back at the information kiosk from mile 0.4. Turn right to the southeast to head back to the trailhead.

5.4 Arrive back at the trailhead.

PUPPY PAWS AND GOLDEN YEARS
National Take a Dog on a Hike Day
You don't need an excuse to go out and enjoy hiking with your dog, but if you'd like one, then leash up and head out to a local trail on National Take a Dog on a Hike Day. The day is held the third weekend of November in conjunction with National Take a Hike Day.

15 WATERFALL LOOP

You wouldn't imagine it, but in the middle of an upscale subdivision in the town of Hoover, there is an amazing water feature and boulder-strewn preserve that seems a million miles from civilization: Moss Rock Preserve. Both you and your dog will enjoy this hike along the clear, cool waters of Hurricane Creek, where they can frolic and splash a bit while you relax next to the soothing sounds of the many—and I mean many—seasonal waterfalls.

THE RUNDOWN

Start: From the trailhead on the east side of the parking lot at the kiosk
Distance: 3.9-mile loop
Approximate hiking time: 3 hours
Difficulty: Difficult on the east side loop
Trailhead elevation: 801 feet
Highest point: 805 feet
Best season: Fall and Nov–May, when Southern rains fill the creek; open year-round sunrise to sunset
Trail surface: Dirt, rock, sand
Other trail users: Trail runners
Canine compatibility: Leash required
Land status: City preserve
Fees and permits: None
Trail contact: Moss Rock Nature Preserve, 617 Preserve Way, Hoover; (205) 444-7777; www.hooveral.org

Nearest town: Hoover
Trail tips: I don't think it has to be said, but bring that camera! Waterfalls, remarkable boulders and outcroppings, and sparkling streams are images you won't want to forget. The eastern loop of the hike to Turtle Rock may be a challenge to some. When I hiked it I thought the climb uphill was a bit steep. Talking to local hikers they said, "Didn't you know? We call it the Cardio Trail." As always, be careful on the slippery rocks at the waterfalls, and make sure your pup is safe.
Maps: USGS: Helena, AL
Other maps: Available online at www.hooveral.org/219/Hiking-Map-Trail-Guide

FINDING THE TRAILHEAD

From the intersection of I-65 and I-459 in Hoover, take exit 250 from I-65 to get onto I-459 S. Travel 0.7 mile and use exit 13A (AL 150 / Galleria Boulevard). In 0.7 mile, turn right onto Chapel Lane. Travel 0.7 mile and turn left to stay on Chapel Lane. In less than 0.1 mile, Chapel Lane becomes Al Seier Road. Travel 1.9 miles and turn right onto Sulphur Springs Road. Travel 0.5 mile; the trailhead will be on the right. The Sulphur Springs parking lot is a good-size gravel lot with enough room for about 15 cars. Trailhead GPS: N33 22.585' / W86 51.201'

THE HIKE

Driving up to the Sulphur Springs trailhead of the Moss Rock Preserve, you will find it hard to believe that you're about to enter a wonderland of geology and water features. The drive in takes you through a very nice upscale residential area, past a shopping area, then there you are in an amazing 250-acre preserve that is seemingly miles away from civilization. It's an extraordinary place for you and your dog to spend an incredible afternoon exploring.

The Waterfall Loop I describe here is a subset of the 12 miles of trail that can be found at Moss Rock Preserve. It includes the very patriotic sounding Red, White, and Blue Trails, all of which are blazed in the color of the trail's name.

As you can guess by the name, the highlights of this 3.9-mile loop are the waterfalls.

For most of the trek, you and your pup will be following the banks of Hurricane Creek, a beautiful clear stream that tumbles over its rocky bed, creating many shoals and several beautiful waterfalls. There are many places where your dog can visit the creek and splash a bit and you can take in the sound and beauty of the sparkling cascades. But remember, as with many waterfalls in Alabama, they are seasonal, and summertime droughts tend to dry them up to a trickle. The best time to visit is between November and May, when spring rains and melting winter snow fill the creeks.

The hike begins on the Red Trail, which crosses Preserve Parkway twice (be careful crossing the highway). Along this stretch you will begin your walk above the creek, traveling up and down rolling hills. Several side trails lead you down the hill to the creek for a view of a couple of small shoals.

The real water show begins once you cross the highway for the second time and join the White Trail. Hurricane Creek now widens and really starts flowing. You will encounter at least six waterfalls along this hike, including my personal favorite, Tunnel Falls, which flows from beneath the rocks out of a small tunnel, near the sandstone glade that you will encounter on the return trip.

It's not only waterfalls that make this trip special. As you walk the trail through a forest of basswood, hickory, sweet gum, and winged elm trees, you will be treated to a spectacular rainbow of wildflowers, like blazing star, spiderwort, and bird-foot violets from spring through summer.

Then there is the geology. After you leave the Red Trail and join the White, you will see tall rock bluffs on your right and large boulders scattered all around, one of which on the left has a hole straight through the middle of it, a result of weathering.

As the trail swings to the north and begins to loop around for the return trip, you will come to Turtle Rock. Yes, it really does look like a turtle. Personally, I think the "head" of the rock looks like the giant Japanese movie turtle Gamera, but maybe that's just me.

You will also encounter the Sandstone Glade, a remarkable flat, pavement-like outcropping with a smattering of trees, including natural bonsai, as well as many rare and endangered plants and wildflowers. You can visit the glade, but keep your dog close at hand and only step on rocks. This is a very fragile landscape that is easily killed off by walking on it.

Finally, the White Trail links up to the Blue Trail for the return to the trailhead, but before you get there, it links to the White Trail one more time for a trip to the Frog Pond, where you will be able to hear a chorus of frog song, even though it's near Preserve Parkway.

One note about this hike: It can be quite difficult for some, as it swings north away from Hurricane Creek and starts to head to Turtle Rock. On my last visit I was told that this section is known as the "Cardio Trail" by locals, and for good reason. If you don't want to make the climb, simply turn around at the bridge at mile 1.8 and continue on the White Trail back the way you came, picking up from mile 2.7 in the Miles and Directions (below).

CREATURE COMFORTS

RESTING UP

Days Inn Galleria–Birmingham, 1800 Riverchase Dr., Birmingham; (205) 208-1461; www.wyndhamhotels.com/days-inn

A maximum of two pets (any size) is allowed with a $25 per pet, per night fee charged. A pet sanitation fee of $50 may be requested. Make your reservations online.

CAMPING

Oak Mountain State Park, 200 Terrace Dr., Pelham; (205) 620-2527; alapark.com/oak-mountain-state-park

Plenty of campsites and plenty of trails can be found at Oak Mountain State Park in Pelham, just south of Birmingham. Make reservations by phone or online. The park has eighty-five improved sites with water and electricity and sixty primitive sites. Improved sites are $26.40 per night, primitive $17.60. There is also a $4.50 transaction fee plus tax. Weekends require a two-night minimum stay, holidays between Mar and Oct require a three-night minimum. The campground is outfitted with seven nice, clean bathhouses. If you want to pack in to a campsite, Oak Mountain offers backcountry camping atop the twin mountains for $6 per person per night. Park rules say that dogs must be tethered with a 6-foot leash at campsites.

FUELING UP

Vecchia Pizzeria & Mercato, 610 Preserve Pkwy., Hoover; (205) 637-3036; www.vecchiabirmingham.com

Do you crave Italian cuisine? Then let us recommend Vecchia Pizzeria and Mercato. Their name is the Italian world for "old," the perfect name for a restaurant that believes in cooking the traditional old Italian way: brick ovens with real, freshly made (not shipped in from a franchise headquarters) and hand-tossed dough. For authentic Italian pizza, try Vecchia's Margherita D.O.P. that's smothered in San Marzano tomato sauce, basil, olive oil, and certified Italian bufala mozzarella cheese. Vecchia's also has indescribably delicious antipasto, panini, and pasta dishes as well, not to mention calzones. Well-behaved dogs are welcome in their outdoor patio seating area.

MILES AND DIRECTIONS

0.0 Start from the east side of the parking lot at a small kiosk on the other side of a short split-rail fence. There is a directional sign indicating distances to different trails. This short approach trail is a 5-foot-wide dirt and rock path. In less than 0.1 mile, come to a marker with a blue #2 on it. This is the intersection with the blue-blazed Blue Trail. Turn to the right (south) onto the Blue Trail.

0.1 Come to a Y intersection with the White Trail. Take the right fork to the south onto the white-blazed White Trail. In less than 0.1 mile, arrive at Patriot Junction where the Red, White, and Blue Trails meet (get it?). From here, continue straight to the south on the red-blazed Red Trail.

Facing page: **The best time to visit Moss Rock Preserve is between fall and April when rain fills the creeks and make for spectacular and soothing water displays.**

Waterfall Loop

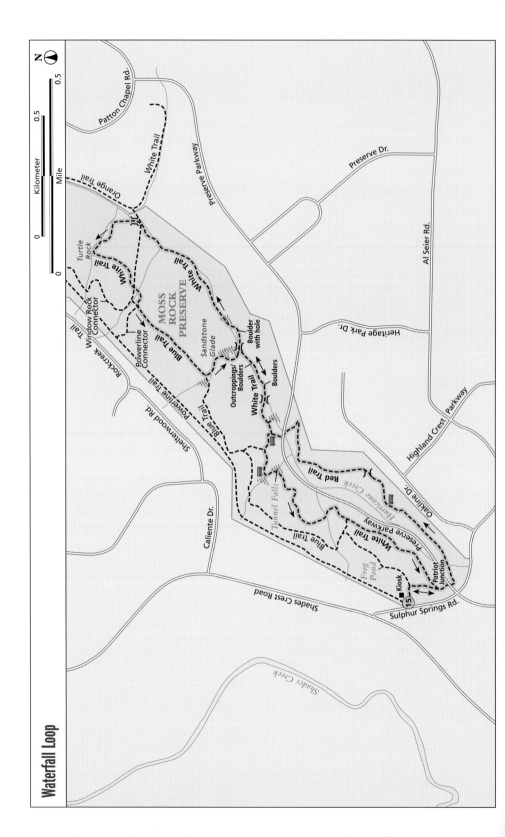

N

0   0.5   Kilometer
0   0.5   Mile

Patton Chapel Rd.

White Trail

Orange Trail

Preserve Parkway

Preserve Dr.

Al Seier Rd.

Turtle Rock

White Trail

Window Rock Connector

Rockcreek Trail

Powerline Connector

Blue Trail

MOSS ROCK PRESERVE

White Trail

Sandstone Glade

Shelterwood Rd.

Powerline Trail

Blue Trail

Outcroppings/ Boulders

White Trail

Boulder with hole

Boulders

Heritage Park Dr.

Highland Crest Parkway

Red Trail

Hurricane Creek

Oakline Dr.

Caliente Dr.

Tunnel Falls

Blue Trail

White Trail

Preserve Parkway

Patriot Junction

Shades Crest Road

Frog Pond

Kiosk

15

Sulphur Springs Rd.

Shades Creek

0.2 Come to Preserve Parkway and carefully cross the road to the south. Pick up the Red Trail again on the other side. The trail narrows to about 2 feet wide. Houses will be seen on top of the ridge to your right. In less than 0.1 mile, you'll cross a small creek.

0.3 Pass the red #2 trail marker on a 4x4 post.

0.4 Cross a deep runoff channel.

0.5 Pass a bench on the right and see the beginnings of Hurricane Creek downhill on the left.

0.6 Cross a bridge over a runoff; there may be a small waterfall after a rain.

0.7 Come to a Y. Take the right fork to the northeast to stay on the Red Trail. You can take the left fork that will lead you down to the creek. A path there will lead you back to the Red Trail at mile 0.8.

0.8 The side trail to the creek rejoins the Red Trail. Continue straight to the east.

0.9 There are some small boulders on your right behind a black material used for erosion control. The Red Trail turns sharply to your left (west) and starts to head downhill. In less than 0.1 mile, cross Preserve Parkway once again. Across the street you will see a sidewalk with guard rails. Pick up the Red Trail where the guard rails end to your left and head back into the woods to the west.

1.0 Pass a bench on your left. In a few feet come to the intersection with the White Trail. Turn right (east) onto the White Trail. In less than 0.1 mile, come to a short side trail that leads to a nice little cascade in Hurricane Creek.

1.1 Cross over Hurricane Creek and a nice cascade using a bridge. The path becomes rockier as it parallels the creek.

1.2 Begin walking through a small boulder field. In less than 0.1 mile, a side trail takes you to some impressive boulders and outcroppings on the right. When done viewing retrace your steps to the White Trail and turn right (northeast).

1.3 Pass a bridge on the left that was Nathan Hatch's Eagle Scout project (Boy Scout Troop 93) in March 2003. Continue straight to the east on the White Trail. The clear, fairly wide creek flows directly next to you on the right as you meander around boulders. You'll pass another directional sign here and a white #6 marker. *FYI:* The bridge you just passed will be part of the return trip to complete the loop on this end of the trail.

1.3 Pass a large boulder with a good-size hole or "window" straight through it.

1.4 On your left, you'll hear a really nice waterfall in the creek. It's a short off-trail walk to get there but worth it when it's running. In less than 0.1 mile, pick your route and rock-hop across Hurricane Creek to the north. Watch out for slippery rocks. The water may get deep here. The creek will now be running to your right.

1.5 Pass a white #7 marker.

1.7 Cross a runoff into the creek. In less than 0.1 mile, start walking around and between boulders.

1.8 Come to another bridge. Do not cross it. Make a sharp left to the north to continue on the White Trail. The trail is narrow, maybe 2 feet wide, and brushier as it begins a steady incline. In less than 0.1 mile, come to a creek. The trail makes a sharp left turn to the west.

2.0 Arrive at Turtle Rock. There is a directional sign here and White Trail marker #11. In less than 0.1 mile, pass White Trail marker #12.

2.1 Come to a Y at a directional sign with a White Trail marker #13. Go straight to the southwest to begin the blue-blazed Blue Trail (the sign points the way to the Great Wall). In a few feet you'll cross another creek with a small cascade. As you climb to a small ridge, the trail is smooth rock and the path looks like it is a runoff. At the top, the path becomes dirt and sand.

2.2 A trail that connects to the Powerline Trail splits off to the right. Keep going straight to the southwest on the Blue Trail. In less than 0.1 mile, pass Blue Trail marker #12 on the left. You'll be walking through more pines than hardwoods for a bit. The trail is littered with pine needles.

2.4 Pass some interesting rock outcroppings and boulders, one with a small rock shelter, on the right. In less than 0.1 mile, come to another directional sign showing the miles and directions to the Great Wall, Waterfall Trail, White Trail, Turtle Rock, and Boulder Field. Go straight to the west for just a few yards to view another great waterfall. When done retrace your steps and turn right at the directional sign to the south to continue on the Blue Trail. The trail is rocky going downhill. A nice creek will be on your right with several cascades and a small rock shelter carved into the rock.

2.5 Pass Blue Marker # 11 on the left.

2.6 Come to a sign that reads SANDSTONE GLADE—RARE PLANTS, DO NOT DISTURB. (See the text for rules regarding the glade.) You'll hear the sound of a waterfall. Turn right (south) at the sign to continue on the Blue Trail. Immediately cross the creek to pick up the trail on the other side. In less than 0.1 mile, get a great view of a waterfall next to the trail.

2.7 Arrive back at the bridge we passed at mile 1.3. Another nice waterfall will be on your left. Cross over the creek on the bridge and turn right (southwest) onto the White Trail.

2.9 Pass the Red Trail we came in on and continue straight to the west on the White Trail.

3.0 Pass White Trail marker #4. In less than 0.1 mile, cross a nice, wide stream over a bridge built as a Boy Scout Eagle project by Andrew Judson Wills of BSA Troop 119. A waterfall will be on the right. After crossing there is a bench on the right.

3.1 Pass Tunnel Falls on the left.

3.3 Cross another creek.

3.4 Come to a Y. Take the left fork to the south and pass a bench on the right.

3.5 Come to the Frog Pond Trail on the left. You'll hear the frog song when the pond is full. Either take the Frog Pond Trail to visit the pond or continue straight on the White Trail. The two rejoin in 0.1 mile.

3.6 The Frog Pond Trail reunites with the White Trail at a directional sign and White Trail marker #1. Take the left fork to the southwest to continue on the White Trail. The trail is a gravel path for a short distance.

3.7 Returning to Patriot Junction, turn right (north) onto the Blue Trail.

3.8 Turn left (west) to head back to parking lot.

3.9 Arrive back at the trailhead.

16 TANNEHILL IRONWORKS HISTORICAL STATE PARK

Follow four trails back in time to revisit the days of Birmingham's iron and steel glory on this loop at Tannehill Ironworks Historical State Park. The trail is a relatively easy walk that will take you and your pup past a slave cemetery and the amazing stonework of the restored Tannehill blast furnace, which was built by slaves; down an old stagecoach road; and along the beautiful turquoise waters of Roupes Creek. You and your dog will uncover plenty as you explore the trail.

THE RUNDOWN

Start: Behind the Iron & Steel Museum of Alabama
Distance: 4.1-mile lollipop loop
Approximate hiking time: 2.5 hours
Difficulty: Moderate with some short climbs
Trailhead elevation: 486 feet
Highest point: 622 feet
Best season: Year-round; open sunrise to sunset, visitor center and museum open 10 a.m.–4 p.m.
Trail surface: Dirt and gravel
Other trail users: Cyclists
Canine compatibility: Leash required
Land status: Alabama historic state park
Fees and permits: Day-use fee: adults $5, seniors 62 and older

$4, children 6–11 $3, under 6 free; museum admission free with day-use fee
Trail contact: Tannehill Ironworks Historical State Park, 12632 Confederate Pkwy., McCalla; (205) 477-5711; www.tannehill.org
Nearest town: McCalla
Trail tips: Restrooms available at the visitor center and museum; a small camp store and snack bar is located near the campground
Maps: USGS: Halfmile Shoals, AL
Other maps: Trail maps are available at the visitor center or online at www.tannehill.org/activities.html

FINDING THE TRAILHEAD

From the intersection of I-459 and I-20 W / I-59 S, take I-20 W / I-59 S for 5 miles. Take exit 100 (Abernant/Bucksville) and turn left onto AL 216 E. (Shortly after turning onto AL 216, it becomes Bucksville Road.) Follow AL 216 / Bucksville Road for 0.6 mile and make a slight right onto Tannehill Parkway. Travel 1.9 miles and turn right onto Eastern Valley Road. In less than 0.1 mile, turn left onto Confederate Parkway. The park entrance is ahead in 0.7 mile. Trailhead GPS: N33 14.970' / W87 04.297'

THE HIKE

Once again you and your pup will take a walk back in time to the days of Birmingham's amazing iron and steel history along the trails of the Tannehill Ironworks Historical State Park.

This 1,500-acre park features forty historic structures from the period 1830 to 1870, which have been brought in and restored for the public to view. There are churches, blacksmith shops, and even an old grist mill with working water wheel.

The path parallels a row of historic cabins that have now been repurposed to showcase the work of local artisans.

But the centerpiece of Tannehill is the completely rebuilt furnace. The giant stone structure was originally built in 1830 by Daniel Hillman. Unfortunately, two years after starting the operation, Hillman passed away and never saw the fruits of his labor. Local farmer Ninian Tannehill purchased the forge and, with slave labor, built three tall furnaces, all made by hand-carved and hand-placed sandstone bricks.

By 1862, the furnace was producing pig iron for the Confederate army but was quickly put out of business as Union troops moved in and destroyed the foundry.

Fastforward to the 1970s, when the state of Alabama and several colleges resurrected the site. Archaeologists uncovered the old blower house and the main furnace and set about rebuilding it to its former glory. Today, you can visit their work, which is now on the National Register of Historic Places.

This loop hike begins directly behind the Iron & Steel Museum of Alabama (which is free to visit with your paid day-use fee) and uses four trails to do a sprawling loop through this history and the beautiful Tuscaloosa county landscape. For the most part, the loop uses well-maintained dirt, gravel, and clay roads, but remember that after a good rain some of the route, especially the Iron Road Trail, can be quite muddy with several water runoffs crossing it.

The trail has a moderate canopy, so be sure to pack plenty of water for both you and your dog during the hot summer months. Your dog will enjoy the walk and visiting the banks of Roupes Creek on the return leg of the hike.

We begin on the Furnace Trail, where you'll stroll behind the trade cabins, structures from the 1800s that were relocated to the park and now showcase the craftsmanship of local artisans who demonstrate crafts such as quilt making and blacksmithing. The trail parallels the beautiful turquoise water of Roupes Creek. This wide and swift-flowing stream once powered the massive stone Tannehill furnace.

The Furnace Trail ends at the remarkable furnace itself. Take your time to explore the structure—it is an unbelievable highlight of the park. By the way, just after starting the hike you will cross a creek and come to a three-way intersection. The trail on the far right simply loops back onto the middle trail. The middle trail leads to the furnace as well, but it takes you to the top of a ridge and a walkway for another look at the furnace from a different perspective. We'll take this trail on the return trip.

From there we hook up with the Slave Quarters Road. This is a wide dirt road along which the housing for the slaves who built the furnace once stood. The trail ends at its intersection with the Old Bucksville Stage Road. As its name implies, this path was the main highway into the region during the mid-1800s.

As you near the end of the trail, a short side trail off to the right will lead you to the old slave cemetery. All that remains here are unmarked rocks that identify the graves.

Continuing on from the cemetery, the trail joins the Iron Road. This is a nice walk in the woods through an oak and dogwood forest and along the banks of several creeks, including Roupes, a good chance for your pup to cool off.

I've rated the hike as moderate due to small inclines, but they are nothing the average hiker and conditioned dog couldn't handle. It's borderline easy.

The park is usually buzzing with activity as many events take place on the weekends, but none are as big as the park's Trade Days, which are held the third weekend of each month from March through November.

And a friendly reminder: Artifacts, including bricks and stone, are protected by the state of Alabama and cannot be removed.

CREATURE COMFORTS

RESTING UP

Comfort Inn, 5051 Academy Ln., Bessemer; (205) 428-3999; www.choicehotels.com/al/alabama/bessemer/comfort-inn-hotels

You can make reservations online or by phone, but it's best to call the hotel directly to verify there are pet rooms available. One pet up to 20 pounds is allowed per room. There is a $20 per night pet fee charged.

CAMPING

Tannehill Historical State Park, 12632 Confederate Pkwy., McCalla; (205) 477-5711; www.tannehill.org/camping.html

Need a campsite? Tannehill has them: 195 improved campsites with power and water, 100 primitive campsites. Campsites are on a first come, first served basis. Reservations are not accepted, and since the campground can be a bit crowded, be sure to get there early on the day you arrive. Halloween and Tannehill Trade Days are the busiest dates of the year (visit their website for exact dates). Improved campsites are $25 per night for a family of four, with a $3 fee for each additional person. Primitive sites are $20 per night

Tannehill Ironworks Historical State Park

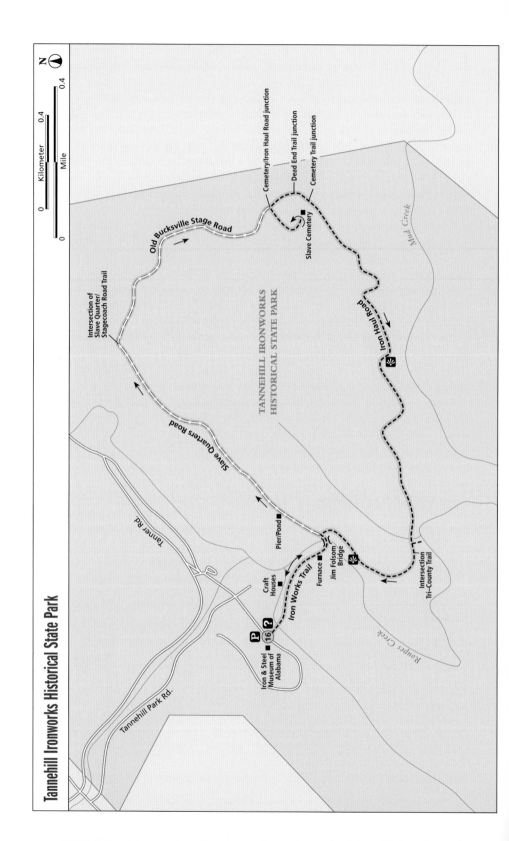

for a family of four, with a $4 fee for each extra person. Seniors 62 and over receive a 15 percent discount, except on holidays.

FUELING UP

Full Moon BBQ, 408 Colonial Promenade Pkwy., Alabaster; (205) 620-4442; full moonbbq.com/

With outdoor seating where you and your well-behaved pup can dine together, Full Moon serves up some great Southern barbecue, slow smoked over hickory-wood fire pits. But it's not just barbecue. They have American favorites as well: hamburgers and hot dogs, as well as salads and soup.

MILES AND DIRECTIONS

0.0 Start from behind the Iron & Steel Museum of Alabama. Head down a set of cement stairs toward the creek to the southeast. Cross the creek on a small wooden bridge (a playground is on the opposite side of the creek on your right; a picnic area is to the left). There is a Y after the bridge. Take the left fork to the east (a sign here reads IRON WORKS TRAIL). This trail takes you behind the craft buildings and to great views of the creek.

0.4 Come to the furnace. Cross the creek to the left (east) over the wood and steel Jim Folsom Bridge. On the other side come to the intersection with the Iron Haul Road. A sign here points to the left (northeast), showing the way to the cemetery and Stagecoach Road. Turn left here onto the Slave Quarters Road.

0.5 Pass a short pier that juts into a pond to the left (west).

0.9 Cross a stream that flows under the road.

1.2 Come to the intersection with the Old Bucksville Stage Road. A sign here points to the cemetery (to the right) and to the furnace (the way you just came). Turn right (southeast) onto the Old Bucksville Stage Road Trail.

1.9 Come to the intersection of the Iron Haul Road Trail and Cemetery Trail. Turn right (southwest) onto the Cemetery Trail.

2.0 Arrive at the slave cemetery. A chain-link fence encircles the site. You can enter through a gate that is tied shut with a rope. From the cemetery the trail continues to the southeast.

2.3 Turn right (southwest) on the Iron Haul Road Trail.

2.8 Start getting good views of Roupes Creek to the left (south).

3.3 A nice grassy, 30-foot-long side trail leads to the banks of the creek.

3.4 Pass the Tri-County Trail coming in from the right (north). Continue straight to the west.

3.6 Good views of Roupes Creek to the left (west).

3.8 Return to the Jim Folsom Bridge. Retrace your steps to the parking lot.

4.1 Arrive back at the parking lot.

17 LAKESIDE TRAIL

You and your family—that includes Fido—will love hiking this 4.0-mile out-and-back along the banks of Lake Lurleen especially if you catch it when there is a crystal-clear blue sky that reflects off the 250-acre lake. There are a couple of places your pup can grab a cool drink from the lake. The turnaround is at the dam that creates the lake. It's a tranquil place to sit and contemplate.

THE RUNDOWN

Start: From the south side of the picnic pavilion
Distance: 4.0-mile out-and-back
Approximate hiking time: 2 hours
Difficulty: Easy over dirt footpaths with some light climbs
Trailhead elevation: 253 feet
Highest point: 308 feet
Best season: Year-round; open 7 a.m. to sunset
Trail surface: Dirt and sand, root studded in places
Other trail users: Cyclists
Canine compatibility: Leash required
Land status: Alabama state park
Fees and permits: Day-use fee: adults $4, children 4-11 and seniors 62-plus $2, children under 4 free

Trail contact: Lake Lurleen State Park, 13226 Lake Lurleen Rd., Coker; (205) 339-1558; www.alapark.com/lake-lurleen-state-park
Nearest town: Tuscaloosa
Trail tips: Restrooms are located at the park office just a little north of the trailhead. If you love to fish, get your Alabama freshwater fishing license and pack your fishing pole for bream, largemouth bass, and catfish. Remember: Dogs are not allowed on the lake's beach, and do not climb on the dam that forms the lake—it's dangerous.
Maps: USGS: Lake Lurleen, AL; available at the park entrance gate or online at www.alapark.com/lake-lurleen-state-park-trail-map

FINDING THE TRAILHEAD

From the intersection of US 43 / Lurleen B. Wallace Boulevard and 5th Street in Tuscaloosa, head west on 5th Street. Travel 1.4 miles and turn right onto Robert Cardinal Airport Boulevard. Travel 1.4 miles and turn right onto Airport Road. In 0.2 mile, turn left onto McFarland Road. Travel 2.7 miles and turn right onto Upper Columbus Road. Travel 2.3 miles and turn right onto Lake Lurleen Road. Continue on Lake Lurleen Road for 2.2 miles and arrive at the entrance gate. After paying your day-use fee, make a left turn immediately past the gate and circle around to the large parking lot adjacent to the building. Park here; the trailhead is at the picnic pavilion on the southwest side of the parking lot. Trailhead GPS: N33 17.823' / W87 40.627'

THE HIKE

Located just north of Tuscaloosa, Lake Lurleen State Park is another serene state park that boasts a huge lake and plenty of amenities for you and your dog to enjoy for a day or more.

The Lakeside Trail that we'll be hiking is part of the park's Tashka Trail System. The system has 24 miles of winding hiking and mountain-biking trails that begin and end at either the north or south trailhead. The Lakeside Trail begins at the south trailhead behind the entrance gate.

Archer checks out the ducks and turtles along the trail.

This 4.0-mile out-and-back is just a gem of a hike along the banks of the beautiful, clear Lake Lurleen, a 250-acre lake that is 0.5 mile wide and 1.5 miles long at its longest points. The deepest part of the lake is 48 feet.

To get to the south trailhead, after paying your day-use fee, simply circle around the entrance gate for parking. You will see a picnic area to the south. That's the trailhead for many of the trails in the park.

For the most part, you and your pup will be walking right alongside the banks of the lake with some stunning views of the shimmering water. As with most parks, dogs are not allowed to swim at the beach area, but you will find a couple of access points along the route where they can splash a bit. As always, use caution with them in the water and watch for snakes.

For the most part, the path is sand and dirt littered with rocks and roots. The path ranges from 4 to 5 feet wide to a narrow 2-foot path. Colorful wildflowers, including red cardinals, downy phlox, spiderwort, and blooming dogwood brighten your walk in season, as do the pink and white flowers of the numerous mountain laurel bushes dotting the path.

On a short, grassy patch from the trailhead, you will undoubtedly be greeted by a couple of geese as well as wood and mallard ducks looking for a handout. Later, as you head into the woods, keep watch for logs in the water where you might see box turtles lined up, taking in the warm sun.

A highlight of the trip comes at the hike's turnaround at the dam that forms the lake. It's a good spot to sit and relax with the soothing sounds of the falls. It goes without saying: Do not climb on the dam.

Overall, the trail has a good canopy with just the right amount of shade and sun. As you walk, keep your eyes open for mountain bikers. All of the trails at Lake Lurleen State Park are shared.

Remember that the park can get very—and I mean *very*—busy at certain times of the year. It is a hot spot for fishermen who wet their lines from boats and the banks of the lake trying to snag bream, catfish, and largemouth bass. On almost any given weekend, you will see boats lining up at the launch. The park also holds fishing tournaments, which add to the traffic at the entrance. Check the park's event calendar (see Trail Contact, above) to find out when any tournaments are taking place.

And you're in Tuscaloosa, friends. You know, SEC football? University of Alabama? Crimson Tide? The trails can get busy with visitors and campers, and the campgrounds will more than likely be booked solid well in advance for weekends when the Tide have a home game. Check in advance before heading to the park.

CREATURE COMFORTS

RESTING UP

Wingate by Wyndham Tuscaloosa, 4918 Skyland Blvd. E, Tuscaloosa; (205) 553-5400; www.wyndhamhotels.com/wingate

Make your reservations online, but, as always, you may want to call the hotel first to make sure they have pet-friendly rooms available. Two pets of any size are allowed. There is a single $20 first-night fee, $10 each additional night.

CAMPING

Lake Lurleen State Park, 13226 Lake Lurleen Rd., Coker; (205) 339-1558; www.ala park.com/lake-lurleen-camping

Pitch your tent in the cozy confines of Lake Lurleen State Park's campground. The park has ninety-one improved sites and a primitive or "open" area. Make your reservations by phone. Site fees from Mar through Nov are $27 per night, $37 during the University of Alabama Crimson Tide's football team "A-Day" Game (exhibition game) week; from Dec through Feb, $20.63. Primitive sites are $17.49. All fees are charged an additional $4.50 transaction fee plus tax. Seniors (62 and over) receive a 15 percent discount except on holidays and on weekends when the Crimson Tide has a home game. If you plan on putting up a second tent, there is an additional $5 per night fee.

Deerlick Creek, 12421 Deerlick Rd., Tuscaloosa; (205) 759-1591; www.recreation .gov/camping/deerlick-creek/r/campgroundDetails.do?contractCode=NRSO&par kId=71135

This is a beautiful US Army Corps of Engineers campground on the banks of Holt Lake with nice, clean bathhouses, laundry, playground, and more. There are forty-seven sites in all, forty of those are shared with RVs, seven are tent only. The park is open Mar 1 through the last day of Nov. Sites run from $26 to $30 for improved sites, $20 for tent only. Make your reservations on the recreation.gov website.

FUELING UP

Wilhagan's Grille & Tap Room, 2209 4th St., Tuscaloosa; (205) 344-9986; www .wilhagans.com/

A big patio for your pup, a big, delicious menu for you. Start with Wilhagan's Mixed Trips Combo: chicken wings, queso sticks, onion rings, and their broccoli cheddar bites

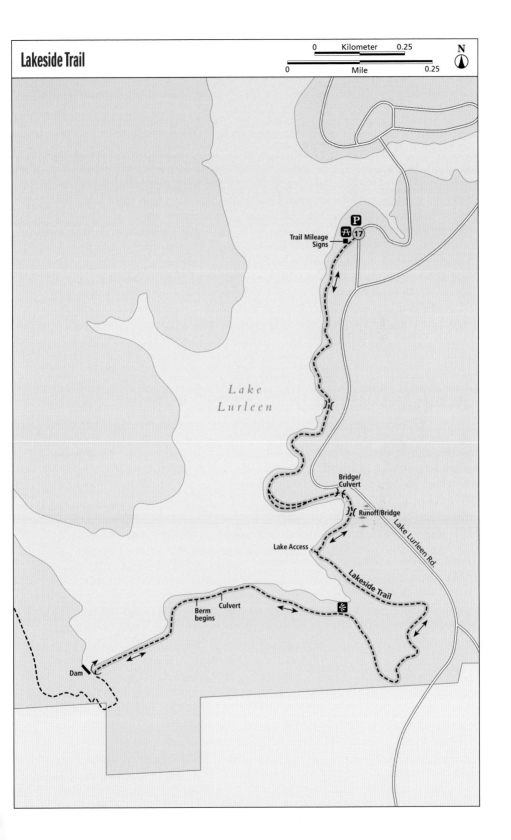

Lakeside Trail

0   Kilometer   0.25

0   Mile   0.25

N

Lake Lurleen

Trail Mileage Signs

P

17

Bridge/Culvert

Runoff/Bridge

Lake Lurleen Rd.

Lake Access

Lakeside Trail

Berm begins

Culvert

Dam

(diced broccoli, onions, and cheddar cheese, battered and fried). After that you will have a hard time deciding what to have for the main meal. The menu is full of delicious salads, wraps, chili, and burgers like the New Orleans burger, a burger blackened with Cajun seasonings and topped with Monterey Jack cheese, mayo, onions, lettuce, tomato, pickle, all on top of a toasted Kaiser roll—unbeatable.

MILES AND DIRECTIONS

0.0 Start in the large parking lot behind the entrance gate to the southwest. In a few yards you will come to the park's picnic pavilion. Walk straight across the facility to the southwest and arrive at a series of trail signs that list the mileage of all the trails accessible from here. Continue to the south. The trail has sandy footing and begins about 3 to 4 feet wide. Mallard ducks swim quietly here and box turtles sun themselves on logs poking out of the water.

0.4 Cross a 50-foot bridge over a runoff.

0.5 At the 0.5-mile marker, the trail splits in two. Take the right fork to stay along the banks of the lake. The path is 2 feet wide and runs just below the park road.

0.7 The two paths rejoin. In less than 0.1 -mile, cross a runoff over a 10-foot bridge and almost immediately after cross a steel culvert directing a spring to the creek.

0.8 Cross a wetland and runoff over a 75-foot bridge. The area is brightened with green ferns. In less than 0.1 mile, cross a runoff over a bridge

0.9 Come to a Y. Take the right fork. It's a short walk to the banks of the lake. This is the best place along the trail where your dog can refresh themselves. When ready, turn around and head back to the trail. Once there, turn right (southeast).

1.0 Pass the 1-mile marker.

1.4 Walk a gradual grade uphill to the top of a ridge with a view of the lake from above.

1.5 Pass the 1.5-mile marker.

1.7 Cross another culvert. In less than 0.1 mile, come out of the woods to an intersection with a wide grass-and-dirt road that is lined with pine needles. Turn right (west) onto the path. Soon you will be walking on a berm next to the lake, which is now on your right.

1.9 Signs indicate that you are at the end of the Lakeside Trail. Continue straight toward the dam.

2.0 Arrive at the lake's dam. Sit awhile and enjoy the soothing sounds. Do not climb on the dam or spillway, and be careful near the edge. The ground is covered with pine needles, making the footing slippery. When ready, turn around and head back to the trailhead.

4.0 Arrive back at the parking lot.

18 PIPER INTERPRETIVE TRAIL

One of the most ecologically diverse rivers in the country, the Cahaba is the setting for this hike through the Cahaba National Wildlife Refuge. You'll begin by hiking down a ridge along an interpretive trail and through a cathedral of towering pines. Slowly you'll make your way up to the top of another ridge for breathtaking views of the river's shoals from high above on several rocky bluffs. And while Fido might not be impressed with the views, they will be intrigued with the exploration.

THE RUNDOWN

Start: From the west side of the parking lot, going around the metal gate
Distance: 2.8-mile out-and-back
Approximate hiking time: 1.5 hours
Difficulty: Moderate with steady climbs to the overlooks
Trailhead elevation: 509 feet
Highest point: 518 feet
Best season: Fall when the hardwoods are blazing with color; open year-round sunrise to sunset
Trail surface: Dirt and rock
Other trail users: None
Canine compatibility: Leash required
Land status: National wildlife refuge
Fees and permits: None
Trail contact: Cahaba National Wildlife Refuge, PO Box 5087, Anniston; (256) 848-7085; www.fws .gov/cahabariver/

Nearest town: Montevallo
Trail tips: For the most part, this is a wonderful walk in the woods for both you and Fido, especially through the longleaf pines. Bring a camera to capture spectacular views of the Cahaba River from high above on the bluffs. The view of the shoals below, where the famous Cahaba lily blooms, is amazing. The parking lot is kind of hidden away, so go slow as you approach it or you might miss it. It is a wide gravel lot that can hold fifty cars easily.
Maps: USGS: West Blocton East, AL
Other: Be careful and keep your pup leashed as you climb the ridge after mile 0.7. There are very high and steep drop-offs straight down to the river.

FINDING THE TRAILHEAD

From the intersection of Middle Street and AL 25 in Montevallo, take AL 25 south for 8.6 miles. Turn right onto Bulldog Bend Road. Travel 5.9 miles and turn left onto Bibb CR 24 / Cahaba River Drive. Travel 1.2 miles. The parking lot and trailhead will be on the left; it's a little hard to see, so keep your eyes peeled. Trailhead GPS: N33 05.291' / W87 02.917'

THE HIKE

The Cahaba River is a tributary of the Alabama River that winds its way through Alabama's largest city, Birmingham, and provides drinking water for one-fifth of the state's population. It is significant because it has been recognized by scientists as one of the most ecologically diverse rivers in the country.

The Cahaba is the longest free-flowing river in the state and plays host to an amazing variety of plant and aquatic life. In fact, the river has been identified as having more species of fish than there are living in the entire state of California—131 to be exact.

The trail rambles through a cathedral of longleaf pine.

In all, 64 rare and unique plants and animals can be found in and around these waters, including 13 that can't be found anywhere else in the world. The most famous plant that grows in the river is the Cahaba lily, with its delicate, snowy-white pedals. The lily requires a special environment to thrive: a fast-moving, rocky river. It is only found in three places—Georgia, South Carolina, and here on the Cahaba River.

Many people love to paddle the Cahaba to see the flowers and the landscape the river flows through, but for this hike, we're going to take you on a journey for a different look at the river—from high above on rocky bluffs.

This hike is located in the Cahaba River National Wildlife Refuge. Established in 2002, the refuge protects almost 3,000 acres of the Cahaba and its watershed. Thanks to the work of volunteers with the Friends of Cahaba, there are some remarkable hiking opportunities for viewing the wonders of the river, and this hike is one of them: the Piper Interpretive Trail.

The path is a 2.8-mile out-and-back hike that is handicap accessible for the first 0.7 mile or so before it makes some moderate climbs up rocky ridges. The trail begins by heading down a slope to a nice wide and level leaf-covered path under a wonderful canopy provided by the hardwoods that blaze stunning colors in the fall and provide plenty of shade from summer heat. This section was once part of the old Piper #2 Mine railroad bed that used to run through the region.

It won't be long before you find yourself walking through a cathedral of towering pines lining the trail, their needles covering the path and providing soft footing. Many birds, including wood thrushes, Kentucky warblers, and great-crested flycatchers, serenade you as you walk.

Soon you'll notice a change in the terrain as the path gets rockier and steeper as it climbs to the top of a ridge. From here you will come to two platforms with spectacular views of the river itself and its fast-moving shoals.

The second big overlook is the turnaround for this hike. Just past the overlook, it looks like the trail continues farther on, and it does, but if you follow it you'll end up walking a really difficult gravel road back to the trailhead. The gravel is 3 to 4 inches in size. Okay, more like rocks instead of gravel. Either way, it makes for an unpleasant walk, especially for your dog.

There is no water on this trail, so be sure to pack enough for both you and your dog. And be sure to leash them as you start going up the ridge. On the side of the trail, there are sheer drops straight down to the river banks.

CREATURE COMFORTS

CAMPING

Tannehill Historical State Park, 12632 Confederate Pkwy., McCalla; (205) 477-5711; www.tannehill.org/camping.html

Need a campsite? Tannehill has them: 195 improved campsites with power and water, 100 primitive campsites. Campsites are available on a first come, first served basis. Reservations are not accepted, and since the campground can be a bit crowded, be sure to get there early on the day you arrive. Halloween and Tannehill Trade Days are the busiest times of the year (visit the Trail Contact website for exact dates). Improved campsites are $25 per night for a family of four, with a $3 fee for each additional person. Primitive sites

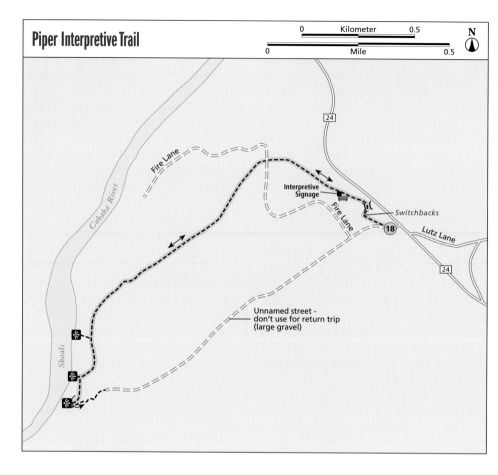

Piper Interpretive Trail

0 — Kilometer — 0.5
0 — Mile — 0.5

N

Cahaba River

Fire Lane

24

Interpretive Signage

Fire Lane

Switchbacks

18

Lutz Lane

24

Unnamed street - don't use for return trip (large gravel)

Shoals

are $20 per night for a family of four, with a $4 fee for each extra person. Seniors 62 and over receive a 15 percent discount, except on holidays.

FUELING UP

Chez Lulu, 1911 Cahaba Rd., Birmingham; (205) 870-7011; chezlulu.us/

You and your pup will be more than welcome at the outdoor seating area of Chez Lulu. The menu leans toward the European side at the restaurant's Continental Bakery, with a lunch menu featuring sandwiches like lox and bagels, a vegan sandwich, and tarragon chicken salad. Or try their *socca,* a savory chickpea crepe served with tapenade (a black olive and caper spread).

MILES AND DIRECTIONS

0.0 Start at the kiosk on the northwest side of the parking lot. There is a metal gate here. You'll see a gravel road heading to the left (west) and a dirt path to the right. Take the dirt path to the northwest. The 6-foot-wide path starts high above a deep ravine with a railing on the right. In less than 0.1 mile, begin heading steeply downhill through a series of switchbacks.

0.1 Cross a 40-foot bridge over a runoff area. You'll see Bibb CR 24 below to the right and rock outcroppings on the left.

0.2 Pass a sign that tells about the songbirds in the area on the right. On the left is a bench that is mounted to a platform of pavers with the names of donors to the refuge inscribed on them. There is also a sign that describes the snakes in the refuge.

0.4 Cross a fire lane to the west (at the sign with the hiker logo and an arrow pointing straight).

0.5 Pass a bench on the left.

0.8 Pass a bench on the left.

0.9 Pass a trail direction sign pointing back the way you came, but keep going straight to the southwest.

1.2 A side trail to the right (west) heads steeply down the hill to a platform for an excellent view of the shoals of the Cahaba River far below. When done viewing turn around and head back to the main trail. At the trail turn right and continue to the south. In less than 0.1 mile, cross a bridge over a seasonal stream.

1.3 Another side trail on the right heads steeply down to a rock bluff for a river view. Use caution on the bluff.

1.4 You will come to a sign pointing to the left and right (north and south, respectively). Turn to the right for a final look at the river. When done, turn around and retrace your steps to the trailhead.

2.8 Arrive back at the trailhead.

19 FLAGG MOUNTAIN LOOP

If you're looking for a hike that offers you and your pup quiet solitude away from maddening crowds, then enjoy a walk on the Flagg Mountain Loop. This hike takes you through a mixed pine and hardwood forest that radiates color in the fall, becomes silent with a blanket of snow in winter, and provides a cooling canopy in the summer. The trail passes a spring and CCC cabins that were built in 1935 and are currently being brought back to life, and with a short detour, visits the amazing stonework of the CCC Flagg Mountain fire tower. You can also extend the hike into a nice overnighter.

THE RUNDOWN

Start: From the northern Yellow Trail trailhead on Weogufka Forest Road
Distance: 2.4-mile lollipop loop with an out-and-back
Approximate hiking time: 2 hours
Difficulty: Moderate up and down rolling hills; one steep climb up a power line to the fire tower
Trailhead elevation: 885 feet
Highest point: 1,087 feet
Best season: Year-round; open sunrise to sunset; hunting is allowed in the fall (see Other, below)
Trail surface: Dirt and rock footpath, some old dirt road
Other trail users: Hunters
Canine compatibility: Voice control
Land status: State forest
Fees and permits: None
Trail contact: Alabama Hiking Trail Society (AHTS), PO Box 691, Montgomery, 36101 ; hikealabama.org
Nearest town: Weogufka
Trail tips: The fall colors are simply beautiful along this loop, so bring

the camera. As of this writing, the cabins are being renovated, and by the time you read this, there may be restrooms available. Be sure to check in and chat with the new caretaker, hiking legend M. J. "Nimblewill Nomad" Eberhart, to let him know you're there and to hear some of his amazing hiking stories. Remember, hunting is allowed in the fall (see Other, below, for more information).
Maps: Flagg Mountain, AL
Other maps: Available at the trailhead kiosk and online at hikealabama.org/joomla/index.php/trails-and-maps/weogufka-state-forest-flagg-mountain
Other: Hunting is allowed in the fall. Please visit the Alabama Department of Conservation and Natural Resources website for information at www.outdooralabama.com/hunting/seasons-and-bag-limits.

FINDING THE TRAILHEAD

From the intersection of US 231 and CR 29 in Wetumpka, take US 231 north 10.2 miles. Turn left onto Buyck Road. Travel 7.7 miles (after 5 miles Buyck Road becomes CR 31). Turn right on CR 29. Travel 12.8 miles and turn left onto CR 16. Travel 0.7 mile and turn right onto CC Camp Road. Travel 3.4 miles. The trailhead is on the right, tucked away in the woods just off the road. A diamond-shaped yellow and green AHTS sign is here. You can park on a narrow strip of shoulder only a few yards before the trailhead on the left. Trailhead GPS: N32 59.084' / W86 21.274'

THE HIKE

It's known as the "state park that never was," a park started by the Civilian Conservation Corps (CCC) in the 1930s that was abandoned as World War II began. Today there is renewed interest in Flagg Mountain, and work has begun to make it the destination it could have been.

Flagg Mountain was to be another amazing Alabama state park built by the CCC. High atop the mountain, which is recognized as the southernmost mountain over 1,000 feet tall in

Just a few of the "amenities" you'll spot along the trail.

the Appalachians, the young men of the Corps hand-split logs for cabins and cut thick stone for the cabin foundations and what would be the centerpiece of the park, a 52-foot-tall observation tower completely built out of hand-cut and hand-laid stone. Similar towers can be seen along the Appalachian Trail, like Perkin's Memorial Tower at Bear Mountain State Park in New York or the tower atop Alabama's highest mountain, Cheaha.

The cabins and tower were built but, as I said, the war curtailed the construction, and the property reverted to the Alabama Forestry Commission (AFC), who manned the tower to watch for fires until the early 1980s. The handiwork of the CCC was left in the hands of nature.

Off and on in the mid-2000s, a statewide hiking group worked to build trails around the mountain, but the state halted the effort until it could figure out exactly what should be done with the property.

With the hard work of local trail volunteers like Callie Thornton, Joe Jones, Barbara Murchison, and so many more that I can't possibly mention them all here, plus the foresight of the AFC management and staff, a plan was put into place in which the cabins and tower would be restored to their former glory and a live-in caretaker would manage the property.

Today, Flagg Mountain in the Weogufka State Forest is beginning to show signs of life. Many of the cabins have been restored, and plans are in the works to stabilize the tower so visitors can once again visit. By the way, when they do open it, on a clear evening from the top you can see the lights of Montgomery to the south and Birmingham to the north.

The site also has a new caretaker, our good friend and hiking legend M. J. "Nimblewill Nomad" Eberhart. "Nomad" is one of about one hundred people to do the Triple Crown hikes (Pacific Crest, Appalachian, and Continental Divide Trails) and probably a hundred more hikes. When you visit the mountain, be sure to stop and say hi and ask him about his adventures. He's had a few.

I've said it before and it still holds true today—probably more so now that the mountain is more easily accessible—but Flagg is one of my favorite hiking destinations. The mountain is the perfect place to explore, with its hardwoods blazing color in the fall, snow-dusted silence and stillness in the winter, and a thick canopy overhead during the hot months of summer. Your pup will love it, too, with the chance to roam free (if they have a solid training with voice commands) and do some exploring.

The Flagg Mountain Loop will take you through that beautiful forest and to the cabins and tower. The loop uses two trails, the Yellow and White Trails, 1- to 2-foot-wide dirt and rock footpaths with either white or yellow paint blazes. At the southern intersection of the two trails, you will leave the blazed trails and head out on an old unmarked CCC road to visit the cabins. At the cabins you will see a long, cleared power line heading straight up the mountain. This is the path you will take to reach the tower. It's a steep climb, but there is an alternative if you don't want to make the jaunt (see Miles and Directions, below).

There are one or two creeks on the hike, but they are seasonal. Pack plenty of water for both you and your dog. There is water on top of the mountain at the cabins and the tower, but remember, as of this writing, you cannot go inside the tower.

CREATURE COMFORTS

RESTING UP

Comfort Inn, 2945 US 280, Alexander City; (256) 234-5900; www.choicehotels.com/alabama/alexander-city/comfort-inn-hotels

Make your reservations online. The hotel allows three pets per room up to 75 pounds total. There is a $10 per pet, per night fee charged. Be sure to call the hotel to see about pet-friendly room availability before making your reservation.

CAMPING

Wind Creek State Park, 4325 AL 128, Alexander City; (256) 329-0845; www.alapark.com/wind-creek-state-park; reserve online at guestrez.megahotel.com/Campground/Home/Index/P3R53

Wind Creek is touted as the largest state-run campground in the country, and it's hard to argue that. The park has 586 improved campsites with 157 on the banks of Wind Creek, a finger of Lake Martin. Prices range from $22 per night Sun through Thurs, $25 Fri, Sat, and holidays; add $3 for waterfront sites. There is a $4.50 transaction fee plus tax, and a 3.5 percent lodging fee. Make your reservations online.

Flagg Mountain, CC Camp Road, Sylacauga; hikealabama.org

Yes, you can now tent camp atop Flagg Mountain, the southernmost mountain over 1,000 feet in the Appalachians. As of this writing, camping is free. All that is requested is a donation to help maintain the cabins, tower, and trails. You must also check in with the caretaker, "Nimblewill Nomad," before pitching camp. Contact the Alabama Hiking Trail Society by e-mail (ahts@hikealabama.org) for more details.

FUELING UP

Catherine's Market, 17 Russell Farms Rd., Alexander City; (256) 215-7070; www.catherinesatcrossroads.com/

A beautiful old barn transformed into a wonderful market and café, Catherine's has a full line of fresh dairy, meat, seafood, and a bakery. But it's their café you'll want to try, with everything from their Eggs Benny (eggs Benedict with Creole hollandaise) to their mouthwatering Reuben, with fresh corned beef and sauerkraut on rye, to a brimming salad bar.

Flagg Mountain Loop

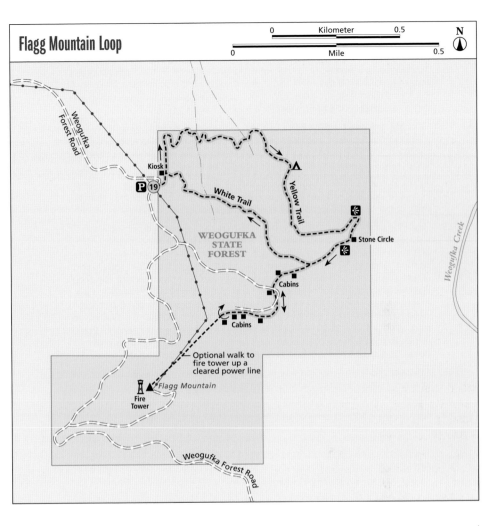

MILES AND DIRECTIONS

0.0 Start at the trailhead on Weogufka Forest Road (formerly CC Camp Road). The trail is a dirt and rock footpath covered with pine straw or leaves and is generally 1–2 feet wide. In less than 0.1 mile, come to the trail's kiosk, where there is a large map of the trail, information about AHTS, and a registry. This is also the northern intersection with the White Trail, which we will use for the return trip. The White Trail comes in from the east. Continue straight on the Yellow Trail to the north.

0.3 Cross a short 15-foot bridge, built as an Eagle Scout project, over a seasonal creek. Immediately after crossing the trail turns left (north).

0.5 Cross another seasonal stream. The trail immediately turns to the left (north) after crossing.

0.7 Pass a campsite with steel fire ring to the right.

1.0 Get some views of surrounding mountains to the left (east). You may see Weogufka Creek far below in the valley when the leaves are down.

1.1 Pass a circle of stone on the left. In less than 0.1 mile, there is another nice view of the mountains to the left (east).

1.2 Come to the southern intersection of the Yellow Trail with the White Trail. The White Trail heads off to the right (northwest). The Yellow Trail turns left (southeast). An old dirt road continues straight to the southwest. We'll come back to this spot again later. Right now, continue straight on the unmarked dirt road uphill to the southwest.

1.3 Pass the first cabin built by the CCC to your right. It is simply a rundown frame with a fireplace and chimney. In less than 0.1 mile, pass a second CCC cabin on your right that, again, is a shell of its former self. At this second cabin turn left (southwest) and head down the power line.

1.4 At the bottom of the power line, do not yet continue straight up the steep opposite side. Instead turn left (south) onto a wide dirt road. In less than 0.1 mile, come to a Y. Take the right fork to the west.

1.5 Pass one of the CCC cabins on the right that has been restored and shows the beautiful handiwork of the CCC. In less than 0.1 mile, pass the second and third restored cabins on the right. Be sure to check in with "Nimblewill Nomad" and say hi. To your left you will see the Flagg Mountain tower high atop the mountain. There is a cleared power line here that leads to the top. Head southeast and follow the power line to the top of the mountain. It's a pretty steep climb. *OPTIONS:* If you don't want to make the climb but still want to see the tower, do not climb up the mountain. Turn around here and retrace your steps to the White and Yellow Trails intersection at mile 1.2, then return to the trailhead on the White Trail. Get in your car and drive south down CC Camp Road 0.9 mile and turn left onto the tower road.

1.8 Arrive at the fire tower. Remember, as of this writing, people are not allowed inside for safety reasons. When you're done, turn around and start retracing your steps to the intersection at mile 1.2.

2.3 Back at the intersection with the White and Yellow Trails, turn left (northwest) onto the White Trail.

2.7 Cross a seasonal creek.

2.8 Arrive back at the kiosk at the north intersection with the Yellow Trail. Turn left (south) onto the Yellow Trail and retrace your steps to the trailhead.

2.9 Arrive back at the trailhead.

PUPPY PAWS AND GOLDEN YEARS

Hiking the Appalachians from Alabama to Maine

How about a real hiking adventure for you and your dog? How about hiking the entire Appalachian Mountains, not just from Georgia to Maine but from Alabama to Maine?

The southern end of the Appalachian range is actually in Alabama. Many recognize Flagg Mountain as being the southernmost Appalachian mountain over 1,000 feet tall.

With that in mind, groups of volunteers and nonprofit organizations, as well as state and local governments, have made this adventure a reality by connecting Alabama's long trail, the Pinhoti Trail (which winds through the Talladega National Forest), to Flagg Mountain. The northern end of the Pinhoti was connected to the Appalachian Trail via the Benton MacKaye Trail in Georgia back in 2006.

The result? A true Appalachian hike along the ridges of the entire range, from Alabama to Maine—and beyond.

20 LAKE TRAIL

This loop hike is a subset of the beautiful and peaceful nature trails on the campus of the University of West Alabama. It's a nice little walk in the woods to get your pup out and acclimated to hiking or just a chance for both of you to get out and stretch those legs. The hike is an easy 2.4-mile loop around Lake LU as it passes little coves on the banks of the lake where beautiful, fragrant wildflowers grow spring through summer and your dog will be interested in the squirrels and chipmunks darting in and out of the brush.

THE RUNDOWN

Start: From the north side of the parking lot near Tartt Stadium at the wetland
Distance: 2.4-mile loop
Approximate hiking time: 1.5–2 hours
Difficulty: Easy over rolling dirt paths and flat grassy trails at the lake
Trailhead elevation: 154 feet
Highest point: 179 feet
Best season: Year-round; open 6 a.m. to 30 minutes before sunset, closed Mon and Tues
Trail surface: Dirt, rock, grass footing; short amount of road walk
Other trail users: Fishermen
Canine compatibility: Leash required
Land status: College recreation area
Fees and permits: None
Trail contact: University of West Alabama, UWA Station 30, Livingston; (205) 652-9266; http://

legacy.uwa.edu/Lake_LU_Nature_Trails.aspx
Nearest town: Livingston
Trail tips: This is a short but fun little walk around the lake, where spring through summer you'll find yourself snapping pictures of the many wildflowers. Be sure to pack along the bug spray during those seasons, too. You will be walking through some wetlands and crossing streams where mosquitoes are sure to find you. Restrooms are located in Tartt Field (the baseball field) near the trailhead. No swimming is allowed in the lake.
Maps: USGS: Livingston, AL
Other maps: Available at the trailhead kiosk or online at http://legacy.uwa.edu/Lake_LU_Nature_Trails.aspx

FINDING THE TRAILHEAD

From Demopolis at the intersection of South Cedar Avenue and US 80, take US 80 west 14.3 miles. Turn right onto AL 28 West. Travel 12.3 miles and turn right onto North Washington Street. Travel 1.2 miles and turn left onto University Drive. In 0.4 mile, turn right into the Tartt Stadium parking lot. Continue straight behind the stadium, and in less than 0.1 mile, you'll be at the parking lot and trailhead. Trailhead GPS: N32 36.179' / W88 11.387'

THE HIKE

If your pup has never been hiking before, or it's been a long time for both your dog and you, you want to start off nice and easy on a trail that is interesting. The Lake Trail on the campus of the University of West Alabama is just the ticket.

The lake itself is called Lake LU (pronounced just like you see it: El Yoo). It is a 54-acre man-made lake that was constructed in 1976. Just as it was over forty years ago, the lake is a hub of activity, with regular events scheduled at the picnic pavilions, and rodeos and

A greeting for hikers just after the start of the Lake Trail hike.

horse barrel racing in the nearby arena. The lake is stocked with bass and bream, so if you love to fish, bring along that rod and reel. Just be sure that you have the appropriate Alabama fishing license (see Trail Contact, above, for details).

The parking lot and trailhead are located on the east side of the college's baseball park, Tartt Field. It is a very small parking lot that can comfortably hold five cars. If it's full, just park on the side of the road out of the way and try not to block anybody.

The trail starts to the north, crossing a bridge over a nice wetland and creek where cattails and wildflowers blow in the wind. Once across you'll arrive at the trailhead kiosk. The first part of the trail is an interpretive nature trail, so be sure to take a brochure.

At the kiosk, two trails begin. The Forest Trail, as the college's map calls it, and the Prairie Trail. These names can be confusing because on the ground the two trails have signs labeling them the Nature Trail and the Meadow or Blackland Prairie Trail. Just know they are one and the same. We'll begin the hike described here by heading north on the Nature (Forest) Trail. You'll cross the Prairie Trail twice more, once at about 0.2 mile and then again at about 0.3 mile.

Just after passing the kiosk you will be greeted with an old, dead tree that has been carved with the word *Nature* on it. An appropriate welcoming if ever there was one.

The trail begins as a wide 7- to 8-foot dirt and small gravel road. There are some interesting orange mushrooms growing here, almost the size of softballs. Eventually the Nature (Forest) Trail becomes the Lake Trail as it narrows down to a standard 2- to 3-foot-wide dirt and root-strewn path.

Along the Lake Trail you will be shaded by the thick canopy and walk through some nice wetlands before coming out to the banks of the lake itself. You'll pass several little coves where wildflowers bloom and songbirds serenade you. Don't be surprised if you round a bend and come upon a fisherman in a small boat trying to land a catch. Blue herons love to sit and wait in these little coves for their own catch.

The trail ends with a short road walk back to the trailhead.

CREATURE COMFORTS

RESTING UP
Comfort Inn, 141 Truckers Blvd., Livingston; (205) 652-4839; www.choicehotels .com/alabama/livingston/comfort-inn-hotels

Make your reservations online but be sure to call the hotel first to make sure they have pet-friendly rooms available before booking. Two pets are allowed per room. There is a $20 per pet, per night fee.

CAMPING

Forkland Campground, 1365 Forkland Park Rd., Forkland; (334) 289-5530; www .recreation.gov/camping/campgrounds/232590

This is a beautiful little US Army Corps of Engineers campground on the banks of Demopolis Lake, the largest lake along the Black Warrior River, and you may be treated to bald eagles soaring over your campsite. Forkland has forty-two improved sites with water and electricity for $26 per night. Most of the sites are located on or very close to the lake. Make your reservations online.

FUELING UP

Sonic Drive-In, 407 US 80, Demopolis; (334) 289-5905; www.sonicdrivein.com/

You know it, you love it. Sonic Drive-In is just a good, old-fashioned drive-in with burgers, hot dogs, breakfast burritos, amazing hand-mixed shakes, and roller-skating carhops. Of course, you can eat in your car with your dog or sit under the covered outdoor patio.

MILES AND DIRECTIONS

0.0 Start from the trailhead on the north side of the parking lot. Head north, crossing a 200-foot bridge over a wetland with tall cattails. At the end arrive at a kiosk with information about the environment you are walking through, wildlife you'll see, and directional signs that point to the Prairie Trail (to the right and left), and the Nature Trail (Forest) / Lake Loop (straight to the north), Head straight on the Nature (Forest) Trail / Lake Loop. Behind the kiosk you'll see a neat old tree trunk with the word *Nature* carved into it.

0.2 Pass a bench on the left. In less than 0.1 mile, come to a T intersection with a bench. You'll see the Prairie Trail to your right. Turn left to stay on the Nature (Forest) Trail / Lake Loop and immediately cross a stream over a 150-foot-long bridge.

0.3 The Nature (Forest) Trail splits off to the left; take the right fork to continue on the Lake Loop. In less than 0.1 mile, cross a 75-foot boardwalk with lots of wildflowers. At the end come to an intersection. The Meadow Trail is to the left, Blackland Prairie Trail to the right. Continue straight to the northwest to stay on the Lake Loop trail. The path is wide and grassy here.

0.4 You'll be walking next to a cow pasture with a barbed wire fence to the right. Watch for a sharp right turn down a gully at the end of the fence. And be prepared. There are cows and bulls in the pasture; your pup could get spooked.

0.6 Pass the Beaver Lodge Trail to the left. Continue straight and cross a 21-foot-long bridge.

0.7 Pass a picnic table on right as the trail bends to the left and crosses a wide, deep creek over a bridge. In less than 0.1 mile, pass a sign that shows the way to the Alpha Center on the right. Turn left (southwest) to stay on the Lake Trail.

0.8 Cross a footbridge over a runoff. You will start to see the lake through the trees on the left.

0.9 Come out to a clearing and your first good view of the lake. The horse stables are to your right. You'll be walking alongside the lake for the remainder of the hike.

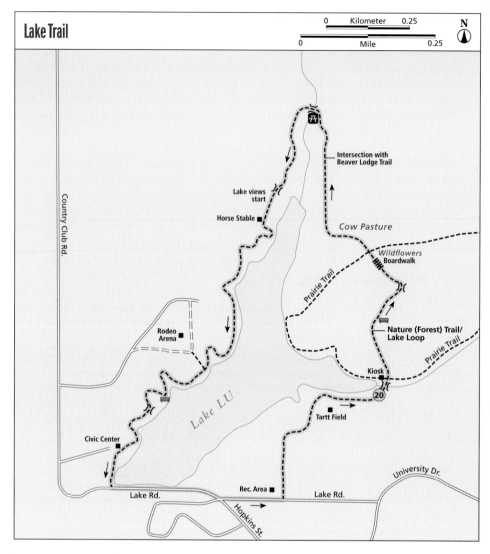

1.3 Pass a cutoff on the right that leads to the rodeo arena. Continue straight. The trail is grass and dirt from here on until you come to the road. Signs dot the trail indicating horses are not allowed. In less than 0.1 mile, pass a second cutoff to the rodeo arena on the right.

1.6 Pass a bench on the left next to the lake. In less than 0.1 mile, cross a 30-foot bridge over a runoff.

1.7 Pass the college's Civic Center on the right.

1.8 Come to Lake Road. Turn left (east) and walk the shoulder of the road.

2.0 Come to a Y in the road. Take the left fork, walking on the wide grassy shoulder.

2.1 Turn left through the gates of the recreation area and follow the edge of the parking lot back to the trailhead, passing behind Tartt Field.

2.4 Arrive back at the trailhead.

21 CHEROKEE RIDGE ALPINE TRAIL

Get a grand tour and view of Lake Martin from the Cherokee Ridge Alpine Trail. The trail is a nice, winding walk through the pine and hardwood forest, bedecked in mountain laurel from spring through summer. The highlight is the beautiful clear waters of the lake itself, with several places you can just sit and reflect and Fido can cool off.

THE RUNDOWN

Start: From the overlook on Overlook Drive. The trail begins from the northeast corner of the overlook.
Distance: 3.3-mile loop
Approximate hiking time: 2 hours, but you will want to linger at the lake.
Difficulty: Moderate over a dirt and rock footpath made a little easier by multiple switchbacks
Trailhead elevation: 730 feet
Highest point: 732 feet
Best season: Year-round; open sunrise to sunset
Trail surface: Dirt and rock footpath
Other trail users: None
Canine compatibility: Leash required
Land status: Alabama Power-leased property
Fees and permits: None

Trail contact: Cherokee Ridge Alpine Trail Association, PO Box 240503, Eclectic, AL 36024; www.crata.org/
Nearest town: Wetumpka
Trail tips: Of course, you'll need your camera for some excellent shots of Lake Martin. Also, bring your bug spray. Every time I've hiked this trail, the insects weren't bad, but when you're around water, well, you know. There are several places where your dog can get a drink in the clear water and maybe cool off. You will find others but be careful; many of the banks are steep and fairly high. Those areas are not safe to let your pup slide down. Two portable johns are available at the overlook and trailhead.
Maps: USGS: Red Hill, AL

FINDING THE TRAILHEAD

From the intersection of US 231 and AL 170 in Wetumpka, take AL 170 east 14.8 miles (in 11.8 miles AL 170 becomes AL 63 N / Kowaliga Road). Turn right onto E. Cotton Road / CR 407 and travel 4.9 miles. Turn left onto AL 229 N / Red Hill Road. Travel 0.6 mile and turn right onto AL 50 E. Travel 2.8 miles and turn left onto Overlook Drive and travel 1.2 miles. The parking lot and overlook will be on the left. The trail begins at the wooden sign on the northeast corner of the overlook. Trailhead GPS: N32 41.472' / W85 53.988'

THE HIKE

It really wasn't that long ago that the only hiking trails around the cool, clear waters of Lake Martin were at Wind Creek State Park. But a group of local volunteers led by a man named Jimmy Lanier changed that and created a series of remarkable trails around the lake that climb its craggy banks for spectacular views.

The inventory of trails now includes the Smith Mountain Fire Tower Loop (see Appendix E: Bonus Hikes at a Glance), the John B. Scott Forever Wild Trail (Hike 22) which opened just as I was putting this book together, and the Deadening Trail. But this trail is the one that started it all: the Cherokee Ridge Alpine Trail.

The trail builders made sure that major intersections are well marked.

That group of volunteers, collectively known as the Cherokee Ridge Alpine Trail Association (CRATA) built this trail soon after the organization was established in 2004. Since its opening, the trail has become a very popular destination. The overlook at the trailhead is a beautiful stone and cement facility offering what is touted as the best panoramic view of the lake and surrounding hills. You may just want to sit here for a while and take it in. When you drive up, you can't miss its large engraved granite sign.

That overlook now has several picnic tables, informational nature signage, and his and hers vault toilets.

From the overlook the trail heads off to the northeast under the tall wooden trailhead sign. The white-blazed trail is moderate in difficulty, using several switchbacks to navigate down from the top of the ridge to the lake below. The path is hard-packed dirt studded with rocks and roots, and it can get very rocky at times. Sometimes the path is thick with a covering of pine straw.

On the way down you will be passing some interesting rock outcroppings and bluffs that show the signs of the weathering that Mother Nature has put them through. Brilliant green lichen clings to the boulders that line the path, and from spring through summer you will pass through a couple of short "tunnels" of mountain laurel.

Once you reach the lake you will see just how clear the water is. The path weaves its way around the shoreline, sometimes right on the water's edge and other times a good 15 feet above it. It goes without saying but, as always, use caution with your pup along the trail and these bluffs. I've indicated a couple of places where Fido can get a drink and maybe splash around a bit, and, depending on your dog, I'm sure you'll find more.

As mentioned, the trail uses white paint blazes to keep you on track. CRATA uses the "dit-dot" method of blazing. Normally you will see only one blaze on a tree or a rock to keep you going in the right direction. Where the trail makes a sharp turn, there will be two blazes, one on top of the other. This is known as a "dit-dot." The top blaze shows you the direction of the turn: If it's offset to the left, the trail turns left. Offset to the right, it turns right.

One thing I was glad to see was a sign CRATA posted along the downhill switchback asking hikers not to reroute the trails. For example, you're going down a series of switchbacks, weaving back and forth downhill. You see the lake below. Instead of following the trail and the switchbacks, you head straight downhill, walking off the trail. Then others do it. This causes the main trail to erode and causes a lot of heartache and heavy work for the volunteers who maintain the trail. Please, stay on the path.

CREATURE COMFORTS

RESTING UP

Clarion Inns and Suites University Center, 1577 S. College St., Auburn; (334) 821-7001; www.choicehotels.com/alabama/auburn/clarion-hotels/al416

Make your reservations by phone. Be sure to let them know that you are traveling with a pet. You can make your reservations online, but you should still call ahead to make sure that pet-friendly rooms are available before booking. Two pets of any size are allowed. There is a $25 per night, per pet plus tax fee. Dogs must be crated if left unattended in a room.

CAMPING

Wind Creek State Park, 4325 AL 128, Alexander City; (256) 329-0845; www.alapark.com/wind-creek-state-park; reserve online at guestrez.megahotel.com/Campground/Home/Index/P3R53

The largest state-run campground in the country is right here in Alabama at Wind Creek. The park has 586 improved campsites with 157 on the banks of Wind Creek, a finger of Lake Martin. Prices range from $22 per night Sun through Thurs, $25 Fri, Sat, and holidays. Add $3 for waterfront sites. There is a $4.50 transaction fee plus tax, and a 3.5 percent lodging fee. Make your reservations online.

FUELING UP

Jim 'n Nick's Community Bar-B-Q, 1920 S. College St., Auburn; (334) 246-5197; www.jimnnicks.com

It's good Southern cookin' at Jim 'n Nick's. Bring your pup to one of their outside tables for hickory grilled catfish, the Southern burger (smothered in barbecue sauce), or the Piggie Express BBQ pork sandwich.

MILES AND DIRECTIONS

0.0 Start from the Cherokee Ridge parking lot and overlook to the north. In a few yards come to the Cherokee Ridge Alpine Trail trailhead.

0.1 Come to a T intersection. A sign here points to the left (west), the direction of the South Loop and Cherokee Ridge Alpine Trail. Turn left (west) onto the South Loop.

0.2 Cross a rocky runoff that looks like it could become quite a waterfall during a good rain.

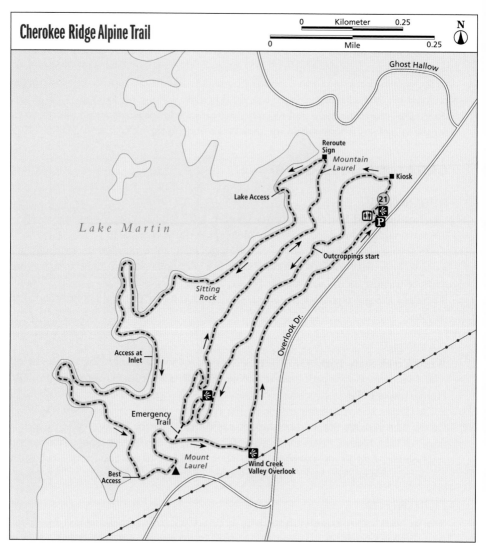

0   Kilometer   0.25
N
0   Mile   0.25

Ghost Hallow

Reroute
Sign
Mountain
Laurel
■ Kiosk

Lake Access

21
P

Lake Martin

Outcroppings start

Sitting
Rock

Overlook Dr.

Access at
Inlet

Emergency
Trail

Mount
Laurel

Wind Creek
Valley Overlook

Best
Access

0.3 Big rock outcroppings start on your left. You will also begin seeing the lake through the trees on the right.

0.6 Pass a side trail to a rock outcropping and, when the leaves are down in late fall and winter, a nice overlook of the lake. The trail narrows considerably here and is very rocky.

0.7 At the end of a switchback, a sign points the direction of the Emergency Trail on the left (south); the South Loop continues to the right. Turn right (north) to continue on the trail. *FYI:* The Emergency Trail is a 0.6-mile path that allows for a quick exit back to the parking lot.

0.9 You'll find yourself walking between boulders and outcrops. In less than 0.1 mile, pass a large rock outcropping that nearly stretches out over the trail. The trail is now leaf covered and levels out for a bit.

1.2 Cross 2 deep runoffs almost back to back. In less than 0.1 mile, pass through a nice section of mountain laurel.

1.3 Pass a sign warning you not to reroute the trails. In less than 0.1 mile, trail arrives at the lake. The path is about 25 feet above the water on a high bank that is lined with bright green moss.

1.4 Come to a good access point for your dog to get a drink and maybe cool their paws.

1.6 Come to a nice sitting rock and possibly lake access for your dog. It is rocky and a bit of a climb down; just be careful.

1.8 Pass another lake access point for your pup.

2.1 The trail narrows again and is a bit brushier with an uphill on the left, a sharp drop off to the right—be careful. In less than 0.1 mile, walk through a short "tunnel" of mountain laurel.

2.5 Cross another big runoff. In less than 0.1 mile, come to a small inlet on your right, another good access point for your pup.

2.6 Pass through another short mountain laurel tunnel.

2.7 Pass a trail coming in from the left (north); this is the opposite end of the Emergency Trail you passed at mile 0.7. A sign here shows that the parking lot is straight ahead to the east. Continue straight to the east. In less than 0.1 mile, pass through a beautiful section of pines and a brilliant green fern glade.

2.8 Arrive at the Wind Creek Valley Overlook. Beyond the road there is a nice view of the hills surrounding the trail.

3.0 Pass another sign that shows that the parking lot is straight ahead to the north. The trail is now a 10- to 15-foot-wide dirt road.

3.1 Turn left (northeast) to continue on the trail into the woods as it as it veers off the dirt road.

3.3 Arrive back at the trailhead.

22 JOHN B. SCOTT FOREVER WILD TRAIL

A beautiful loop hike awaits you on the newest hiking trail built by the Cherokee Ridge Alpine Trail Association along the banks of the Tallapoosa River at Lake Martin Dam. This hike weaves its way back and forth across a sparkling creek that has several small cascades and feeder springs that your dog will love to explore and play in. Your trek culminates in a spectacular view of the surrounding tree-covered hills and valleys from the boulder-strewn summit of Saddle Rock Mountain.

THE RUNDOWN

Start: Under the trailhead sign at the south side of the parking lot
Distance: 4.1-mile loop
Approximate hiking time: 2.5 hours
Difficulty: Moderate due to a rather steep climb and descent on Saddle Rock Mountain
Trailhead elevation: 390 feet
Highest point: 770 feet
Best season: Year-round; open sunrise to sunset
Trail surface: Dirt and rock with a small sandy section and a bit of a gravel road walk
Other trail users: None
Canine compatibility: Voice control
Land status: Alabama state land conservation property
Fees and permits: None
Trail contact: Alabama Forever Wild, State Lands Division, 64 N. Division St., Montgomery; (334) 242-3484; www.alabamaforeverwild.com
Cherokee Ridge Alpine Trail Association, PO Box 240503, Eclectic, AL 36024; www.cherokeeridgealpinetrail.org
Nearest town: Tallassee
Trail tips: The gravel parking lot is large and can hold plenty of vehicles. It's located right on the banks of the river, which makes it a great place to relax and take in the sparkling waters after a good hike. You definitely need your camera; the view on Saddle Rock Mountain is spectacular. The first 0.9 mile can be hot in the summer with little to no shade, so wear a hat and sunscreen (for both you and your dog), and pack that water.
Maps: USGS: Redhill, AL

FINDING THE TRAILHEAD

From the intersection of Old US 231 and US 231 (Tallassee Highway) in Wetumpka, take AL 14 E 0.8 mile and turn left onto AL 170 E / Georgia Road. Travel 10.7 miles until AL 170 becomes AL 63 N / Kowaliga Road. Travel 3.0 miles and turn right onto E. Cotton Road. Travel 4.9 miles and turn left onto AL 229 N / Redhill Road. In 0.6 mile, turn right onto AL 50 E. Travel 2.2 miles and turn right onto Martin Dam Road. In 0.3 mile, the road makes a very sharp right turn and becomes Gold Mine Road. Follow the road 0.1 mile to the parking lot. Trailhead GPS: N32 40.375' / W85 54.516'

THE HIKE

Lake Martin is a beautiful lake to say the least. With over 750 miles of shoreline rimmed by picturesque forests and rocky hillsides, the lake is a magnet for outdoor recreationists of all kinds. Of course, hiking is also wildly popular here, and it's all thanks to the Cherokee

The picture doesn't do the view from the top of Saddle Rock Mountain justice.

Ridge Alpine Trail Association (CRATA) and its volunteers who have worked tirelessly to build some remarkable trails including this hike, the John B. Scott Forever Wild Trail.

The trail's namesake is a local attorney who has worked hard on behalf of the state's environment, having served on the Alabama Environmental Council, as a board member with Alabama's Nature Conservancy, and as the chairman of the State Bar Committee of Environmental Law. To top it off, he was the first lifetime member of CRATA.

This 4.2-mile white paint-blazed loop hike will lead you and Fido through a couple of transitioning environments. It begins on an old, wide dirt-and-gravel road, Goldmine Road, along the banks of the Tallapoosa River. The river is wide and peaceful with only an occasional motorboat cruising by. You'll pass a side trail with a unique sign you don't normally see—a special trail for rock climbers to try their hand at scaling a huge rock outcropping and bluff.

The only drawback to this trip is that the first 0.9 mile has very little shade, so be prepared in the summer months to wear a hat and sunscreen (both you and Fido), and don't forget to pack plenty of water for you and your pup. The breezes that kick up from the river help out some.

The trail then moves away from the river and turns into a narrow 2- to 3-foot-wide dirt, rock, and root-studded path that zigzags its way back and forth across a beautiful clear, sparkling creek, its waters tumbling down a rocky bed and creating several small cascades. Your dog is sure to love splashing in it and will be intrigued by the small fish and tadpoles.

You'll follow the creek for almost 1.1 miles, crossing over it several times as you make your way along the relatively flat trail. The path is lined with blooming and fragrant mountain laurel, dogwoods, and bigleaf magnolias.

Soon you will notice that the rocks are turning into boulders. You are now beginning the climb up the ridge. You will start seeing some nice views until, before long, you find yourself on top of Saddle Rock Mountain. The mountain is strewn with boulders and a great rock outcropping that gives you a panoramic view of the surrounding hills and valleys. It's a great place to sit back, relax, take in the view, and catch a little sun.

Of course, it goes without saying—but I will—be safe on the bluffs, both you and your dog. And be careful walking the trail through here. The path is covered with pine straw, and there are a few holes covered up by it. You could find yourself sprawled on the ground if you step into one. Not that I did that. The pine straw is also slippery, so you may have a slow go climbing up and down the mountain.

From here it's a nice walk in the woods back to the trailhead. You will have to climb down off the ridge using a set of switchbacks as you near the trailhead. Please use the switchbacks and don't create a shortcut straight down. It causes erosion that makes more work for the volunteers.

CREATURE COMFORTS

RESTING UP
Microtel Inn & Suites, 2174 S. College St., Auburn; (334) 826-1444; www.wyndham hotels.com/microtel/auburn-alabama/microtel-inn-and-suites-auburn/overview

Pets under 25 pounds are allowed. There is a $10 per night pet fee charged. Make your reservations online, but contact the hotel first to make sure there are pet-friendly rooms available.

CAMPING
Wind Creek State Park, 4325 AL 128, Alexander City; (256) 329-0845; www.alapark .com/wind-creek-state-park; reserve online at guestrez.megahotel.com/Campground/ Home/Index/P3R53

Wind Creek has 586 improved campsites with 157 right on the banks of Wind Creek, a finger of Lake Martin, making this the largest state park campground in the country. Prices range from $22 per night Sun through Thurs; $25 Fri, Sat, and holidays. Add $3 for waterfront sites. There is a $4.50 transaction fee plus tax, and a 3.5 percent lodging fee. Make your reservations online.

FUELING UP
Little Italy Pizzeria, 129 E. Magnolia Ave., Auburn; (334) 821-6161; littleitalyau.com
Authentic Italian flavors await you at Little Italy. Snag a table in their outside dining area for you and Fido and finisci di mangiare! On the menu are hot Italian sandwiches like meatball, sausage, and eggplant Parmesan as well as garden salads, calzones, and stromboli.

MILES AND DIRECTIONS

0.0 Start on the south side of the parking lot. A wooden portal proclaims the trailhead. The path starts off as a narrow, 2-foot-wide dirt and rock path strewn with pine straw that takes you around a yellow gate that blocks a gravel road. In a few yards you will climb up a short set of stone stairs, then the path joins the road in a few yards.

John B. Scott Forever Wild Trail

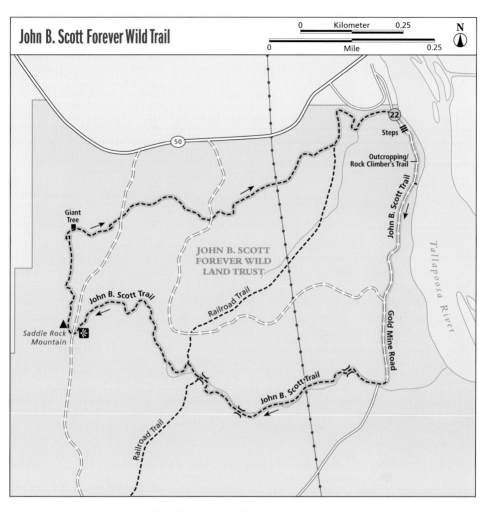

0.2   Pass a side trail on the right that heads up to an impressive rock outcropping. A sign here indicates the trail is for rock climbers. What looks like an old abandoned deer stand is just ahead on the left next to the river. In less than 0.1 mile, pass a small side trail on the left that leads you to the banks of the river. Continue straight to the south. Shortly the trail will start to turn away from the river.

0.6   Pass a sign that points the direction to the north parking lot (back the way you came), Double Bridges Ferry Road Trail (to the right), and the John B. Scott Trail straight ahead to the south. Continue straight to the south.

0.9   The gravel road starts to peter out. In less than 0.1 mile, a sign points the way as the trail moves off the road and into the woods to the west. White blazes begin. The trail begins to parallel a nice creek on the left with many small cascades along the way. The canopy is thicker from here to the end.

1.0   Cross a feeder spring to the creek.

1.2   Cross a 6-foot bridge over a spring feeding the creek and under some power lines.

1.4 Cross a 15-foot bridge over a runoff. Pass a grove of river cane. In less than 0.1 mile, a felled tree blocks the trail. Turn left here to the west and cross the creek, picking up the trail on the opposite side.

1.5 Cross an 18-foot bridge over a feeder spring.

1.6 Come to a sign that reads John B. Scott Trail / Railroad Trail Straight, but actually, turn left here (south then northwest). The trail is now a combination of the white-blazed Scott Trail and the yellow-blazed Railroad Trail. In a few yards, cross a 15-foot bridge over the creek. The creek is now on your left.

1.7 A sign shows that the Railroad Trail and the north parking lot are straight ahead. Turn left (south) to continue on the John B. Scott Trail.

1.8 Cross the creek again; it is now on your right. You will cross the creek again another five times in the next 0.2 mile.

2.2 Topping a ridge, the trail takes you through pines. The footing is covered with pine straw.

2.3 Start getting some views through the trees to your left of the surrounding hills and valley. In less than 0.1 mile, come to an intersection with a dirt road. Cross it to the west. The trail starts up a small hill. At the top is a double blaze indicating the trail turns to the right (north).

2.4 Come to the top of Saddle Rock Mountain with beautiful views from the rock outcropping. When ready, continue to the north. You will start heading down the ridge.

2.8 The trail again parallels a small creek on the left.

2.9 Cross an old dirt road to the northwest.

3.0 Cross another dirt road to the northwest. There are many bright green ferns and deer moss here.

3.1 Cross a small creek. You'll be passing through an area of river cane next to the creek that's on your right.

3.2 Cross the creek. In less than 0.1 mile, cross the creek again over a 15-foot bridge.

3.3 Cross an old dirt road to the northeast. A sign here points the direction to the north parking lot.

3.4 Cross another dirt road to the northeast.

3.5 Cross under power lines.

3.8 Come to a sign that points the to the left and reads Railroad Trail and to the north indicating the direction to the parking lot. Turn left (north) here. The Railroad Trail and John B. Scott Trail rejoin at this point with both yellow and white blazes.

3.9 The trail makes a sharp right turn and heads steeply downhill using a series of switchbacks. You will see the trail blazes near the bottom, but please use the switchbacks and don't create a new path straight down. In less than 0.1 mile, cross a small spring at the bottom of the descent.

4.0 Cross the spring again as it feeds a larger creek with a nice cascade. In less than 0.1 mile, come to a sign that points back the way you came for the Highland Railroad Trail and Saddle Rock Mountain and the Low Line Railroad Trail to the left. Turn left (north) and cross the creek. On the opposite side is a sign showing the direction to the north parking lot. The trail is once again a wide dirt and gravel road.

4.1 Arrive back at the trailhead.

23 **WOOD DUCK TRAIL**

Coon Creek is a wide feeder of the Tallapoosa River. Here you'll find the Wood Duck Trail, a 4.3-mile out-and-back with a loop on the Forever Wild Coon Creek Tract property. The hike hugs the banks of the creek for most of the trip. On the east side the creek narrows with a beautiful wetland before you begin a roller-coaster walk up and down the rolling hills to a scenic view of the creek from above on a ridge. Your dog will love to frolic a bit at the trailhead, which is located at the boat launch.

THE RUNDOWN

Start: East side of boat ramp (opposite side from the kiosk)
Distance: 4.3-mile out-and-back with small loop
Approximate hiking time: 1.5 hours
Difficulty: Moderate with a few climbs up ravines on the north side
Trailhead elevation: 396 feet
Highest point: 463 feet
Best season: Year-round; open sunrise to sunset; hunting is allowed in the fall (see Other, below)
Trail surface: Dirt and rock
Other trail users: Hunters
Canine compatibility: Leash required
Land status: State wildlife management area
Fees and permits: None
Trail contact: Alabama State Lands ADCNR, 64 N. Union St., Montgomery; (334) 242-3484; www.alabamaforeverwild.com
Nearest town: Tallassee
Trail tips: Bring a camera for some great pics of the wetland, lake, and a wide variety of birds like blue herons and, of course, wood ducks.

But bring the bug repellent in warm weather; the wetland and slough can get a bit buggy. The road into the parking area is not well maintained, so be ready for a rough ride. The one drawback is that along the 0.5 mile, as you're in a cove like this, trash from boaters tends to wash up. Consider bringing a trash bag to pack some out.
Maps: USGS: Tallassee, AL
Other maps: Online at on the Alabama Forever Wild website, www.conservationgis.alabama.gov/fwlt/
Other: Alligators are being reported farther and farther north away from the Gulf. Now none has been reported here, but you should still be cautious around the wetland area with your dog and keep them leashed there. Also watch for snakes. Hunting is allowed in the fall. Please visit the Alabama Department of Conservation and Natural Resources website for information: www.outdooralabama.com/hunting/seasons-and-bag-limits

FINDING THE TRAILHEAD

From Tallassee, at the intersection of AL 14 (East Barnett Avenue) and AL 229 (Jordan Avenue), take AL 14 east 2.3 miles. Turn left onto Macedonia Road and travel 3.1 miles. Turn left onto Hicks Store Road and travel 1.0 mile. Turn right onto Gravel Pit Road and, in 400 feet, turn right onto Coon Creek Landing Road. Follow the road to the boat ramp / parking area. The kiosk and trailhead are on the west side of the parking lot. Trailhead GPS N32 35.838' / W85 52.831'

THE HIKE

We head now to the town of Tallassee and the banks of the Tallapoosa River and Yates Reservoir. Here you will find the 320-acre Coon Creek Tract, another state-owned

A picturesque view of Coon Creek along the Wood Duck Trail.

and state-managed property that was purchased, protected, and opened for recreational opportunities by the state's Forever Wild program, which protects historic and environmentally significant land and waterways. Those recreational opportunities include fishing, birding, paddling, and, of course, hiking.

For hikers, Forever Wild built two trails here back in 2009: the Overlook Loop, which is a nice 1.0-mile loop that climbs steeply up a ridge to the top then back down to the river, and the hike we're going to take here, the 4.3-mile Wood Duck Trail.

Much of the red paint blazed trail hugs the banks of the creek, starting at the boat launch on the south side of the waterway. The path heads east to a point where the creek becomes narrower and you cross a short wooden bridge before the path follows the banks of the creek again on the northern side. Basically the trail can be considered sort of a lollipop loop with the "stick" bending around the creek before looping back around and returning the way you came.

The narrow 2- to 3-foot-wide dirt and pine-straw-strewn footpath is a beautiful journey through a mixed hardwood and conifer forest where for most of the hike you will have excellent views of the water. At the wetland crossing where the creek narrows, the water is filled with snowy white lily pads, hyacinth beds, reeds, and a rainbow assortment of wildflowers in season. In the evening, sit still and listen for the chorus of frog song.

Also through this section you'll notice wood duck houses and will undoubtedly see some of the trail's namesake birds. Wood ducks are unique when it comes to the duck family. They have broad wings that make them very nimble and allow them to thread their flight through the trees. They also have a greater buoyancy than any other duck species, which means they sit higher in the water.

If you are into birding, you're in for a treat. The property has been added to the Alabama Birding Trail for good reason. You can really check off some bird species from your list here, like osprey, bald eagles, belted kingfishers, and northern bobwhites. All along the hike you will be serenaded by a wide variety of songbirds.

As for wildlife, don't be surprised if you kick up a whitetail deer or wild turkey, or see a beaver working on his latest construction project.

The only drawback to this hike is, unfortunately, trash along the first 0.1 to 0.5 mile. Think of the creek as a big, wide cove off of the Tallapoosa River. Because of this, trash from boats, whether intentional or dropped accidently, tends to float up to the shore line. Please consider bringing along a trash bag or two and pack some of the trash out with you. You will be helping to keep the area beautiful and aiding the wildlife that lives here.

CREATURE COMFORTS

RESTING UP

Clarion Inns and Suites University Center, 1577 S. College St., Auburn; (334) 821-7001; www.choicehotels.com/alabama/auburn/clarion-hotels/al416

Make your reservations by phone. Be sure to let them know that you are traveling with a pet. You can make your reservations online, but you should still call ahead to make sure that pet-friendly rooms are available before booking. Two pets of any size are allowed. There is a $25 per night, per pet (plus tax) fee charged. Dogs must be crated if left unattended in a room.

CAMPING

Wind Creek State Park, 4325 AL 128, Alexander City; (256) 329-0845; www.alapark .com/wind-creek-state-park; reserve online at guestrez.megahotel.com/Campground/ Home/Index/P3R53

The largest state-run campground in the country is right here in Alabama at Wind Creek. The park has 586 improved campsites with 157 on the banks of Wind Creek, a finger of Lake Martin. Prices range from $22 per night Sun through Thurs, $25 Fri, Sat, and holidays. Add $3 for waterfront sites. There is a $4.50 transaction fee plus tax, and a 3.5 percent lodging fee. Make your reservations online.

FUELING UP

1220 Café, 1220 Gilmer Ave., Tallassee; (334) 252-1220; www.1220cafe.com/

You name it, they got it at the 1220 Café, everything from a menu page full of specialty salads to sandwiches to burgers to amazing desserts. While you're there, be sure to try one of the specialty coffees like the Turtle Latte with hazelnut, chocolate, caramel, espresso, steamed milk, and topped with homemade whipped cream. There is an outdoor patio where you and your pup can dine together.

Wood Duck Trail

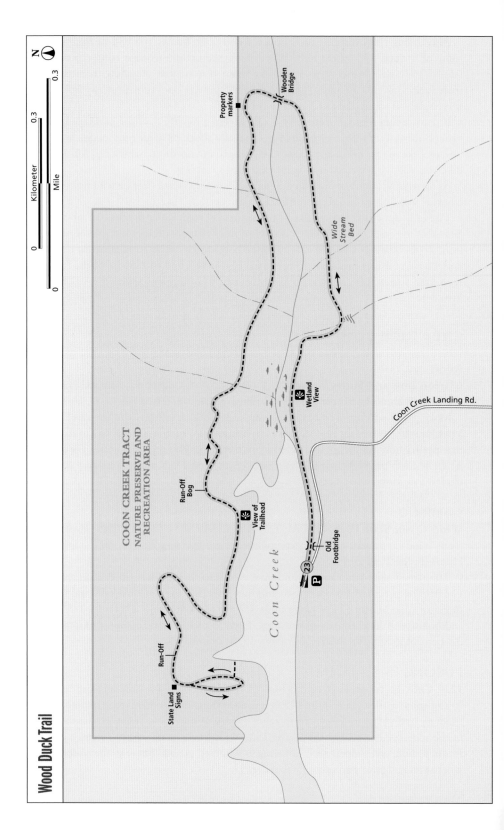

MILES AND DIRECTIONS

0.0 Start on the east side of the boat ramp across from the information kiosk. For this first section you will be walking just a few feet from the banks of the creek on your left with numerous side trails (10 feet or less) to the creek.

0.1 Come to a footbridge that is supposed to help you across a runoff but (as of this writing) was washed off to the side by heavy rains. In 100 feet a dirt road enters from the right. The trail is directly on the creek's bank. Just after the road there is a 50- to 75-foot rocky section with some quartz rocks.

0.2 The trail is running parallel to Coon Creek Landing Road on your right for a short distance and around the east end of the slough and wetland.

0.3 Come to a T intersection with a dirt service road. Turn left (northeast) onto the dirt road. In 200 feet, you will have great views of the slough and wetland.

0.5 Cross a 4-foot-wide stream with a nice little cascade down smooth rocks on your right.

0.6 Cross a 6-foot-wide stream bed. In less than 0.1 mile, you will be walking directly alongside the wetland. The brush is a little thicker here with plenty of smooth palmetto.

0.8 The trail turns right (east) onto an old dirt road. In just under 0.1 mile, cross a nice wooden bridge over a pretty wide stream.

0.9 You will see the yellow property boundary markers painted on trees to your right.

1.2 You will be heading up and down ravines as you cross a few runoffs. This one is a deep gully. From the top of the hills you will have nice views of the wetlands in late fall through winter.

1.3 There is a nice view of wetland below.

1.6 Cross a runoff, then 50 feet later cross a wide bog. This could be deep water after a heavy rain.

1.7 You will be directly across the creek from the trailhead and can see your vehicle on the other side. In less than 0.1 mile, the trail is alongside the creek with good views.

2.1 The path heads uphill on what looks like an old logging road but is now more of a runoff. In less than 0.1 mile, pass a sign on the left—No Off-Road Vehicles Allowed, State Lands—then come to a T intersection with a dirt road. Turn left (west) onto the road.

2.2 Come to a Y. Take the left fork; this is the end of the trail's short loop. In less than 0.1 mile, come to a T intersection with a dirt road. The left fork takes you to the creek. Turn right.

2.3 Come to a T intersection with another dirt road. The left fork takes you to the creek. Turn right. In less than 0.1 mile arrive back at the Y at mile 2.2. Retrace your steps to return to the trailhead.

2.4 Keep your head up and watch for a right turn (it's easy to keep walking straight past it.) You will see the signs from mile 2.1 on the right.

4.4 Arrive back at the trailhead.

OPTION: If you would like more, try the 1.0-mile Overlook Trail loop that begins at the same boat ramp behind the kiosk to the west. The loop is short but much steeper as it uses a set of switchbacks to reach the top of a hill, where you get a few views of the creek during the winter months when the foliage is sparse.

SOUTH REGION

When you get down to it, there really isn't much of a difference, geologically speaking, between the South Region and the Gulf Coast Region. You will encounter a few bigger hills in the South Region, sometimes up to 300 feet above sea level, but again, the region is a relatively flat coastal plain.

The Alabama Department of Tourism used to call this the River Region, and for good reason: *lots* of rivers! The region is a network of streams, creeks, and rivers crisscrossing as they head south toward the Gulf. All of this water makes this very rich and fertile land.

When hiking the region in the summer, you can expect days with extremely high heat and humidity, which make for dangerous heat indexes. In this weather, it's best to reschedule the hike for another day, or at least hike in the early morning. Be sure to carry extra water for you and your dog and keep safety first.

In the spring, the temperature moderate between the mid-60s to low 70s. The hot, humid summer gives way to great hiking weather from fall through winter. It does get a bit colder in this region than in the Gulf Coast, with temperatures averaging in the 40s in January. Cold snaps of below 30 degrees are more frequent here than in the Gulf Coast region.

Speaking of weather, be watchful of sudden severe summertime thunderstorms. These pop-up storms can produce torrential rain, flooding, and dangerous lightning. Longleaf pines are perfect lightning rods, so get off trails as quickly as possible if storms are approaching.

Oh, and don't forget the insect repellent. Many of the trails I will take you to in this section are near swamps and ponds, so expect mosquitoes.

As for hiking the South Region, there are many standout trails. A few of my favorites include the trails of Chewacla State Park (Hike 24) where your dog will love splashing in Moore's Mill Creek that fills Chewacla Lake.

Two other notables are the Conecuh Trail North Loop (Hike 29) and the Five Runs Loop (Hike 28). The North Loop is a long 13-mile trek that can be done as a full day hike or an overnighter. It leads you through the dogwood, holly, magnolia, cypress, and towering longleaf pine forest to numerous cedar ponds, including Mossy, Gum, and Nellie, where brilliant wildflowers light up the path in season and frog song fills the air.

The Five Runs Loop will take you to the banks of the trail's namesake as well as a beautiful crystal-clear blue spring. The spring is a favorite swimming hole of locals; just remember it is very deep and there are no lifeguards here, so swim at your own risk. A life jacket is a good idea for your pup.

This is a good time to remind you that even the South Region has alligators lurking in many of its ponds, wetlands, and swamps. Be safe! When hiking around these water features, keep your dog and kids close at hand and out of the water. Leash your dog through these areas.

24 CHEWACLA STATE PARK

The centerpiece of this loop hike is its water features, the sparkling cascading waters of Moore's Mill Creek and the beautiful shimmering waters of the park's 25-acre lake. Your dog will find the waters of Moore's Mill Creek a blast and will be mesmerized by the small fish swimming around them. Before rounding the bend and heading back to the trailhead, you'll make a stop and take in the soothing sounds of the tumbling waters flowing over the lake's tiered spillway.

THE RUNDOWN

Start: From the east side of the park's nature center

Distance: 3.7-mile hike with 2 loops

Approximate hiking time: 2.5–3 hours

Difficulty: Moderate along the rocky Troop 30 Trail with a stream crossing and one steep climb from the dam to the top of a ridge at a picnic area

Trailhead elevation: 488 feet

Highest point: 589 feet

Best season: Spring; open year-round 8 a.m.–7 p.m.

Trail surface: Dirt and rock, short section of roadway and a rocky, wide stream crossing

Other trail users: Cyclists

Canine compatibility: Leash required

Land status: Alabama state park

Fees and permits: Day-use fee: adults $4; children 4–11 and seniors 62 and over $2

Trail contact: Chewacla State Park, 124 Shell Toomer Pkwy., Auburn;

(334) 887-5621; www.alapark.com/chewacla-state-park

Nearest town: Auburn

Trail tips: Restrooms and water are available at the trailhead near the nature center and playground and also at mile 2.3 near a picnic area. Use caution with your dog at the stream crossing; the water can be swift flowing at times and the rocky bottom slippery. Can't forget the camera on this one. The trees have beautiful color in the fall, while pink and white mountain laurel and dogwoods brighten the path in the spring and summer, and, of course, there is that waterfall and cascades on the stream.

Maps: USGS: Auburn, AL

Other maps: Available at the entrance gate or online at www.alapark.com/chewacla-state-park-hiking-trails

FINDING THE TRAILHEAD

At the intersection of I-85 and S. College Street in Auburn, head south on S. College Street. Travel 0.2 mile and turn left onto Lee Road 674 / Shell Toomer Parkway. Travel 1.8 miles and come to a 4-way stop. Continue straight across Wrights Mill Road onto Murphy Drive to enter the park. In 500 feet you'll come to the main gate and pay your entrance fee (you can also get a trail map here). Continue straight on Murphy Drive 0.2 mile and turn right into a parking area. Drive to the very southern end of the parking lot near the playground and park. To find the trailhead, take the walkway on the left side of the restrooms to the stone CCC Nature Center building. The trail starts here, heading down hill to the southeast and the banks of Moore's Mill Creek. Trailhead GPS: N32 33.140' / W85 28.565'

Archer is ready to ford Moore's Mill Creek.

THE HIKE

In the town of Auburn, just south of Auburn University, you'll find Chewacla State Park, a beautiful 696-acre park where, once again, water features are the highlight of this hike that your dog will love. I especially enjoy this park because of its rustic charm and feel, and history is all around you as you walk its trails. Throughout the park you will see the handiwork of the Civilian Conservation Corps (CCC), who built Chewacla back in 1935; it is now lovingly cared for by the park's staff.

Throughout the park you will see the CCC's craftsmanship in the impressive stacked hand-cut stone cabins, picnic pavilions, and bathhouses. Along this hike you will also see more examples of their stonework in the beautiful arched stone bridges you'll pass.

But, as I said at the beginning, the highlights of this hike for you and your pup are the water features: Chewacla Lake and Moore's Mill Creek.

The hike begins by the old CCC building that has been turned into a nature center. From here, head downhill and take the easy-walking Boy Scout and Sweet Shrub Trails along the banks of the creek at its widest point before it spills into the lake. Fragrant and colorful mountain laurel and wildflowers bloom here, as well as tall stalks of river cane, as the creek gets narrower and narrower, passing a remarkable beaver pond along the way and the amazing stone bridges of the CCC, as mentioned before.

A beautiful cascade tumbles down the spillway of Chewacla Lake.

The trail eventually comes to the main park road. After carefully crossing you'll pick up the Troop 30 Boy Scout Trail on the other side for a wonderful 1.0-mile loop on both sides of the Moore's Mill Creek. The creek is wide, clear, and cold and always has a good flow in it as it tumbles down its rocky bed that forms some beautiful, glistening cascades. There are plenty of access points so your pup can enter the creek and get a little wet.

After hiking 0.5 mile, it's time for you to get wet, too. You will have to ford the creek to continue the loop on the other side. Be careful crossing; after rain the creek can be fast, and the rocky bottom is slippery. They say there are stepping-stones here, but I didn't see a good path and ended up just wading through the water.

On the other side, the trail heads back to the road again, and once there, carefully cross it again and pick up the Mountain Laurel Trail. A portion of this path is gorgeous in season as you walk through a cave of blooming laurel. The trail is a bit more rugged than the one we started on, as it goes up and down ridges that provide some nice views of the lake on your right.

The trail finally comes out to the dam that was built by the CCC to form the park's lake. There's a rushing 30-foot-tall cascade down the multitiered cement spillway. It's a great place to sit on the rocks below the falls and just take in the soothing sounds and the spectacle.

The dam is where you'll make the steepest climb of the hike, straight up to the top of a ridge where you'll begin your return trip.

The entire hike has plenty of canopy providing much needed shade during the hot summer months. The old, faded paint blazes that used to be on the trails have been replaced with fiberglass 4-inch-by-3-foot signs that have stickers on them indicating what trail you're on and also a number so that, in case of emergency, you can call for help and tell rescuers exactly where you are. The only exception to this is the Troop 30 Trail, which uses green metal signs that are mounted to metal T-posts and proudly announce that you're still on the right path.

A couple of reminders before heading out: Some of this hike shares short sections of mountain-bike trails with cyclists. Keep your eyes open for them. And the park is very, I mean *very*, busy during college football season when the SEC's Auburn Tigers have home games.

CREATURE COMFORTS

RESTING UP

Clarion Suites and Inn University Center, 1577 S. College St., Auburn; (877) 411-3436; www.choicehotels.com/alabama/auburn/hotels

The Clarion is a very pet-friendly hotel. Two pets of any size are welcome. They must be crated if left unattended in the room. There is a $25 per pet, per night fee. Make your reservations online or call, but be sure to specify you're booking a pet-friendly room.

CAMPING

Chewacla State Park, 124 Shell Toomer Pkwy., Auburn; (334) 887-5621; www.ala park.com/chewacla-state-park-tent-camping

Chewacla has nine primitive tent camping sites available on a first come, first served basis. They do not take advanced reservations, which can be an issue during college football season when the Auburn Tigers are at home. Get there *really* early. Campsites are $25.96 per night.

Wind Creek State Park, 4325 AL 128, Alexander City; (256) 329-0845; www.alapark .com/wind-creek-state-park; reserve online at guestrez.megahotel.com/Campground/Home/Index/P3R53

Wind Creek is touted as the largest state-run campground in the country, and it's hard to argue that. The park has 586 improved campsites with 157 on the banks of Wind Creek, a finger of Lake Martin. Prices range from $22 per night Sun through Thurs; $25 Fri, Sat, and holidays. Add $3 for waterfront sites. There is a $4.50 transaction fee plus tax, and a 3.5 percent lodging fee. Make your reservations online.

FUELING UP

Island Wing Company, 200 W. Glenn Ave., Auburn; (334) 501-9555; www.islandwing .com/

Bring your well-behaved pooch to the outdoor dining area of Island Wings and get ready for some chicken wings. What makes them great are their sauces that are rated on their spicy thermometer, starting with the mild "30s" (teriyaki, orange ginger, and garlic Parmesan) and going up the scale to the hot "95," Island Inferno, and the scale-breaking "98," Scorpion. But it's not just about wings. Island Wings has an amazing menu with something for everyone, like the Bangin' Buffalo Mac & Cheese, What-a-Jerk grilled

Chewacla State Park

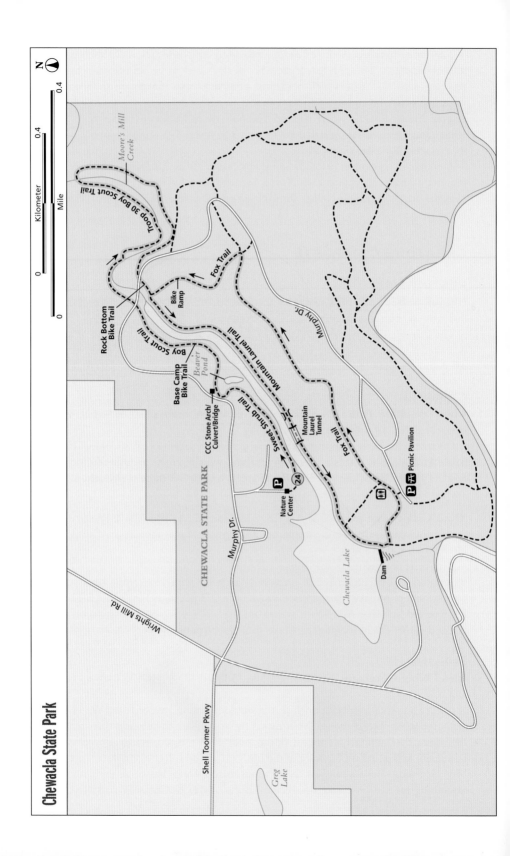

chicken sandwich, and the Bandito South of the Border Burger. And that's only a few from the menu.

MILES AND DIRECTIONS

0.0 Start from the south end of the parking lot. Just beyond the playground is the stone nature center building. From the left side of the building, head down a short hill. You will run into the Sweet Shrub Trail at the bottom. Turn left (northeast) onto the trail. You will be walking just below a CCC stone picnic pavilion on a hill to your left. You will also see some small CCC stone pillars as you walk along the banks of the lake.

0.2 Pass a beaver pond on the right. In less than 0.1 mile, pass a sign that reads SWEET SHRUB TRAIL.

0.3 As you near Murphy Drive, the trail bends to the right (east) and becomes the Base Camp Bike Trail. Immediately cross over a creek on a wooden bridge. Here you will see the CCC's beautiful stonework in an arch bridge. The path begins to circle around to the opposite side of the beaver pond and the creek.

0.5 Pass a side trail on the right to a small sandbar, perfect for access to the creek for your dog. In less than 0.1 mile, pass a side trail to a picnic pavilion on the left and a bench alongside the creek and another great access point. In a few yards, pass a CCC stone culvert on the left, then cross a short bridge before carefully crossing Murphy Drive.

0.6 On the opposite side of the road you'll see the sign for the Troop 30 Boy Scout Trail. Continue to the northeast on the Troop 30 Boy Scout Trail. In less than 0.1 mile, cross a runoff that may be pretty muddy and slick after a good rain. The creek is on the right.

0.7 Get a nice view of an upcoming cascade. You can see the return trail on the other side. In less than 0.1 mile, arrive at the cascade. Continue to the south.

0.8 Pass another quick-moving shoal in the creek. In less than 0.1 mile, pass a bench on the left.

1.0 Come to the north end of the Troop 30 Trail. Carefully ford the creek to the other side and pick up the southbound section of the Troop 30 Trail. *OPTION:* If the crossing seems daunting, don't worry; many people have turned around here. Turn around and head back to mile 0.5. When you arrive at Murphy Drive, turn left (southeast) onto the road and pick up the route directions at mile 1.4.

1.4 Cross Murphy Drive to the southwest and pick up the Rock Bottom Bike Trail on the opposite side. Be sure to take a look at the stone handiwork of the CCC in the double arch bridge to your right. In less than 0.1 mile, come to a multiple intersection. A sign shows that the Mountain Laurel Trail begins here. Continue straight on the Mountain Laurel Trail to the southwest. Moore's Mills Creek will be on your right. The trail becomes hilly and rocky.

1.8 Cross a 10-foot bridge over a runoff.

1.9 The trail narrows considerably, maybe 1 to 2 feet wide, with a moderate drop-off to the lake on the right.

2.1 Arrive at the dam. Use caution on the rocks and stay off the dam. After visiting head straight up the hill to the east.

2.2 Pass a split-rail fence. Continue straight to the east. In less than 0.1 mile, just before arriving at a picnic pavilion and parking lot, come to a cement picnic table. Turn left (northeast) to continue on the Mountain Laurel Trail. You will be walking just below a parking lot.

2.3 Pass a restroom on the left. Pick up the Fox Trail on the left side of the building (there is a sign for the trail there).

2.8 You'll be walking through a pine cone–strewn forest. In less than 0.1 mile, pass a trail coming in from the left (north).

2.9 The Rock Bottom Bike Trail comes in from the left (north) at a kiosk with a trail map on it. Turn left (north) here onto the Rock Bottom Bike Trail.

3.0 Come to a wooden bike ramp. Walk under—or around—the ramp to the north.

3.1 Arrive back at the beginning of the Mountain Laurel Trail. Turn right (east). In less than 0.1 mile, arrive back at Murphy Drive. Turn left (west) and carefully walk along the shoulder of the road across the bridge. On the other side of the bridge, pick up the Sweet Shrub Trail and follow it to the trailhead.

3.7 Arrive back at the trailhead.

PUPPY PAWS AND GOLDEN YEARS
Thank the CCC

The Civilian Conservation Corps (CCC) was part of an effort by President Franklin D. Roosevelt and the US Congress to get the country back on its feet during the Great Depression. Young men between the ages of 18 and 25 were put to work creating state and national parks, like Chewacla, planting billions of trees, and building vital national infrastructure to help the country grow. In return, the men had room and board, meals, and earned $30 a month. Of that amount, it was required that $22 to $25 be sent home to help support their families.

25 BARTRAM NATIONAL RECREATIONAL TRAIL

You and your dog can explore the same forest, streams, and creeks that William Bartram, famed botanist to King George III, visited in the mid-1700s on this hike through what is today the Tuskegee National Forest. This hike will lead you into a forest of blooming magnolias and dogwoods as well as hardy pines on a trail that is dotted with beautiful wildflowers and seasonal streams that your dog can splash in. You can make this a long full-day out-and-back or a half day point-to-point hike with shuttle. It's a great trail for training your dog to hike with you and for you to shake down that new gear.

THE RUNDOWN

Start: From the western trailhead on US 29 heading west
Distance: 9.2-mile out-and-back with shorter option
Approximate hiking time: 5.5–6 hours
Difficulty: Moderate due to length
Trailhead elevation: 552 feet
Highest point: 560 feet
Best season: Year-round; open sunrise to sunset
Trail surface: Dirt footpath, wooden bridges and boardwalks
Other trail users: Cyclists, hunters
Canine compatibility: Leash required
Land status: National forest
Fees and permits: None
Trail contact: Tuskegee National Forest, Tuskegee Ranger District, 125 National Forest Rd. 949, Tuskegee; (334) 727-2652; www.fs.usda.gov/ detail/alabama/about-forest/ districts/?cid=stelprdb5152167

Nearest town: Tuskegee
Trail tips: If you have just started hiking and are looking for a longer trek, if you want to do more training with your pup on the trail, or if you have new gear you want to try out, this is the trail for you. Bring along the insect repellent. You will be walking past some slow-moving streams, bogs, and swamps, so mosquitoes can be expected.
Maps: USGS: Little Texas, AL
Other maps: Available online at www.fs.usda.gov/recarea/alabama/ recarea/?recid=30181
Other: Hunting is allowed in national forests. Please contact the Trail Contact (above) or visit www.fs.usda .gov/activity/alabama/recreation/ hunting for dates and restrictions.

FINDING THE TRAILHEAD

Eastern Trailhead (Start of Hike): From the intersection of I-85 (exit 42) and AL 186 E in Tuskegee, take AL 186 E 3.7 miles. Turn left to get on the ramp and then left onto US 29 N. Travel 1.0 mile. The well-marked trailhead will be on your left directly across the street from the Little Texas Volunteer Fire Department. The trailhead has enough room for about 15 cars. Trailhead GPS: N32 28.727' / W85 33.834'

Optional Western Trailhead (Pleasant Hill) for Shorter Point-to-Point Hike (Requires Shuttle Vehicle): From the intersection of I-85 (exit 42) and AL 186 E in Tuskegee, take AL 186 E 1.2 miles. Turn right onto FS 900. The trailhead will be on the right. Trailhead GPS: N32 28.682' / W85 37.107'

THE HIKE

As I pointed out in my book *Hiking Through History Alabama*, just about every state in the southeast has a Bartram Trail. There's the loop in northern Georgia that connects to the Appalachian Trail, and on the Alabama Gulf Coast there is the Bartram Canoe Trail. And then there is the hike we are about to take along the Bartram National Recreational Trail (NRT) of the Tuskegee National Forest near Auburn.

One would think that these trails were all named just to honor the eighteenth-century botanist William Bartram, but actually there is evidence, or as close as can be determined from his records, that Bartram's travels actually used what would become portions of these routes as he documented the amazing biodiversity of the South back in the late 1700s. If you want to view all of Bartram's walks through the region, I recommend visiting the Bartram Trail Conference website at bartramtrailconference.wildapricot.org.

The trail here in the Tuskegee National Forest was the first in Alabama to be designated a National Recreational Trail. Along this path you will be treated to colorful wildflowers, like the white milkweed and trillium, as well as flowering and fragrant dogwoods and magnolias. You will cross over several seasonal creeks and a few bogs that your dog will love and appreciate. They will also love exploring the understory, investigating every nook and cranny of the forest.

The Bartram National Recreational Trail is much like the Conecuh Trail North Loop (Hike 29) in that it is a great place for training and gear shakedowns. If you or your dog is just starting out in hiking, the Bartram is a good intermediate trail to continue learning on. The trail is veined with forest service roads that crisscross the forest, giving you plenty of opportunities to exit in case of emergency.

The trail is also a good place to try out your new day-hiking or backpacking gear. It makes for an easy overnighter and will put your gear through its paces.

The trail itself has a dirt and rock footing and is laced with several bridges and boardwalks over creeks and bogs. The trail is marked intermittently with white metal diamond blazes, but even if you can't find them, the trail is still pretty easy to follow.

There are several different options available for hiking the Bartram NRT. The first is what I describe here: a 9.2-mile out-and-back that makes a good full-day trip. The Miles and Directions section (below) takes you from the eastern trailhead on US 29 to the Pleasant Hill Mountain Bike Trailhead at the intersection of AL 186 and FS 900. You can cut the mileage in half to 4.6 miles if you park a shuttle vehicle at the Pleasant Hill Trailhead.

What I describe here isn't all there is to the Bartram National Recreational Trail, however. From where I mark this hike's turnaround at Pleasant Hill, you can make the hike an 8.5-mile point-to-point by continuing on an additional 4.2 miles through some nice bogs over boardwalks to the westernmost trailhead at the intersection of CR 53 and FS 913. Again, you would need a shuttle vehicle parked there, or you will have to make it a 16-plus-mile out-and-back.

You also have the option of camping in the forest to make it an overnighter. There are fourteen primitive campsites available scattered about the forest, one of which is an easy 0.5-mile walk using the Destiny Horse Trail. I have indicated how to get there in the Miles and Directions section below. This is a primitive campsite, basically a clear and leveled area where you can pitch a tent. There are no other amenities so please, use Leave No Trace practices. Camping is free.

A long-abandoned fireplace just past the Pleasant Hill Trailhead.

CREATURE COMFORTS

RESTING UP

Microtel Inn & Suites, 2174 S. College St., Auburn; (334) 826-1444; www.wyndham-hotels.com/microtel/auburn-alabama/microtel-inn-and-suites-auburn/overview

This establishment allows pets under 25 pounds. There is a $10 per night pet fee charged. Make your reservations online, but contact the hotel first to make sure there are pet-friendly rooms available.

CAMPING

Chewacla State Park, 124 Shell Toomer Pkwy., Auburn; (334) 887-5621; www.ala
park.com/chewacla-state-park-tent-camping

Chewacla has nine primitive tent camping sites available on a first come, first served
basis. They do not take advanced reservations, which can be an issue during college
football season when the Auburn Tigers are playing a home game. Get there *really* early.
Campsites are $25.96 per night.

Wind Creek State Park, 4325 AL 128, Alexander City; (256) 329-0845; www.alapark
.com/wind-creek-state-park; reserve online at guestrez.megahotel.com/Campground/
Home/Index/P3R53

Wind Creek is touted as the largest state-run campground in the country, and it's hard
to argue that. The park has 586 improved campsites, with 157 on the banks of Wind
Creek, a finger of Lake Martin. Prices range from $22 per night Sun through Thurs; $25
Fri, Sat, and holidays. Add $3 for waterfront sites. There is a $4.50 transaction fee plus
tax and a 3.5 percent lodging fee. Make your reservations online.

FUELING UP

Little Italy Pizzeria, 129 E. Magnolia Ave., Auburn; (334) 821-6161; littleitalyau.com

Authentic Italian flavors await you at Little Italy. Snag a table in their outside dining area for you and Fido and finisci di mangiare! On the menu are hot Italian sandwiches, like meatball, sausage, and eggplant Parmesan, as well as garden salads, calzones,
and stromboli.

MILES AND DIRECTIONS

0.0 Start from the western side of the parking area. The trail throughout, for the
most part, is a good 2- to 3-foot-wide dirt footpath. It begins covered in a
thick layer of pine duff then slowly changes to a leaf-covered trail as the
environment changes. A little ravine will be viewed to the right. The trail parallels US 29 for a bit, so you will hear highway noise for a short time at the
beginning. Just after you head out, one of the old benches carved with the
sayings of William Bartram can be seen on a small hill to your left (south).

0.2 Come to an old logging road. Turn right (north) and in 50 feet pick up the
trail again into the woods on the left (west). In less than 0.1 mile, pass a sign
indicating a wildlife food plot on the right. Very young bamboo plants alongside the trail are visible.

0.3 Cross an aging 30-foot wooden bridge over a creek. *FYI:* At the time I visited,
the wood on this bridge had rotted in spots, so cross carefully. Volunteers,
however, were in the process of fixing these. You may lose the trail for a bit
after crossing, but just head straight to the south and you will pick it up again.

0.4 Cross a 10-foot bridge over a creek.

0.6 Come to a Y. Take either fork. They rejoin in less than 0.1 mile at the bottom
of a hill, where you will cross another creek over a wooden bridge.

0.7 Cross a creek over a 10-foot bridge.

0.8 Cross a creek over a 10-foot bridge.

0.9 Cross a small creek over a short bridge. A small pine savannah is to your
right (north).

1.1 Pass another wildlife food plot on the right.

Bartam National Recreation Trail

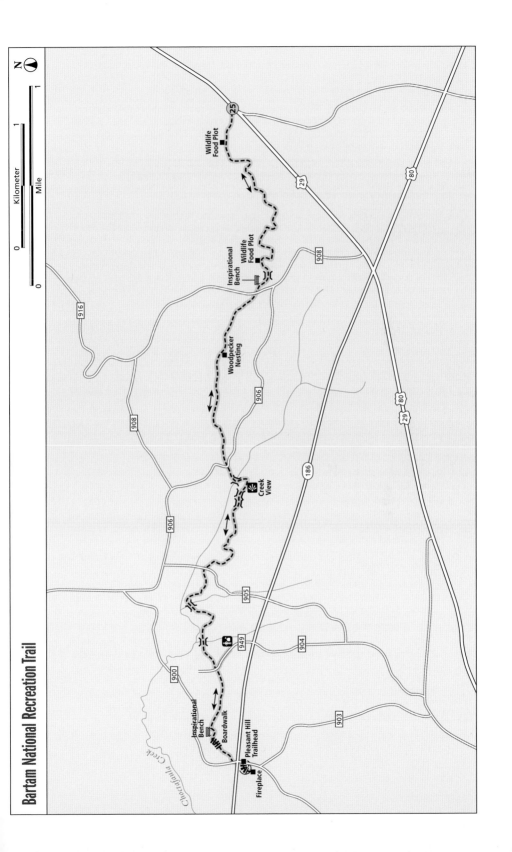

1.3 Cross another creek over a short 4-foot bridge. In less than 0.1 mile, pass another one of the inspirational benches on the left. It was recently pretty badly burned during a prescribed burn, but, again, volunteers are working to rectify that. It is inscribed "Erect stems, arise from its roots."

1.4 Arrive at the dirt FS 908. As you approach the road, a flat fiberglass sign points to the right (northwest). Turn right onto the road. In 100 feet you will see a diamond marker on a tree to the left (west). Turn right here and proceed back onto the trail and into the woods.

1.8 Pass an interesting-shaped tree and next to it, in a unique burned-out 5-foot-tall pine-tree stump, is a sort of a "duplex" woodpecker home (2 holes).

2.1 Top out on a small hill and walk the ridge line for a bit.

2.4 Arrive at FS 906. The trail comes out at a hairpin turn in the road. Go straight across the road to the southwest and pick up the trail on the other side (it's marked with a flat brown fiberglass sign letting you know who can use the trail). *OPTION:* If you want to camp for the night, head north on FS 906 only a few yards and pick up the Bold Destiny / Bedford Cash Memorial (Horse) Trail. Turn right onto the horse trail and in about 0.5 mile you will come to the forest's Primitive Campsite #6. The next morning, just retrace your steps back to the Bartram NRT and continue on.

2.5 Cross a 10-foot boardwalk over a creek. As of this writing some boards were missing.

2.6 Top a hill for a nice view of the creek you just crossed to your right (north).

2.7 Cross a seasonal creek and bog over a 60-foot-long bridge.

2.8 Cross a seasonal creek over a 20-foot-long bridge. Soon after, look up and see a lone bigleaf magnolia among the pines.

3.2 Walk straight across FS 905 to the north.

3.4 The trail parallels a creek on the left with deep banks. In a few feet cross the creek over a wooden footbridge.

3.7 Cross another creek over a 25-foot-long boardwalk. There are more magnolias through this section.

3.9 Come to FR 949 at the historic marker and a NRT (National Recreational Trail) sign. Go straight across the road to the southwest and pick up the trail on the other side. *OPTION:* You can make this into a 4.0-mile point-to-point by parking a shuttle vehicle at the ranger station and ending the hike here by turning left (southeast) onto the road. The ranger station will be on your right in 0.1 mile.

4.3 Pass an inspirational bench on the right. In less than 0.1 mile cross a bog over a 50-foot boardwalk and, soon after, cross another bog over a 70-foot boardwalk, then a few feet later a shorter 20-foot boardwalk.

4.5 Arrive at FS 900. Turn left and *cautiously* cross AL 186 / US 80 (it's a very busy highway). After crossing you'll arrive at the Pleasant Hill Mountain Bike Trail trailhead. Go past the trailhead for just a bit to visit some of the area's past at an old house location. Turn right to continue on the Bartram NRT. Just after making the turn, cross a bog over a 100-foot boardwalk. There is a distinct change in the ecosystem here as you make your way into a bog, wetland, and bottom land area. *OPTION:* You can park a shuttle vehicle at the Pleasant Hill trailhead to make this a 4.5-mile point-to-point.

4.6 Pass an old stone fireplace just off the trail on the left. If you chose to do the 9.2-mile out-and-back, this is your turnaround. Retrace your steps to the eastern trailhead.

9.2 Arrive back at the trailhead.

26 **PINES TRAIL**

The Pines Trail at the Forever Wild Wehle Tract and Nature Center is a beautiful rolling path over hills covered with waving pine savannah grass and dotted with young, brilliant-green longleaf pines and wildflowers. The trail crosses several creeks that your pup can frolic in and passes two shimmering lakes.

THE RUNDOWN

Start: From the south side of the parking lot at the trailhead kiosk
Distance: 6.5-mile loop
Approximate hiking time: 3.5–4 hours
Difficulty: Moderate due to length and some areas that are thick in mud from equestrians and tractors
Trailhead elevation: 616 feet
Highest point: 616 feet
Best season: Feb–Nov; open 8 a.m.–4 p.m. on the following days: first and third Sat in Feb, first and third Fri and Sat Mar–May and Sept–Nov, third Sat in June and July; closed Jan, Aug, and Dec; the Day-Use Hiking Trail is open 7 days a week
Trail surface: Grass, dirt, sand
Other trail users: Equestrians
Canine compatibility: Leash required
Land status: State wildlife management area
Fees and permits: None
Trail contact: Alabama State Lands ADCNR, 64 N. Union St., Montgomery, AL 36130; (334) 242-3484; www.alabamaforeverwild.com/wehle-tract
Nearest town: Union Springs

Trail tips: Restrooms are available at the Nature Center itself or at the campground. Don't forget to slather on the bug spray in the warmer months. You'll be hiking around ponds, lakes, and some standing water. Your pup will enjoy a refreshing dip in any of the several streams you will cross. If you love to fish, get your Alabama freshwater fishing license, bring the pole, and bank fish the beautiful Blue Heron Lake, where you'll spy many different species of waterfowl, including its namesake.
Maps: USGS: Comer, AL
Other maps: Available at the trailhead kiosk or online at www.alabamaforeverwild.com/wehle-tract
Other: Several stream crossings can be difficult after a hard rain due to flooding. And while there are sections of the trail that can be boggy and muddy, as of this writing the worst section is at mile 4.4 just before the campground, where tractors use the old dirt road, creating deep ruts and mud that can be more than ankle-deep.

FINDING THE TRAILHEAD

From the intersection of I-65 and I-85 in Montgomery, take I-85 N 13.6 miles to exit 15 / AL 108. Take exit 15 and turn right onto AL 108. Travel 1.9 miles and turn left onto AL 110. Travel 26 miles and turn left onto US 82 E. In 0.3 mile, bear right to stay on US 82 E, and in 0.2 mile, turn left to stay on US 82 E / Martin Luther King Jr. Boulevard. In less than 0.1 mile, turn right to stay on US 82 E. Travel 13.4 miles and bear right onto Bullock CR 47. Travel 0.6 mile, and turn left to stay on Bullock CR 47 / Pleasant Hill Road. Travel 4.1 miles. The trailhead and parking will be on the right. Trailhead GPS: N32 02.759' / W85 28.158'

THE HIKE

Once again we visit another example of the great work the Alabama Forever Wild program does in protecting the state's ecologically and historically significant lands from development, then opening them to the public for outdoor recreation. The property is called the Wehle Tract, and it is located midway between Auburn and Dothan in the town of, not coincidentally, Midway.

The tract where this hike is located is open only on specific days throughout the year (see Best Season, above, for the schedule). On those days, the Nature Center is open with exhibits showing the area's wildlife and an occasional educational program. There is a day-use hiking trail here that is open year-round, seven days a week. You will cross that path several times on this hike. It can be accessed from the same trailhead.

As soon as you step out of the car, you'll be greeted by a chorus of frog song coming from the wet, brushy grounds near the parking area. From here the hike heads off over rolling hills covered with amber savannah grass waving in the breeze. Beautiful, young longleaf pines dot the hillsides, adding a brilliant bright green color to the picture. The pines are part of a reforestation effort by the state.

Keep your eyes to the skies here for red-tailed hawks and turkey buzzards catching thermals as they soar above you looking for a meal. And as you head into the mature pine forest, be on the lookout for whitetail deer foraging close by.

Along this hike you'll encounter three big water features. The first is Wehle Pond, where turtles sun themselves on logs and frogs sing merrily from the banks.

Next up is Blue Heron Lake, with brilliant white lily pads adorning the banks and where fishermen wet their lines. If you plan to fish, you will need an Alabama freshwater license. On the days the Nature Center is open, you can also rent canoes to paddle around the lake.

Finally, right next to the lake is Alligator Pond. The placid waters of the pond are rimmed with colorful wildflowers. Wood ducks float serenely on top of the water, and herons stand stoically but cautiously watching you walk by.

Remember that alligators could be present in these ponds, so do not allow your dogs in the water. They have plenty of chances to get wet along the trail in the streams and creeks the trail crosses. After a good rain these waterways can have a strong flow with some nice little cascades; the best comes at mile 4.2 when the water is deep and flows down a long rock slide into a deeper pool. When the water is up, you'll have to do a little rock hopping to get across.

Overall the trail is a wide, grassy path using old dirt roads, some of which appear to still be used for maintenance. It is blazed with either yellow diamond markers with directional arrows or diamond markers with a combination of either a horse and hiker on them, or just a horse or a hiker emblazoned on them. This trail is shared with equestrians, so keep an eye out for them.

The trail follows a rolling countryside. The swales at the bottom of these hills can retain water after a rain, so you may get wet. There are a few areas where horses have dug up the footing, and after a rain it becomes muddy. For the most part, though, it is easy to walk around these areas.

There is one section, however, just before the campground at mile 4.4, where things get dicey after a rain. It's not because of horses; it's because tractors use that short section and dig the bed to the point that, when it's muddy, you could be walking ankle-deep in the mud. You can bushwhack around this, but watch for thorn bushes.

An egret waits for a meal in Alligator Pond.

And a word about parking at the trailhead: It is a narrow gravel lot that is on an incline and can hold about six cars comfortably, but if there are more than that, it is easy to get blocked in. Please leave room for others.

CREATURE COMFORTS

RESTING UP

Quality Inn, 631 E. Barbour St., Eufaula; (334) 687-4414; www.choicehotels.com/alabama/eufaula/quality-inn-hotels

Once again, you can make your reservations online, but it is a good idea to call the hotel first to make sure they have pet-friendly rooms available. Two dogs up to 25 pounds each are allowed per room. There is a $20 per night, per pet fee charged. You will also be required to put down a $50 refundable deposit upon registering.

CAMPING

Lakepoint State Park, 104 Lakepoint Dr., Eufaula; (334) 687-6026; www.alapark.com/Lakepoint-state-park-camping

Now this is the way to camp, at Lakepoint, one of the beautiful Alabama State Park resorts. The park boasts 192 improved campsites with water and electricity, laundry, Wi-Fi, clean bathhouses, and of course, all of the amenities you'd expect, like tennis courts, playgrounds, and swimming. Waterfront sites are $28, other sites $22, plus a $4.50 transaction fee and tax. Make reservations online at www.alapark.com/Reservations.

FUELING UP

Phil's Barbecue, 534 S. Randolph Ave., Eufaula; (334) 687-3337; philsbbq.org/

Great south Alabama barbecue is the fare at Phil's, which is located in the heart of historic downtown Eufaula. Their motto is "Best Butts in Alabama," and you'll be hard-pressed to argue that. Since 1991, Phil's has been serving up delicious barbecued chicken, pork, and ribs and some of the best chicken, ham, and turkey salads to boot. Fido is welcome to dine with you in the outdoor seating area.

MILES AND DIRECTIONS

0.0 Start from the south side of the trailhead on Pleasant Hill Road. This is the beginning of the Day-Use Hiking Trail. There is a kiosk here with a map and additional maps to take with you. The trail is a wide 6- to 10-foot grassy path. Listen for frog song coming from the wet bottoms between the hills.

0.1 Come to an intersection. The Day-Use Hiking Trail continues straight, the Pines Trail heads off to the northwest/southeast. Turn right onto the Pines Trail. You'll start walking through a mature pine forest.

0.4 Come to Wehle Pond on your left, an old barn to your right. A little peninsula juts out into the pond so you can get a better view. When done retrace your steps and head toward the barn.

0.5 At the barn turn right (north) to stay on the Pines Trail (look for the yellow diamond-shaped horse marker on the trees). Stay out of the barn; it's in serious disrepair.

0.7 Cross your first swale. They've used gravel to try to stabilize it, but it still can be muddy and full of water at times.

1.0 Cross a stream.

1.1 Come to a Y. The left fork is the Day-Use Hiking Trail. Take the right fork to the south to stay on the Pines Trail. You should see the next marker after the turn.

1.3 Come to a T intersection at a FOREVER WILD sign. Turn left (southeast). The creek you just crossed will be on your left. In less than 0.1 mile, cross another creek. This one could be over a foot deep when it's running. Be careful heading down the rather steep and muddy banks. Right after crossing there is an intersection with a sign pointing to the Firebreak Trail straight ahead and the Pines Trail to the left. Take a left (southeast) to continue on the Pines Trail. The creek continues on your left.

1.4 Cross another creek with steep banks going down.

1.5 Come to an intersection with the Day-Use Hiking Trail, which crosses to the left and right (northeast to southwest). The creek you've been paralleling

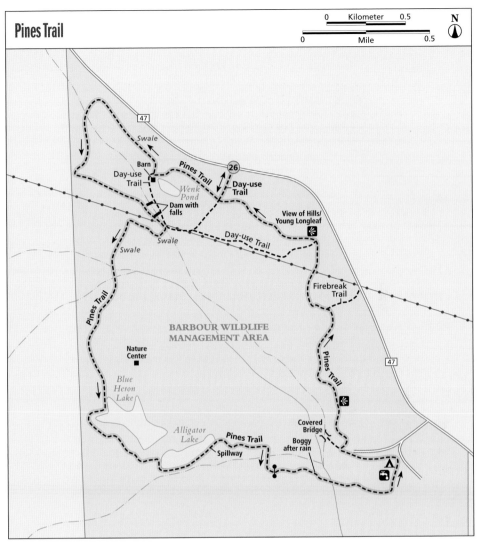

0   Kilometer   0.5

0   Mile   0.5

N

47

Swale

Barn

Day-use Trail

Pines Trail

26

Day-use Trail

Wenk Pond

Dam with falls

View of Hills/ Young Longleaf

Swale

Swale

Day-use Trail

Pines Trail

Firebreak Trail

BARBOUR WILDLIFE MANAGEMENT AREA

Nature Center

Pines Trail

47

Blue Heron Lake

Alligator Lake

Covered Bridge

Pines Trail

Boggy after rain

Spillway

has a nice little falls to the left over an old dam. Continue straight to the southeast.

1.6   You'll see what looks like an old, abandoned outhouse across the creek on the left.

1.7   Cross under a power line. In less than 0.1 mile, come to a 3-way fork with a sign. This is another intersection with the Day-Use Hiking Trail, which goes to the left and crosses over the creek you've been paralleling and straight to the southeast. The Pines Trail turns to the right (southwest). Take the right fork to continue on the Pines Trail. Before you do, though, take a look at the creek on the left and the waterfall over a small dam.

1.8   Pass another swale that holds a considerable amount of water after a rain.

1.9   The trail follows the power line. There is a long swale here that can be deep in water and mud after rain.

2.1 Pass another swale. In less than 0.1 mile, come to a T intersection. Turn left (southwest) to stay on the Pines Trail and follow the power lines.

2.2 Cross another narrow creek. In less than 0.1 mile, the trail turns to the right (south) and leaves the power line. You'll see the Nature Center at the top of the hill.

2.4 Come to an intersection. The trail to the right dead-ends. The trail to the left leads to the Nature Center (a sign here shows the way). Continue straight to the south to stay on the Pines Trail. In less than 0.1 mile, come to a Y. Take the right fork to the south. You'll be climbing up to a small ridge with a nice view of the surrounding hills and valley.

2.7 Arrive at Blue Heron Lake. Head to the banks of the lake and follow it around. Some pretty good-size fish will be jumping and frogs hopping in as you pass.

2.8 Pass a bench on the right, a great place to relax and take in the serenity of the lake. In less than 0.1 mile, cross a small creek over a culvert where you'll meet up again with the Pines Trail. You can either continue to follow the banks of the lake to the south to mile 3.1 or follow the Pines Trail up a ridge for nice lake views from above. This description takes you up the ridge.

3.1 Come to a berm between Blue Heron Lake and Alligator Lake. It's worth your while to walk out on the berm a bit, chat with the many fishermen trying their luck here, and take in the view of both lakes. When you're done, continue straight to the south on the Pines Trail.

3.2 Pass a large live-catch trap on the right.

3.3 Turn left (northeast) off the trail and head down to the banks of Alligator Lake. Follow the banks of the pond to the south. In less than 0.1 mile, rejoin the Pines Trail by turning left (east) onto it.

3.6 Cross a small spillway that will most likely flood after a heavy rain and when the pond fills.

3.7 If you hike this trail after it has rained, be prepared to hike through some extended boggy areas beginning here.

3.8 Come to a dirt and gravel road. Turn right onto the road and cross a nice stream with a small cascade formed by the large rocks used to stabilize the banks. On the other side the gravel consists of 2- to 3-inch rocks. You should walk your dog off to the side of the road through here until the gravel gets smaller.

3.9 Come to a gate that's clearly marked Private Property. Turn left (east) to stay on the trail. The path narrows to about 4 or 5 feet wide. The bands of wide yellow paint around the trees to the right indicate the Forever Wild property line.

4.0 Cross another creek and come to another long boggy swale on the other side. In less than 0.1 mile, you will see the campground through the trees on your left.

4.1 Cross another creek and another swale on the other side.

4.2 Cross the best creek of the hike. It's wide and can be deep with sandy banks. The highlight is a wide rocky shoal to the left with its waters cascading over. After the creek, climb a short hill. At the top cross a dirt road east. The path becomes sandy at this point.

4.4 As of this writing, tractors or bulldozers have gouged the path so that it collects more water after a rain and can be ankle-deep in mud, making this quite a slog.

4.5   Finally come out of the bog. In less than 0.1 mile, arrive at the campground, which is used mainly for horses. Turn left (north) here off the rutted dirt road and head toward a 10-stall paddock. There is a spigot here and a hose where you can get water, plus a restroom to the right. Continue straight to the north.

4.6   Turn left to the west and walk down the shoulder of the gravel road.

4.9   The trail turns right (northeast) to cross the road, but first, continue straight down the road a few yards to take a look at the Twin Creek Covered Bridge. When done retrace your steps and cross the road.

5.1   Come to a Y. Take the right fork to the northwest. Once again this area can be boggy after rain.

5.4   Cross a creek over a culvert, then come to an intersection with a sign pointing to the Bottom Land Cutoff to the left and the Pines Trail straight. Continue straight to the north.

5.4   Climb a small hill where you'll start getting some nice views of the grass-covered hillsides dotted with young longleaf pines.

5.7   Come to a T intersection. A sign points to the Firebreak Trail to the right. Turn left (west) to stay on the Pines Trail. In less than 0.1 mile, there is another great view of the rolling hills, savannah grass, and young longleaf pines.

5.8   Cross a creek over a culvert.

5.9   The trail crosses under a power line.

6.0   Come to an intersection with the Day-Use Hiking Trail. Continue straight to the north. In less than 0.1 mile, you'll pass a couple of live traps on the left.

6.4   Arrive back at the intersection with the Day-Use Hiking Trail you crossed at mile 0.1. Turn right (northeast) to head back toward the trailhead.

6.5   Arrive back at the trailhead.

PUPPY PAWS AND GOLDEN YEARS

When doing an overnight (or longer) backpacking trip with your dog, remember these tips:

- Check with your vet about your dog's readiness before heading out.
- Keep your dog's pack light and load it evenly.
- Bring along plenty of power snacks for them like TurboPup Bars or Dogsbar.
- Rest often.
- Be aware of their condition on the trail at all times: Watch for signs of stress and fatigue, remove ticks, and keep them from eating plants that could be harmful.

27 FRANK JACKSON STATE PARK

One of Alabama's smallest state parks offers up a unique hike that takes you across a long wooden bridge to an island where the path loops around, giving you great views of W. F. Jackson Lake. Snowy-white water lilies and wildflowers bloom along the banks as well as in an amazing wetland thick with beautiful, fragrant flowers.

THE RUNDOWN

Start: At the boat ramp parking lot
Distance: 2.4-mile double loop
Approximate hiking time: 1.5 hours
Difficulty: Easy over level dirt or grass footpaths and boardwalks
Trailhead elevation: 260 feet
Highest point: 266 feet
Best season: Year-round; open 6 a.m.–7 p.m.
Trail surface: Dirt, sand, grass, boardwalk
Other trail users: Cyclists
Canine compatibility: Leash required
Land status: State park
Fees and permits: Day-use fee: adults $4; children 4–11 and seniors over 62, $2; children under 4, free

Trail contact: 100 Jerry Adams Dr., Opp; (334) 493-6988; www.alapark .com/frank-jackson-state-park/
Nearest town: Opp
Trail tips: Restrooms and picnic area are located on the northeast side of the parking lot near the trailhead. The creek has a nice little beach for swimming, but alligators are known to live here. A sign warns you to keep your kids close at hand and your puppy on a leash. Be sure to visit in Oct and Nov when the town gets together for "Scarecrows in the Park" and they line the trails with homemade scarecrows.
Maps: USGS: Opp West, AL

FINDING THE TRAILHEAD

From the intersection of AL 134 and US 84, take AL 134 west 21.6 miles. Turn right onto US 331 N. Travel 2.7 miles and turn left onto Ellis Road. Travel 0.4 mile and turn left onto N. Main Street. Travel 1.1 miles and turn right onto W. Jeffcoat Road. Travel 0.2 mile and W. Jeffcoat Road turns into Opine Road. In 0.9 mile, turn right onto Jerry Adams Road. Arrive at the entrance gate in 0.2 mile. After paying the entrance fee, make a right turn and follow the road 0.4 mile. Parking is available at the playground to the left or boat ramp on the right. Trailhead GPS: N31 18.082' / W86 16.258'

THE HIKE

Sometimes you and your pup just need a nice little walk in the woods. A short walk through a forest with birds, maybe some wildlife, wildflowers, and a couple of water features. If that sounds like a prescription you need to fill, then this is a great hike for both of you, and it's found at Frank Jackson State Park.

The park itself is just over 2,000 acres in size with the hub of activity centering around the 1,000-acre W. F. Jackson Lake. This little oasis in Opp, Alabama, is normally a tranquil setting but can get a little busy on weekends, so be prepared. That lake is a very popular destination for anglers.

This hike uses seven different trails to loop your way around the park: Honeysuckle, Magnolia, Nature, Seth Hammett Walkway, Dogwood, Walking, and Azalea Trails. All of

Taking a long walk on a long bridge. Crossing the channel to get to the island at the confluence of Lightwood Knot and Cameron Creeks.

the paths are easy walks over flat, sandy footpaths, narrow dirt and grass trails, and a bit of old dirt and small gravel roads.

What's unique about this hike is that after arriving at the trailhead, you'll walk a long bridge, the G. Cleve Pierce Memorial Footbridge, across the lake and to an island where the Honeysuckle and Walking Trails loop around, giving you some nice views of the lake. Water lilies line the banks, as do several types of wildflowers, like the purple plantain and yellow plantain. Take a seat on one of the many benches and look for large osprey nests or maybe a bald eagle soaring above.

Back on the mainland, the paths wind through a mixed hardwood forest where indigo buntings and blue grosbeaks dart from the brush, while a songbird choir serenades you.

As you approach the campground, the Seth Hammett Walkway crosses a wonderful wetland with a rainbow of wildflowers in season. A sign reminds you here to be wary of snakes like cottonmouth, coral, and even diamond rattlers.

While this is a really nice hike where you can get outside for a quick commune with nature and maybe do a little trail training with your dog, we are in south Alabama and, as the signs at the lake tell you, alligators do live in the water. Be sure when you're near the lake to keep your dog leashed and out of the water.

We have to thank the volunteers of the Lake Frank Jackson Trail Masters for maintaining the trails at Frank Jackson. This seventy-plus-member organization does a little of everything for the park, such as building and maintaining bridges, boardwalks, and gazebos, as well as grooming the trails. They even built a brand new restroom near the playground and swimming area.

If you can make it to the park in October and November, you can be a part of the group's annual "Scarecrows in the Park" event. For two months the trails are lined with beautiful and unique scarecrows designed by local residents, organizations, students, and businesses.

The Trail Masters were recently awarded the Alabama State Park's Eagle Award for their work and partnership with the state.

When you arrive you can park either in the boat ramp parking area or, if it's a big fishing weekend, in the lot next to the playground. Both are near where this hike begins at the G. Cleve Pierce Memorial Footbridge.

The trails are not blazed, but they are well maintained and easy to follow, so it is hard to get lost. There is a nice bathroom located on the east side of the boat ramp parking lot near a picnic pavilion, where you can also find water for your pup. And as mentioned before, another restroom is next to the swimming area you will pass along the way.

CREATURE COMFORTS

RESTING UP

Econo Lodge, 1421 MLK Jr. Expressway, Andalusia; (334) 222-7511; www.choice hotels.com

Make your reservations online but phone the hotel first to verify there are pet-friendly rooms available. Three pets are allowed per room, each weighing a maximum of 50 pounds. There is an additional $20 per pet, per night fee.

CAMPING

Frank Jackson State Park, 100 Jerry Adams Dr., Opp; (334) 493-6988; www.alapark .com/frank-jackson-state-park-camping

The park has thirty-two improved RV campsites with power and water, but these are also available for tent campers. There are also many primitive campsites as well. Tent campers will pay the full RV prices for improved sites: Sun through Thurs $33.37 for water-side sites, $30.03 off water; Fri and Sat $36.71 on water, $33.37 off water. Be sure to phone in advance to check on availability and to make reservations.

FUELING UP

Sonic Drive-In, 306 E. 3 Notch St., Andalusia; (334) 222-1443; www.sonicdrivein .com/

The closest thing to a good old-fashioned drive-in, Sonic Drive-Ins feature everything that makes a drive-in great: burgers, hot dogs, breakfast burritos, and amazing hand-mixed shakes. Of course you can eat in your car with your dog or sit under the covered outdoor patio. You may even be greeted by a roller-skating carhop. Happy days!

MILES AND DIRECTIONS

0.0 Start from the northwest side of the parking lot at the boat ramp. You will see the G. Cleve Pierce Memorial Footbridge straight ahead. Cross the bridge and head to the island.

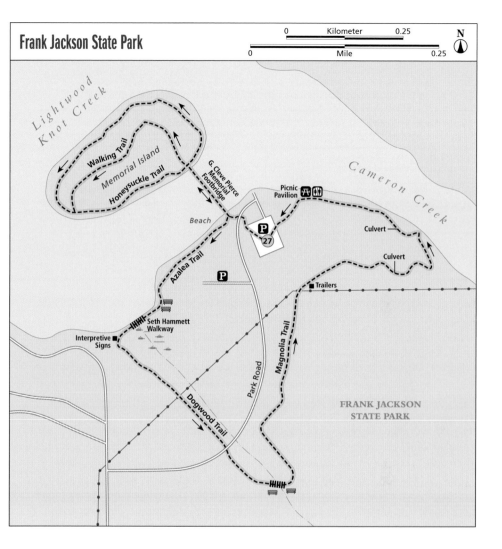

Frank Jackson State Park

0.1   Come to a nice wide deck on the bridge where you can take in the view of the lake. Continue to the northwest on the bridge to the island.

0.2   On the other side of the bridge, arrive at Memorial Island. There is an informative kiosk that tells you about woolly mammoths that used to roam the area. Two trails intersect here: Straight ahead to the northwest is the Walking Trail. The Honeysuckle Trail heads to the left and right (northeast/southwest). Turn right (northeast) onto the Honeysuckle Trail. At this point the path is wide and grassy with sandy footing along the banks of the creek and a couple of picnic tables. In less than 0.1 mile cross a 36-foot-long bridge over a deep runoff.

0.3   Pass the Walking Trail on the left. Continue straight to the southwest.

0.4   Coming out of the woods, the path becomes wide and grassy again with a few picnic tables and a panoramic view of W. F. Jackson Lake.

0.5   Pass a side trail that connects this trail with the Walking Trail on the left. We'll come back to this point again in a minute.

0.6 Cross a 15-foot bridge over a runoff. In less than 0.1 mile, pass an unidentified trail on the left. Shortly after that, you'll pass yet another unidentified trail on left with a bench.

0.7 Back at the bridge and the trail kiosk, you can either turn right (southeast) and cross the bridge to continue at mile 0.8 or turn left to add to the hike on the Walking Trail. Right now, turn left (northwest) onto the Walking Trail for a nice walk in the woods. In less than 0.1 mile, turn left onto a connector trail that will lead back to the Honeysuckle Trail (you can actually continue straight here to the northwest a short distance if you want). Shortly after, come to a T intersection. Take the right fork to the west.

1.0 Come to the intersection with the Honeysuckle Trail. Turn left (east) and continue along the banks of the creek heading toward the bridge. In less than 0.1 mile, arrive back at the bridge. Turn right (southeast) and cross the bridge heading back toward the boat ramp.

1.1 On the other side, turn right (southwest) and walk about 20 feet along a cement sidewalk, then get off the sidewalk and follow the edge of the creek behind a playground. In less than 0.1 mile, pass a beach to your right on the banks of the creek with a sign warning you of alligators and snakes, and to swim at your own risk (there are no lifeguards).

1.2 The Azalea Trail begins. In less than 0.1 mile, come to a sign that points the way to the campground (left) and playground (right). Continue straight to the south. In a few feet pass benches on the right next to the lake with great views. In less than 0.1 mile, cross the Seth Hammett Walkway, a long boardwalk over a backwater wetland with blooming lily pads and wildflowers spring through summer.

1.3 At an intersection at the opposite end of the walkway, there will be interpretive signs about snakes in the area. Turn left (south) onto the Dogwood Trail.

1.4 Cross under a power line.

1.5 Cross the park road to the southeast and pick up the Dogwood / Magnolia Trail connector on the other side.

1.6 Come to a T intersection with a wide gravel path. This is the Magnolia Trail. Turn left (east) onto the Magnolia. In less than 0.1 mile, cross a 30-foot boardwalk over a runoff. Benches are scattered all along this trail.

2.0 The trail comes up behind 3 small trailers. You can see the parking lot to the left (northwest).

2.1 Cross a culvert next to a field on the right.

2.2 Arrive back at the creek, where there's a bench swing. In less than 0.1 mile, cross another culvert.

2.4 Come to a picnic pavilion. Head through the picnic area to the southwest. In less than 0.1 mile, arrive back at the parking lot.

28 FIVE RUNS LOOP

The majestic longleaf pines of Conecuh National Forest form the backdrop for this loop hike around several water features, including Buck and Ditch Ponds, the wide and swift-flowing Five Runs Creek, and the aqua Blue Spring that invites you and your dog to take a dip during the hot summer months.

THE RUNDOWN

Start: From the parking lot at the south bathhouse next to Open Pond
Distance: 5.8-mile loop
Approximate hiking time: 3 hours
Difficulty: Moderate due to length
Trailhead elevation: 280 feet
Highest point: 330 feet
Best season: Early spring to early fall; open sunrise to sunset
Trail surface: Dirt footpath, some sandy service roads
Other trail users: Cyclists, hunters
Canine compatibility: Leash required
Land status: National forest
Fees and permits: $3 per person day-use fee
Trail contact: Conecuh National Forest, 24481 AL 55, Andalusia, AL 36420; (334) 222-2555; www .fs.usda.gov/recarea/alabama/ recreation/picnickinginfo/ recarea/?recid=30107&actid=71

Nearest town: Andalusia
Trail tips: Restrooms are available at the bathhouse near the trailhead. Bring your swimsuit in the summer to take a dip in the icy cold spring, but remember, it's deep and there are no lifeguards. Swim at your own risk. You should also consider a life jacket for your dog. You may be tempted to run your dog off leash here if they're under voice control, but the forest service requires leashes, and alligators are known to live in the ponds and lakes of Conecuh. You should leash them and keep them and your children close at hand near the water features.
Maps: USGS: Wing, AL
Other: Hunting is allowed in Conecuh National Forest. Please visit the Trail Contact (above) for seasons and restrictions.

FINDING THE TRAILHEAD

From Andalusia at the intersection of US 84 (River Falls Street) and US 29, take US 29 south 11.2 miles and turn left onto AL 137 S. Travel 5.4 miles and turn left onto Open Pond Road. Travel 0.3 mile and turn right onto CR 28 (Tower Road). Travel 1.1 miles and come to a Y; there is a self-pay kiosk here. Pay your day-use fee and put the tag in your window. Take the left fork and park in the lot behind the bathhouse. The trailhead is on the south side of the parking lot. There are three 6-inch round creosote poles blocking a short, old dirt road. That is where the hike begins. Trailhead GPS: N31 05.408' / W86 32.675'

THE HIKE

This hike takes us to the 83,000-acre Conecuh National Forest near Andalusia. The forest is a favorite of hikers because of its magnificent longleaf pines that tower above the sandy footpaths and the water features that dot the landscape. You will have a chance to visit some of those on this 5.8-mile loop hike.

The forest itself provides a unique habitat for many species of wildlife, including several rare and endangered species like the gopher tortoise. The sandy soil of the longleaf forest

An inviting swimming hole—the cool, crystal-clear water of Blue Spring. Remember, it's deep and there are no lifeguards.

is the ideal home for the tortoises, who burrow down into it for protection. As you walk the trail, be on the lookout for these small burrows just off the trail.

Another rare reptile that calls Conecuh home is the eastern indigo snake. In just the right light, this beautiful black snake has a blue glow to it. It's a friendly, nonvenomous snake that can be distinguished from black snakes by its scales, which are smooth with no ridges.

The tortoise and the snake are truly an odd couple: The snake actually shares the tortoise's burrow. Just don't ask which one is Felix and which one is Oscar.

Sadly, though, the eastern indigo is coming dangerously close to extinction. The good news is that many state and federal agencies are attempting to bring them back to places like Conecuh.

As for the trail itself, it is brightened in season with many beautiful and colorful wildflowers and plants like pink orchids, red cardinal plants, and plenty of black-eyed Susans. Near the many bogs that dot the landscape, look for the long, slender green tubes of the carnivorous white-top pitcher plants.

And then there are the water features. The Five Runs Loop passes three ponds: the calm, sparkling waters of Buck and Ditch Ponds and the smaller Alligator Pond. Buck and Ditch are favorite places for fishermen to go to wet their lines for bass and bream. If you love to fish, don't forget to pick up an Alabama freshwater license before dropping the hook. You're sure to see plenty of blue herons and egrets along the banks, as well as wood ducks silently floating on the surface.

The final pond is the small Alligator Pond, a tranquil little reflecting pond in the thick forest. As the name implies, alligators have been spotted here—in fact, in all three ponds and in the larger Open Pond at the recreation area. Signs posted near the ponds will give you a chuckle: "Do not molest alligators." Think about that.

But seriously, injuring an alligator can get you jail time and a $5,000 to $10,000 fine, but more than that, alligators are dangerous for you and most especially for small children and your dog. While hiking in Conecuh, even though this hike is listed as allowing your dog to be under "voice control," for safety, leash them and keep them and your kids close at hand when near the ponds.

Just before making the turn to head back to the trailhead, you'll come to what is arguably the best part of the trip. First you'll encounter the trail's namesake, Five Runs Creek, a wide and fast-flowing blackwater creek that feeds the Blackwater River and eventually flows into the Gulf of Mexico. The creek alongside the trail has a few sets of small shoals.

And finally, just past the creek, you will come to Blue Spring, a beautiful crystal-clear, icy-blue natural spring. The spring is so clear you can see the rock formations on the bottom far below the surface. The spring is plenty deep and makes a great place to swim during the hot summer months. But having said that, it is very deep, and there are no lifeguards here. Swim at your own risk and pay close attention to your pup if they decide to swim. A life jacket wouldn't be a bad idea for them.

The trail uses the white diamond blazes of the Conecuh Trail to show the way. If you plan on hiking in the summer, be ready for mosquitoes—and lots of them—along the water features. And remember, hunting is allowed. Call or visit the Trail Contact (above) for dates and restrictions.

CREATURE COMFORTS

RESTING UP
Econo Lodge, 1421 MLK Jr. Expressway, Andalusia; (334) 222-7511; www.choice hotels.com/alabama/andalusia/econo-lodge-hotels

Make your reservations online but phone the hotel first to verify there are pet-friendly rooms available. Three pets are allowed per room, each weighing a maximum of 50 pounds. There is an additional $20 per pet, per night fee.

CAMPING
Open Pond Recreation Area; Off CR 28, Andalusia; (334) 222-2555; www.fs.usda .gov/recarea/alabama/recarea/?recid=30113

Open Pond is a beautiful campground in Conecuh's longleaf forest. There are seventy-four improved campsites, all situated in four camp loops (A through D), with an additional primitive area. If you don't get a campsite near the pond, you're only a short walk from it. The bathrooms are very nice and clean. Conecuh National Forest does not make reservations in advance. All campsites are available on a first come, first served basis. When you arrive, check in with the camp host. Campsites range from $6 for primitive sites to $12 for improved sites with water.

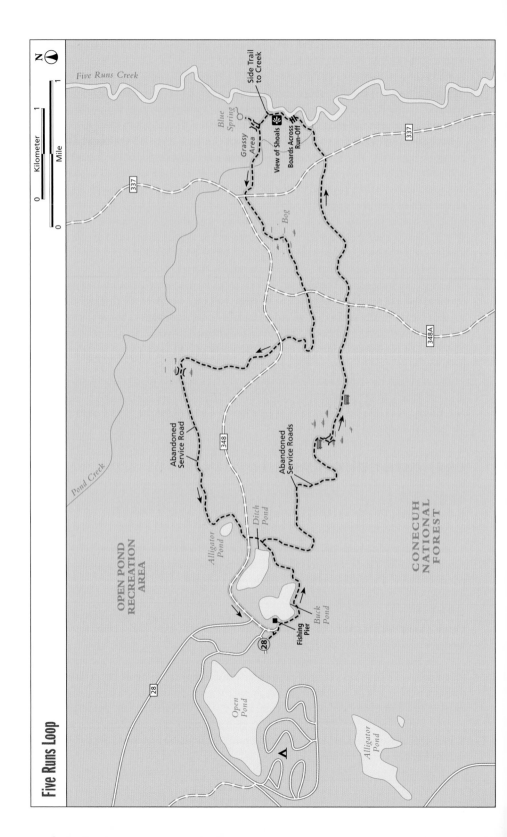

Five Runs Loop

N

Kilometer

Mile

Five Runs Creek

Side Trail
to Creek

Blue Spring

Grassy
Area

View of Shoals

Boards Across
Run-Off

Bog

337

337

348A

Abandoned
Service Road

348

Abandoned
Service Roads

Pond Creek

OPEN POND
RECREATION
AREA

*Alligator
Pond*

*Ditch
Pond*

*Buck
Pond*

CONECUH
NATIONAL
FOREST

Fishing
Pier

28

28

*Open
Pond*

*Alligator
Pond*

FUELING UP

Sonic Drive-In, 306 E. 3 Notch St., Andalusia; (334) 222-1443; www.sonicdrivein
.com/

Who doesn't like a good old-fashioned drive-in complete with roller-skating carhops? Sonic Drive-In is just that, with all that makes a drive-in great: burgers, hot dogs, breakfast burritos, and amazing hand-mixed shakes. Of course, you can eat in your car with your dog or sit under the covered outdoor patio.

MILES AND DIRECTIONS

0.0 Start from the parking area next to the south bathhouse at Open Pond. The entrance to the trail is about 100 yards northwest of the bathhouse. Three 6-inch round creosote poles show the entrance (they are actually used to keep people from driving in on the abandoned dirt road at this point). In 300 feet pass a white-diamond-blazed trail on the right (south). You will see Buck Pond straight ahead to the east. Continue straight toward the lake. In another 200 feet, turn right (south) onto a second white-diamond-blazed trail. The path is now a 2-foot-wide dirt path. You will have nice views of the pond to your left (northeast).

0.5 Ditch Pond will be to your left (west).

0.6 A trail comes in from the north. A sign here points the direction to Blue Spring to the east and the Blue Lake Recreation Area to the north. Turn right onto the side trail and head north. The trail is still blazed with white diamond markers.

1.0 Cross an abandoned service road. You will see an established campsite to left (east). In about 400 feet, cross another abandoned service road.

1.3 Pass a bench.

1.4 Cross a creek and wetland over a 25-foot-long bridge.

1.5 Pass a bench.

1.9 Cross FS 348A to the east.

2.2 The path is grassy here for a short distance. Look for pitcher plants alongside the trail.

2.5 Cross FS 337 to the northwest.

2.6 Cross a narrow creek. After the crossing, Five Runs Creek will be on your right (east).

2.7 Cross a runoff over a small footbridge. There is a pond on your left (west) and Five Runs Creek on your right.

2.8 About a 3-foot section of the trail is washed out. You will need to hop this carefully. A steep bank to the creek is next to the trail. In 100 feet you'll see a line of shoals in the creek and then come to a Y. The right fork to the northeast is a short 20-foot trail to the river with a better view of the rapids. Take the left fork; you will be walking away from the creek.

2.9 Come to a T intersection. Turn right (northeast) and walk across a long wooden bridge. After crossing the bridge, come to another T with a dirt service road. Turn right (east) onto the road. In 200 feet arrive at Blue Spring. When done visiting the spring, turn around and retrace your steps to the bridge and cross it to the southwest.

3.0 After crossing the bridge, continue straight (west) on the wide, hard-packed clay path.

3.1 Come out to a small open grassy area. In 200 feet, come to a Y. Take the left fork to the northeast (a large brown sign here that reads TRAIL points the way).

3.2 Cross FS 337 to the west.

3.5 Pass a small bog with a few pitcher plants.

3.7 Cross FS 348A to the west.

4.1 Cross FS 348 to the north.

4.5 Cross a wetland over a 120-foot-long bridge.

4.7 Pass a wildlife food plot on the right. In 200 feet cross an abandoned service road to the west.

4.9 Cross another abandoned service road. In 500 feet cross a creek over a 20-foot bridge. There may be wildflowers blooming here in season.

5.1 A trail comes in from the left (southeast). A sign here points the direction to the Open Pond Recreation Area (0.7 mile to the left) and Blue Pond Recreation Area (3 miles to the west). Turn left onto the dirt footpath (the blazes are still white diamond markers). You will be walking next to Alligator Pond on your right (west).

5.2 Cross a creek over a 15-foot bridge.

5.3 Come to FS 348. Turn right (west) onto the road. In 200 feet take the left fork of a Y onto a small sandy road that will take you along the banks of Ditch Pond.

5.6 A paved road intersects the dirt road you are walking on. Continue straight on the dirt road to the southwest. A sign here points the direction to both Ditch and Buck Ponds.

5.7 The road crosses over a culvert (there is a short split-rail fence on either side of the road). You are back at Buck Pond where you originally entered. Turn right (northwest) here and follow the dirt road the short distance to the trailhead.

5.8 Arrive back at the trailhead.

29 CONECUH TRAIL NORTH LOOP

This easy walking 13.0-mile loop is actually the north loop of the longer Conecuh Trail. Your dog will love romping through this beautiful longleaf-pine forest, and you'll love the quiet solitude. The loop takes you past several water features, including the cypress Mossy Pond as well as Gum and Nellie Ponds. There is ample canopy over most of the trail for summertime shade, and don't be surprised if you kick up some wild turkeys along the way.

THE RUNDOWN

Start: From the south trail head of the Conecuh Trail on AL 137

Distance: 13.0-mile loop

Approximate hiking time: 7 hours

Difficulty: Easy over flat to mildly rolling hills

Trailhead elevation: 322 feet

Highest point: 346 feet

Best season: Year-round but sections may be closed for hunting; open sunrise to sunset

Trail surface: Dirt footpath or sandy service road

Other trail users: Cyclists, hunters

Canine compatibility: Leash required

Land status: National forest

Fees and permits: None

Trail contact: Conecuh National Forest, 24481 AL 55, Andalusia, AL 36420; (334) 222-2555; www.fs.usda .gov/detail/alabama/about-forest/ districts/?cid=fsbdev3_002554

Nearest town: Andalusia

Trail tips: Head to the ponds early in the evening to hear a joyful frog choir. Don't forget the bug spray in the warmer months. And bring along the camera for brilliant colors of wildflowers in the spring and summer and the moody atmosphere of the cypress-lined Mossy Pond.

Maps: USGS: Wing, AL

Other: Hunting is allowed in Conecuh National Forest. Please contact their office for dates and restrictions (see Trail Contact, above).

FINDING THE TRAILHEAD

From Andalusia at the intersection of US 84 (River Falls Street) and US 29, take US 29 south 11.2 miles and turn left onto AL 137 S. Travel 3.7 miles. The trailhead parking lot will be on the left. Trailhead GPS N31 07 28.9' / W86 34 14.3'

THE HIKE

If you're looking just to get away for a full day hike or for a quick overnighter, then look no further than the North Loop trail.

This 13.0-mile loop is a subset of the longer Conecuh Trail, which is about 20 miles long (one way) and is pretty flat, making it the perfect trail for those who have just started hiking and are looking for a longer hike, if you and your pup are just starting to move into backpacking and looking for an easy "intro" hike, or if you're a veteran hiker looking for a quick overnighter or a place to do a shakedown of your new gear.

But don't get me wrong. The North Loop isn't just a training trail. It is a beautiful circuit through the magnificent longleaf-pine forest of the Conecuh National Forest with visits to some remarkable water features.

Conecuh National Forest's North Loop is a long but easy hike for both beginners and advanced hikers with plenty to see and plenty of exit points in case you need to bail out quickly.

On the west side of the loop you will pay a visit to a Trail and Mossy Pond. The ponds are quintessential southern red cedar swamps with tall, rugged-barked trees draped in flowing Spanish moss and towering into the sky, their roots almost defying gravity as their tops, or "knees," protrude out of the murky water at the base of the trunk.

As you proceed to the eastern half of the loop after crossing AL 137 for a second time, almost immediately you will arrive at Gum Pond. Visit the pond in the early evening to be serenaded by the frog song of pine barren frogs. Their joyful sound echoes through the forest. In the spring the black-eyed Susan, honeysuckle, and an assortment of other wildflowers are gorgeous, and white water lilies blanket the surface of the pond both here and at your next stop, Nellie Pond.

In the spring, the fragrant smell of dogwood and magnolia wafts in the air as you walk the path, and white-top pitcher plants bloom in the bogs just off the trail.

For birders, you're in for a real treat: Dozens of species of birds call the forest home, including blue herons, yellowthroats, yellow-throated warblers, and a number of different songbirds. As for wildlife, don't be surprised if you kick up a wild turkey, whitetail deer, or gray fox from the brush.

Along the trail you will pass through some old cattle gates, and you may wonder why they are there. Not too long ago, farmers grazed their cows in the forest. The farmers earned a living from their cattle, and the forest earned money from leasing the land to the farmers.

This path is a good beginning trail for novice backpackers because it has easy escape routes in case you need to bug out in an emergency or during bad weather. Simply take one of the dirt forest service roads back to the highway and then the highway back to your vehicle.

A lot of people love to do this hike as a quick overnight. They walk the 9.5-mile trail all the way to Nellie Pond, where they spend the night. From there it is a short 3.5-mile trip back to the trailhead the next morning.

Camping is allowed anywhere along the trail using the dispersal method, that is, keeping your campsite at least 100 feet away from the trail. There are some very nice camping spots at Nellie Pond, and you can get a good view of the night sky there. The forest service recommends that you use previously established campsites you come across along the trail to prevent further damage to the land and ecosystem. Remember that campfires are not allowed, so bring the backpack stove.

But, as we all know when it comes to hiking, you take the good, you take the bad. Well, it's not really bad; just be prepared. First, you're walking past bogs and the still water of ponds, so pack along that insect repellent.

You may be tempted to run your dog off leash here if they're under voice control, but remember the forest service requires leashes, and alligators are known to live in the ponds and lakes of Conecuh.

Of course, hunting is allowed in the forest in the fall and winter. Visit the Conecuh National Forest website or contact the ranger station for dates and restrictions on hiking. See Trail Contact (above) for contact information.

CREATURE COMFORTS

RESTING UP
Econo Lodge, 1421 MLK Jr. Expressway, Andalusia; (334) 222-7511; www.choice hotels.com/alabama/andalusia/econo-lodge-hotels

Make your reservations online but phone the hotel first to verify there are pet-friendly rooms available. Three pets are allowed per room, each weighing a maximum of 50 pounds. There is an additional $20 per pet, per night fee.

CAMPING
Open Pond Recreation Area, off CR 28, Andalusia; (334) 222-2555; www.fs.usda .gov/recarea/alabama/recarea/?recid=30113

Open Pond is a beautiful campground in Conecuh's longleaf-pine forest. There are seventy-four improved campsites in all, situated in four camp loops (A through D), with an additional primitive area. If you don't get a campsite near the pond, you're only a short walk from it. The bathrooms are very nice and clean. Conecuh National Forest does not make reservations in advance. All campsites are on a first come, first served basis. When you arrive, check in with the camp host. Campsites range from $6 for primitive sites to $12 for improved sites with water.

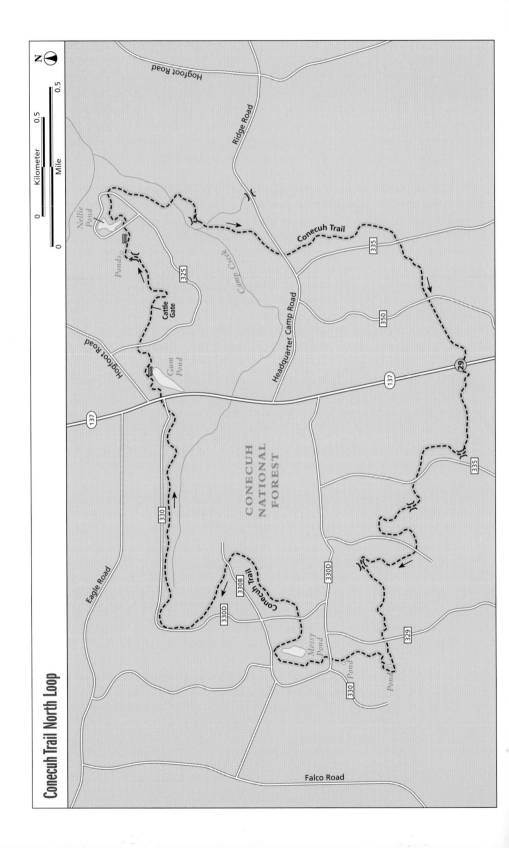

Conecuh Trail North Loop

N

Kilometer
0   0.5

Mile
0   0.5

Hogfoot Road

Ridge Road

Nellie Pond

Ponds

Cattle Gate

Camp Creek

Conecuh Trail

325

335

350

Headquarter Camp Road

137

29

335

CONECUH NATIONAL FOREST

330

Hogfoot Road

Gum Pond

137

Eagle Road

330D

330B

Conecuh Trail

330D

Mossy Pond

Pond

330D

329

Ponds

330

Falco Road

FUELING UP

Sonic Drive-In, 306 E. 3 Notch St., Andalusia; (334) 222-1443; www.sonicdrivein.com/
Who doesn't like a good old-fashioned drive-in complete with roller-skating carhops? Sonic Drive-is just that, with all that makes a drive-in great: burgers, hot dogs, breakfast burritos, and amazing hand-mixed shakes. Of course, you can eat in your car with your dog or sit under the covered outdoor patio.

MILES AND DIRECTIONS

0.0 Start from the Conecuh Trail South Trailhead. From the trailhead head west and immediately—and cautiously—cross AL 137 and pick up the white-blazed trail on the opposite side.

0.8 Cross a bridge.

1.4 Cross a dirt road to the west.

1.6 Cross a bridge.

2.2 Cross a dirt road to the west.

2.7 Cross a bridge.

3.4 Cross a dirt road to the north.

3.6 Pass a small pond and marsh on the left.

4.1 Pass a small pond on the right and, in less than 0.1 mile, cross FS 330D north.

4.5 Come to a sign indicating that the dirt roads (not the trail) are closed Mar 10–Oct 18. Mossy Pond will be on your right.

5.6 Pass a pond on the left and, in less than 0.1 mile, cross another dirt forest service road to the northwest.

8.0 Come to a T intersection with FR 330. Turn right (east) onto the dirt road. In a few yards arrive at AL 137. Once again, carefully cross the highway, picking up the trail on the opposite side.

8.1 You will get your first glimpse of Gum Pond on the right.

8.2 The trail comes right up to the banks of Gum Pond with a view of the pond and a bench.

8.4 The trail passes through an old cattle gate. In about 100 feet cross a dirt forest service road to the east.

8.6 Pass a bench.

8.7 Pass through another cattle gate. In 100 feet the trail narrows as it heads through a tunnel of thick shrubs and hardwoods.

8.9 Cross a 30-foot footbridge over a seasonal creek.

9.2 Cross a 100-foot footbridge over a seasonal wetland. Look for pitcher plants.

9.5 Arrive at the southern end of Nellie Pond

9.7 Get your best view of Nellie Pond. There are some nice places to pitch camp here.

10.6 Cross a bridge over a seasonal creek.

11.8 Cross another seasonal creek over a footbridge.

12.0 Cross a dirt road. A sign on the other side reads HIGHWAY 137 1 MILE, BLUE POND RECREATION AREA ½ MILE.

13.0 Arrive back at the trailhead.

Locals have been flocking to Little River State Forest since 1935, and for good reason. This little out-of-the-way gem has a beautiful glistening lake, Little River Lake, that's perfect for fishing, swimming, and wading in with Fido. There's also a playground and, most importantly, hiking trails. The two trails of this park will take you on a tranquil walk along the wildflower-laden banks of the lake and to the historic gazebo that was built when the park was established by the Civilian Conservation Corps during the Great Depression.

THE RUNDOWN

Start: From the parking lot next to the lake and old bathhouse
Distance: 4.8-mile double loop
Approximate hiking time: 2.5–3 hours
Difficulty: Easy over rolling hills and dirt and grass foot paths; only one steepish climb
Trailhead elevation: 185 feet
Highest point: 338 feet
Best season: Year-round; open 7 a.m.–7 p.m.
Trail surface: Dirt and grass footpath, short walk on dirt road
Other trail users: Cyclists, equestrians
Canine compatibility: Leash required
Land status: Alabama state forest
Fees and permits: Day-use fee: adults $2; children 6–15, $1; children under 6, free
Trail contact: Little River State Forest, 580 H. Kyle Rd., Atmore; (251) 743-2350; www.forestry .alabama.gov/little_river_state_ forest.aspx

Nearest town: Atmore
Trail tips: The trails are fun and relatively easy at Little River. The park staff reminds you that a dog leash is required. If you want to go into the lake with your dog, they ask that you wade in next to the boat ramp on the east side of the lake (on the CCC/Bell Trail). Alligators have been spotted here. The other nuisance you'll find here are the mosquitoes near the creeks in the warmer months and yellow flies in early summer (see Joe's Five Hiking Tips and "Seasonal Nuisances" for information on combatting these little demons).
Maps: USGS: Uriah East, AL; Uriah West, AL
Other: The park reopened in 2018 after being closed for a year. The new managers are deciding if hunting will be allowed in the fall. Contact the park for updates.

FINDING THE TRAILHEAD

From the intersection of I-65 and AL 21 (exit 57), take AL 21 north 11 miles. Turn right onto H. Kyle Road and travel 0.4 mile to the pay station. The old bathhouse and the start of the trail are straight ahead in another 0.2 mile. Trailhead GPS: N31 15.436′ / W87 29.129′

THE HIKE

Another one of the great, but lesser known, Civilian Conservation Corps (CCC) parks in Alabama is located only a few miles north of the town of Atmore—Little River State Forest.

The park was built by the CCC in 1935 during the Great Depression as part of President Roosevelt's New Deal. Companies of young men ages 18 to 23 set out across the

Growl and his human pals check out Little River's lake from the fishing pier.

country to plant millions of trees and build new infrastructure and national and state parks, all for a guaranteed monthly salary of $30, $25 of which the government sent home to their families to help them survive.

The park has had an identity crisis over the years. Originally it was called Little River State Forest, later to be called Little River State Park, only to be renamed to Claude D. Kelley State Park after a local politician, then back to Little River State Forest, although the STATE PARK signs still line the highway as you approach the park. Recently the recreation area was renamed the Claude D. Kelley Recreation Area. Keeping up?

I have combined the park's two trails into one double loop with both connecting in the parking lot at the old bathhouse. This makes it easy to split the trip into two separate hikes if you want.

The first trail is a combination of the CCC and Bell Trails. The Bell Trail was named for a former park ranger, Paul Bell, who built the trail. This path begins by crossing the picturesque spillway of the lake's dam, then hugs the banks of the lake on an earthen berm before heading into the woods, where you'll have views of the lake from the opposite side, away from the recreation area. The path through here is shady, with wildflowers lining the footpath.

By the way, that berm was hand-built by the CCC to create the lake, a monumental, backbreaking task. You can see a film of the workers building the dam as well as park's original cabins in a film titled *Down Mobile Way 1935*. The film is available online at YouTube: www.youtube.com/watch?v=N23Vpy6VTmw. The segment about this forest comes at about the 10-minute mark.

Eventually the path heads rather steeply uphill on an old, rutted dirt road. At the top near a clay pit, turn around for something unheard of in relatively flat south Alabama—a view of the surrounding hills.

At the top of the hill, the Bell Trail connects to the CCC Trail, which is the actual road the workers used to move men and materials into the forest to build the park. As you walk down the wide dirt and gravel CCC Trail, keep a lookout for CCC-built stone culverts that run beneath the road to divert rainwater and prevent erosion.

By the way, you are allowed to wade with your dog on-leash into the spillway at the dam but not in the lake itself. The staff tells me that alligators had been spotted there recently.

The second loop is the Gazebo Trail. The trail is so named because it climbs the rolling south Alabama hills until it reaches a gazebo that was also built by the CCC. Step inside the structure and look up. You'll see the tightly fitted rafters, all hand-built, that have withstood the ravages of time and hurricanes, a testament to the skill of the CCC workers.

There is a really nice but seasonal stream crossing at mile 0.6 that your dog will enjoy; otherwise, bring plenty of drinking water for both you and your dog.

Both trails are blazed with dollar-bill-size yellow paint blazes, a tip of the hat to the state bird, the yellowhammer. The blazes use what is called the "dit-dot" method of marking, which means that whenever the trail makes a sharp turn, there will be two paint blazes one on top of the other; the top blaze will be offset in the direction of the turn.

CREATURE COMFORTS

RESTING UP

Holiday Inn Express, 111 Lakeview Circle, Atmore; (251) 411-3436; www.ihg.com/holidayinnexpress/hotels/us/en/atmore/atmor/hoteldetail

Make your reservations online or by phone, but, as always, it's best to phone ahead to make sure there are pet-friendly rooms available. Two pets of any size are welcome. There is an additional $25 per pet, per night fee charged, as well as a $50 refundable deposit. The deposit is returned when the room is verified to be clean after checkout. Dogs cannot be left unattended in rooms.

CAMPING

Magnolia Branch Wildlife Reserve, 24 Big Creek Rd., Atmore; (251) 446-3423; www.magnoliabranch.com/

The Poarch Creek Indians opened this beautiful and fun-filled campground several years ago, and it's one popular place. The park features zip lines, canoeing, tubing, bike rentals, and, of course, camping. Magnolia Branch has fifteen improved tent campsites with water and electricity and unlimited primitive sites. Improved sites are $20 per day for up to six people. Primitive sites are $10 per day plus $1 per person. Call to make your reservations.

FUELING UP

Sonic Drive-In, 205 McMeans Ave., Bay Minette; (251) 937-4472; www.sonicdrivein.com/

You know it and love it. It's all that makes a drive-in great: burgers, hot dogs, breakfast burritos, and amazing hand-mixed shakes. Of course, you can eat in your car with your dog or sit under the covered outdoor patio.

MILES AND DIRECTIONS

0.0 Start at the park office and bathhouse. We will hike the 2.0-mile Bell/CCC Trails first. Both trails are blazed with the yellow markings of the Alabama Trail. Head southwest along the banks of the lake toward the park's pay station and entrance.

0.1 The trail comes to a 50-foot-long footbridge that spans the lake's spillway. Cross the bridge heading to the south; once across, turn to the east and head back toward the lake. At the lake, turn right and follow the dirt road atop the earthen dam.

0.3 Pass a T fishing pier that extends out into the lake on the left (east).

0.4 Come to a T intersection. To the right you will see a dirt road. This is the CCC Trail, and you will return on it. But now, turn left (southeast) into the woods. The trail is now a dirt footpath.

0.5 Cross a short 20-foot metal-grate bridge over a small stream.

0.6 Come to a Y. Take the right fork to the southwest. (*FYI:* The left fork is a side trail that takes you to a nice walk along the banks of the lake. It will eventually meet back up with the main trail at mile 0.7).

0.7 The side trail to the lake rejoins the main trail from the northeast. Continue about another 20 feet and come to a Y. Take the right fork to the southeast. (*FYI:* The left fork is the forest's property line and is marked with yellow-and-white rings around the trees and has a grass-covered service road along the perimeter.) Soon the trail begins a pretty decent climb up the hill to the intersection with the CCC Trail.

1.0 Come to a Y. Take the right fork up the hill to the southwest. The trail is now a dirt road that is usually well maintained but may have deep ruts after heavy rain.

1.1 Come to a T intersection. Straight ahead is a clay pit. (*FYI:* Be sure to turn around and catch the views of the surrounding hills to the southeast.) Turn right (northwest) at the pit onto the dirt CCC Road. This is the unblazed CCC Trail.

1.7 The trail comes to the end of the loop that you first started at mile 0.4. Turn left (northeast) and retrace your steps over the earthen dam and spillway back to the trailhead.

2.0 Arrive back at the trailhead. You can stop here and do the 2.8-mile Gazebo Trail at a later time, but right now we will continue on from this location. Head away from the lake to the northeast toward the picnic pavilion and picnic area. The trail here is neatly mowed grass.

2.2 Cross the dirt Campground Road to the north. The trail now follows a 3- to 4-foot dirt and grass path through some beautiful pines. Watch for deer in this area.

2.6 Come to a 78-foot-long bridge across a seasonal stream that feeds the lake. Once on the other side of the bridge, turn to the left (northeast).

2.8 Cross a dirt road to the east.

2.9 The trail merges with a dirt logging road that comes in from the left. Keep going straight (north), following the blazes. In about 100 feet come to a

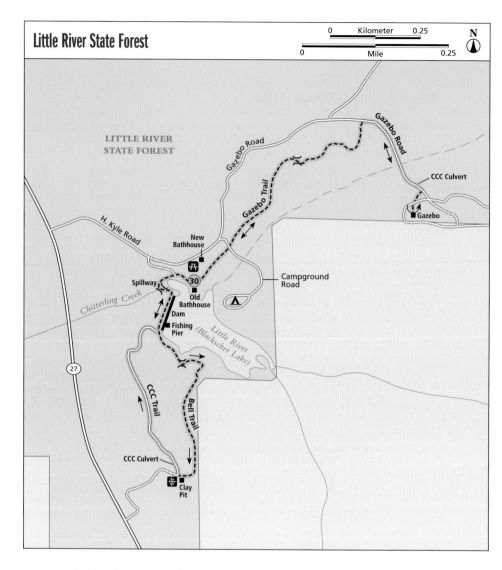

Little River State Forest

LITTLE RIVER
STATE FOREST

H. Kyle Road

Gazebo Road

Gazebo Trail

Gazebo Road

CCC Culvert

Gazebo

New
Bathhouse

Spillway

Chitterling Creek

Old
Bathhouse

Dam

Fishing
Pier

Campground
Road

Little River
(Blackscher Lake)

27

CCC Trail

Bell Trail

CCC Culvert

Clay
Pit

Kilometer

Mile

N

double yellow blaze, indicating a turn. Turn left (north) and leave the dirt road, continuing on a narrow grass and dirt footpath.

3.0 The trail intersects with the dirt Gazebo Road. Turn right here (southeast) onto the road and follow it uphill.

3.3 Pass a stone CCC culvert that funnels water from a stream under the road. This area is beautiful in the spring, with hundreds of blooming white dogwoods. In 200 feet you will come to a double blaze indicating a right turn. Turn right (southwest) onto a narrow dirt footpath back into the woods.

3.4 Cross the dirt Gazebo Road to the southeast and scramble up a short hill. In a few hundred feet, you will reach the gazebo and some nice views of the surrounding hills. Turn around here and retrace your steps to the trailhead.

4.8 Arrive back at the trailhead.

31 ST. STEPHENS HISTORICAL PARK

We're going to take a trip back in time to the site of the first territorial capital of Alabama and a current active archeological site, St. Stephens Historical Park. Your dog will love splashing in the lake at the quarry. You'll love experiencing history at the dig site where you'll see the old town well, walking the rediscovered streets of the city, and visiting the Globe Hotel dig where archeologists are working to bring the past back to life.

THE RUNDOWN

Start: From the trailhead on the west side of the horse trailer parking area
Distance: 3.1-mile loop
Approximate hiking time: 2.5 hours
Difficulty: Moderate, mostly because of the thick mud that may be encountered at the beginning of the hike due to horses
Trailhead elevation: 35 feet
Highest point: 88 feet
Best season: Year-round; open sunrise to sunset
Trail surface: Dirt, some gravel road
Other trail users: Equestrians
Canine compatibility: Leash required
Land status: Historical park
Fees and permits: Day-use fee; adults $3, children 6-11 $2, children 5 and under free
Trail contact: Old St. Stephens Historical Commission, 2056 Jim Long Rd., St. Stephens; (251) 247-2622; www.oldststephens.net/
Nearest town: Jackson
Trail tips: Bring the swimsuit! The swimming is great in the quarry at the designated swimming area near the camp store. And be sure to visit the park's website for special events that bring the history of Alabama's first territorial capital to life. Restrooms are available at the camp store near the trailhead and at a picnic pavilion at mile 1.4.
Maps: USGS: St. Stephens, AL
Other: The first 0.1 mile of the loop is also used by equestrians, and after a hard rain the footing is thick in mud and your dog can actually get stuck. Walk along the outer edges of the path through here.

FINDING THE TRAILHEAD

From Jackson and the intersection of AL 69 and US 43, take US 43 south 8.4 miles. Turn right onto Mobile Cutoff Road and travel 1.9 miles. Turn right onto Gibb Bailey Road / Cement Plant Road. Travel 0.8 mile and come to a fork in the road. Take the right fork onto Old St. Stephens Road. (Cement Plant Road continues on the left fork). The park entrance gate is ahead on the right in 0.2 mile; if it is not attended, please deposit your entrance fee in the honor box here or as you near the trailhead. Continue 1.8 miles and turn left (the second honor box is here). Travel 0.2 mile and park in the wide field by the horse coral. The trailhead is to the southwest and clearly marked. Trailhead GPS: N31 33.695' / W88 02.094'

THE HIKE

The big, wide Tombigbee River is the backdrop for this historical hike through an active archaeological site, St. Stephens Historical Park.

For history lovers, the archaeology site is fascinating, as students, professors, and volunteers uncover the history of the first territorial capital of Alabama, hence the park's motto, "Where Alabama Began."

The story begins in 1789. As with other rivers throughout the south, a sharp bend in the Tombigbee was followed by a set of shallow shoals that boats of the day could not pass through. Passengers had to disembark and goods were unloaded here before their journey continued overland.

The Spanish governor of Mobile, Juan Vincente Folk, realized that this location had economic opportunity written all over it and built a fort high atop the limestone bluffs overlooking the river, making it a sort of a rest area. Sure enough, ships would sail through the Gulf of Mexico to Mobile, then up to this point and use the fort as a hub for transferring.

When the land was signed over from Spain to the United States in 1799, making it part of the Mississippi Territory, the fort expanded exponentially, increasing the population from 190 to 7,000.

According to accounts, it was a bawdy, wild town, causing superior court judge Ephraim Kirby to write to President Thomas Jefferson, describing its citizens as "illiterate, wild, and savage, of depraved morals, unworthy of public confidence or private esteems, litigious, disunited, and knowing each other, universally distrustful of each other."

The town was bustling with streets lined with residential housing, boardinghouses, and the hub of activity—the Globe Hotel. That is, it was bustling until the capital was moved to Cahawba and later Montgomery, and old St. Stephens was reclaimed by nature.

Today, archaeologists have rediscovered many of the streets and identified several house addresses as well as the stories of the families who lived there.

This loop takes you through the archaeological site, where interpretive signs and uncovered artifacts highlight the discoveries. The most impressive is the site of the Globe Hotel, where the foundation has been uncovered. Be sure to visit the park's website (see Trail Contact, above) to learn about special archaeological days with presentations and demonstrations.

Now, I don't think your dog will be impressed with the history, but they will love visiting a couple of streams that flow through here, as well as the glistening, sky-reflecting waters of the old limestone quarry. Get the camera ready as the trail rounds the quarry on the east side for some amazing shots of the limestone walls across the lake, especially in the spring and summer when the wildflowers are in full bloom.

As you wrap up the hike and start heading back to the trailhead, the path narrows to just 1 to 2 feet wide as it parallels the broad green waters of the Tombigbee River, a beautiful view from a bluff high above the flow. Keep your dog on leash through here; there are very steep and dangerous bluffs straight down to the river.

To your left as you walk along the river, you'll pass a wetland with vibrant colors in season, wood ducks floating serenely, and blue herons wading in the shallows. Just past the wetland the trail turns grassy. Many times the grass is deep, so be sure to do a tick check on you and your pup when you're back at the car.

The hike begins at the horse trailer parking lot near a large wooden paddock. It's a unique entrance with two large dead trees holding up a sign made of branches proclaiming Trailhead. The trail has some wooden arrows painted with the specific color of each trail, but otherwise keep your eyes out for the faded paint blazes on trees. The bulk of the trail follows the Yellow Trail, with a short section on the Orange.

A section of the trail parallels the wide Tombigbee River.

The first section of this trail shares the path with equestrians. As more and more horses use the path, they dig up the trail and it becomes very muddy after a rain. Just after beginning the hike the mud can be so deep that your dog could get stuck. Make sure you walk around all of these muddy areas for everyone's sake.

CREATURE COMFORTS

RESTING UP
Best Western Suites, 3218 College Ave., Jackson; (251) 246-6030; www.bestwestern .com

Make your reservations online. Two pets are allowed up to 80 pounds total. There is also a per night, per pet fee charged. Contact the hotel for rates.

CAMPING
St. Stephens Historical Park, 2056 Jim Long Rd., St. Stephens; (251) 247-2622; www .oldststephens.net/cabins-and-camping.html

Be sure to phone ahead to make reservations.

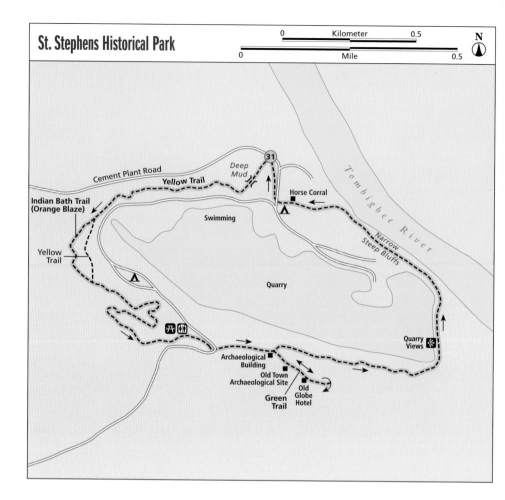

St. Stephens Historical Park

FUELING UP

Sonic Drive-In, 2035 College Ave., Jackson; (251) 246-5491; www.sonicdrivein.com/

How can you go wrong with this iconic American drive-in? You and Fido can eat in your car or on the outdoor patio. The menu is quintessential Americana: burgers, hot dogs, breakfast burritos, and amazing hand-mixed shakes.

MILES AND DIRECTIONS

0.0 Start from the southeast side of the parking area under a tall portal with a large TRAILHEAD sign made from branches. The yellow-blazed trail heads down a rocky hill. In less than 0.1 mile, cross a creek over a cement bridge. Just after the bridge you may encounter a muddy area dug up by horses. After a rain this could be thick enough for your dog to get stuck. Pick your way around it.

0.2 Pass an old cement building on the right.

0.3 Cross a creek; the trail follows alongside it on your left. The trail is now running just beneath the main park road.

0.4 Cross the creek over a steel culvert. The creek is now on your right.

0.5 Come to an intersection. The park road can be seen to your left. The Yellow Trail continues straight to the south. Turn right (southwest) onto the orange-blazed Indian Bath Trail.

0.6 Come to an intersection with the Yellow Trail. Turn left (south) onto the Yellow/Orange Trail. In less than 0.1 mile, turn right (southeast) to stay on the Orange Trail.

0.7 Cross through an area that is normally dry but is a deep bog after rain.

0.8 Come to an intersection with a dirt road. Turn to the left and, in about 10 feet, turn right onto the Yellow Trail. In a few feet you'll see one of the campgrounds through the trees on the left as you parallel the road.

1.0 Turn left (southwest) onto a narrow dirt road.

1.4 Come to the park road. There is a picnic pavilion and restrooms here. Cut across the road to the southeast toward a building.

1.5 Enter "Old Town" through the gate on the right side of a building that touts "Where Alabama Began," picking up the Green Trail.

1.6 Pass the monument to the Kimbrough and Gordy families, who donated the property for the creation of this park. In less than 0.1 mile, come to a Y. We'll take the left fork in a bit, but right now take the right fork (southwest) onto the Green Trail.

1.7 Arrive at the active archaeological site at the old Globe Hotel. Feel free to explore.

1.8 Turn around and retrace your steps to mile 1.6.

2.0 Back at the intersection with the Yellow Trail, turn right (northeast) onto the Yellow Trail.

2.3 Come to a Y. Take the left fork to the north. The path is initially wide with gravel footing.

2.4 Begin to take in nice views of the quarry and its limestone bluffs.

2.5 Cross a 15-foot bridge over a runoff. In less than 0.1 mile, a wetland will be on your left with amazing views of the Tombigbee River beginning on the right.

2.6 Come to a Y. You will see the lower campground to the left. Take the right fork to the northwest to continue on the Yellow Trail. The trail narrows down to 2 feet wide here, and you will soon be walking high above the river with sheer drop-offs on either side of the trail. You should keep your dog leashed through here, and use caution.

2.9 Cross under another trailhead sign that marks the official end of the Yellow Trail. Continue straight to the west.

3.0 Pass a set of horse corrals. You will see the park's camp store to the left. In less than 0.1 mile, arrive at the main park road. Turn right (north) onto the park road.

3.1 Arrive back at the trailhead and the parking lot.

GULF COAST REGION

We finally reach the end of our journeys in the state's Gulf Coast Region. The region is very small in size, only two counties—Mobile and Baldwin—but ecologically speaking, it's one of the most significant biodiverse regions in the state. This is where the myriad of rivers that flow through the state funnel down and form the second largest river delta in the country, the Mobile-Tensaw River Delta, before they end their journeys in the Gulf of Mexico. This brackish mix creates a fertile and wild landscape for migrating birds, waterfowl, mammals, and many endangered wildlife species.

These water features create amazing adventures for hikers and their dogs over a relatively flat landscape. Hiking the trails of the Gulf Region is rarely strenuous; elevations range from sea level to maybe 100 feet at the most.

A unique water feature of the region is its blackwater rivers. These rivers are not actually black; they are cool, clear flows that are tinted a light brown color due to the leeching of tannin from the trees that line their banks. A great hike for experiencing a blackwater river is the Perdido River Trail Section 1 (Hike 37), which will take you through Atlantic white cedar bogs and beautiful white sandbars perfect for swimming—for both you and your dog.

The region also plays host to what is described as the most visually stunning pitcher plant bog in the world, Splinter Hill Bog. You will have three chances to view the beautiful tubular carnivorous plants. The first is along the George W. Folkerts Bog Trail (Hike 32) at Splinter Hill, where you will be surrounded by thousands of the plants. Your other two opportunities will be along the Pitcher Plant Loop (Hike 33) and the Blue Trail (Hike 38).

As I mentioned, this is where many of the state's rivers converge to create the Mobile-Tensaw River Delta, a true wilderness area located only a few miles from the bustling port city of Mobile. The delta has been called "America's Amazon." While there aren't many trails that travel directly through the delta (it's more of a paddling wilderness), you will encounter the lower end of it on Hike 36, the Blakeley Delta Wetland Loop.

Finally, there is the Gulf of Mexico itself, with its turquoise water and sugary white beaches. You and Fido can frolic in the surf on the Audubon Bird Sanctuary trail (Hike 39) and the Pelican Island trail (Hike 40). Both lead to the only dog-friendly beaches on the Alabama Gulf Coast.

Please remember, the American alligator calls this region home. When hiking around wetlands, ponds, and even Mobile Bay, please keep your children and dogs close at hand and out of the water. Leash your dogs. There have been many recent alligator attacks on dogs in the area, and we don't want yours to be on that tragic list.

32 GEORGE W. FOLKERTS BOG TRAIL

It is called the "most visually impressive pitcher plant bog in the world." You'll agree when you visit the Nature Conservancy's Splinter Hill Bog. Literally thousands of the amazing green-and-white tubular plants bloom here in the spring and summer, along with an amazing array of wildflowers. There is plenty for your pup to explore on this hike, but watch for those crawfish; they might not be too happy with your dog nosing around. Fido will also be able to cool off on a hot summer day in the tannin-colored waters of Dyas Creek.

THE RUNDOWN

Start: From the south side of the parking lot at the trailhead kiosk
Distance: 3.1-mile out-and-back
Approximate hiking time: 2 hours
Difficulty: Moderate due to a slog through an optional bog; otherwise easy
Trailhead elevation: 234 feet
Highest point: 241 feet
Best season: Year-round; open sunrise to sunset; closed periodically for prescribed burns
Trail surface: Sand, water and mud in the bog
Other trail users: None
Canine compatibility: Leash required
Land status: Nature Conservancy property
Fees and permits: None
Trail contact: The Nature Conservancy in Alabama, 2100 1st

Ave. N, Birmingham; (205) 251-1155; www.nature.org/ourinitiatives/regions/northamerica/unitedstates/alabama/index.htm
Nearest town: Bay Minette
Trail tips: Bring your camera, especially from April through July, when the pitcher plants are in peak bloom, but also pack your insect repellent. You are walking through a bog after all.
Maps: USGS: Dyas, AL
Other: If you hike with small children or are handicapped, consider parking at the trailhead and venturing out the first 0.4 mile of the trail. This is where you'll see the most pitcher plants. And while your dog will love splashing through the bog at mile 0.8, be wary of snakes.

FINDING THE TRAILHEAD

From the intersection of AL 59 and AL 287 in Bay Minette, take AL 287 north. In 10.1 miles, cross under the interstate and the road becomes CR 47. Continue on CR 47 north 1.7 miles. The trailhead will be on the right. Trailhead GPS: N31 01.512' / W87 41.116'

THE HIKE

There is a remarkable 2,100-acre tract of land in north Baldwin County on the Alabama Gulf Coast that is a must-see: the Ruth McClellan Abronski Splinter Hill Bog. We just call it Splinter Hill for short.

The property is managed and protected by the Nature Conservancy, and for good reason. The land is world renowned for the being the most "visually stunning pitcher

A group of hikers and Archer T. Dog head out on the George W. Folkerts Bog Trail.

plant bog in the world." Each spring and summer the land is overflowing with blooming white-top pitcher plants that turn the fields into a magnificent display.

Pitcher plants are carnivorous plants, much like a Venus flytrap, except pitchers have a long tube, narrow at the bottom and flared at the top, with an upper flap covering the interior. Insects are attracted to the plant by a sweet nectar inside the tube. Once they climb or crawl in, tiny hairs that are bent downward prevent them from escaping, and that nectar turns out to be their demise.

Splinter Hill plays host to five different types of pitcher plants and at least seven other documented carnivorous plants, but the pitcher plants are the standouts.

When most people hear that they are hiking through a bog, they think that they will be walking through a swamp, waist-deep in water, but a bog is the opposite. While a swamp retains water on the surface, a bog retains its water just under ground level, making it feel mushy. You will find this type of environment in longleaf-pine forests, where rainwater seeps down off ridges through sandy soil into the valley below, where it collects underground. This is known as a pine-seepage bog, exactly what you'll find at Splinter Hill.

The pitcher plants hit full bloom anywhere from midsummer to August. But don't get me wrong—that's not the only plant that grows here. In fact, as you walk the trail through the complex of pine and swamp forest, wetlands, and creeks, you'll find an amazing and beautiful array of wildflowers and plants like sundews, butterworts, milkworts, and orchids.

The trail through this wonderland is called the George W. Folkerts Bog Trail, named for the famous biology professor from Auburn University. On this 3.1-mile out-and-back, you'll experience all that Splinter Hill has over wide, relatively flat, sandy paths.

The hike takes you to a couple of nice water features. The first is a walk across a nice little stream where you'll see many of those wildflowers. Later on at the turnaround, you'll come to the cool, tannin-colored waters of Dyas Creek, where your dog can get a drink and cool off a bit. When it's rainy season on the Gulf in the spring and fall, the creek is wide.

There is an optional walk through a swamp to a secondary pitcher plant bog at mile 0.8, that is, if you don't mind getting down, dirty, and wet. At this location you will come to a T intersection with a dirt road. If you want to avoid the wet stuff, turn left onto the dirt road and head to Dyas Creek. If you want an adventure, turn right onto the road and, in a few yards, you'll see the trail head back into the woods on your left.

The trail here heads steeply down the ridge until it bottoms out into a dark swamp. When it rains, this can be ankle- to knee-deep in water. Keep your eyes open and look up to see the trail signs high in the trees—and also keep an eye out for snakes. My dog Archer loved picking his way through this. The trail gradually moves slightly uphill out of the swamp until you come to another pitcher plant bog. From here, keep going straight on the trail until it comes to the dirt road, where you'll turn right and continue to the creek.

For those of you who just want to visit the main attraction, that huge field of pitcher plants, without hiking far, you can park and walk the first 0.4 mile of the trail; the plants are right there. You will see several side trails going into the bog, which were made by others before you. If you want to get closer, take these trails and don't beat down any new ones! And use extreme caution so you don't trample or disturb the plants.

CREATURE COMFORTS

RESTING UP
Log Cabin Inn, 1819 S. US 31, Bay Minette; (251) 494-0234; logcabininn.us

The Log Cabin Inn is a quaint, pet-friendly hotel only a few miles south of the trail. One dog of any size is allowed. An additional per night pet fee is charged. Contact the hotel for rates. Make your reservations online or by phone.

CAMPING
Live Oak Landing, 8700 Live Oak Rd., Stockton; (251) 800-7464; www.liveoakalabama .com

A great little campground located on the banks of the second largest river delta in the country, Live Oak has twenty-eight RV sites, twenty drive-in primitive campsites, plus backcountry and tree camping (actual tents in the trees). There's lots to do here, like

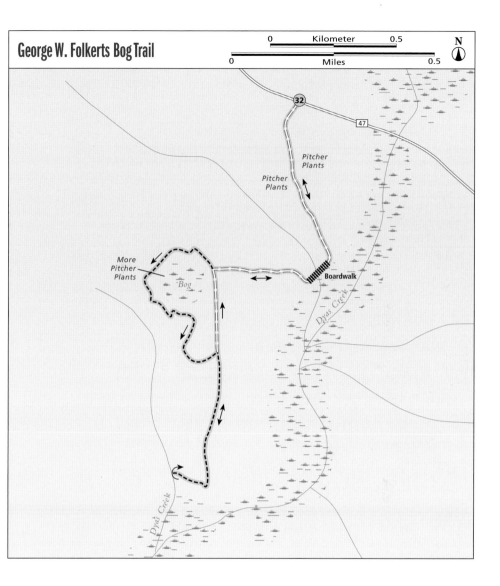

disc golf, kayaking the delta, and hiking on the campground's 4 miles of trails. Primitive and backcountry sites are $20 per night. Book online at www.liveoakalabama.com/accommodations.

FUELING UP

Sonic Drive-In, 205 McMeans Ave., Bay Minette; (251) 937-4472; www.sonicdrivein.com/

How can you go wrong with this iconic American drive-in? You and Fido can eat in your car or on the outdoor patio. The menu is quintessential Americana: burgers, hot dogs, breakfast burritos, and amazing hand-mixed shakes.

MILES AND DIRECTIONS

0.0 Start at the trailhead at the kiosk on the south side of the parking lot. The trail, a nice 4- to 5-foot-wide dirt/sand/grass path, is dotted with informative signs about the ecosystem. During spring and summer you'll be surrounded by thousands of white-top pitcher plants. You'll pass several small, unmarked 1-foot-wide side trails through this section, where you can walk in deeper to view them but walk carefully and stay on the path!

0.4 Two yellow diamond arrow signs point to the right (southwest) to indicate the trail bends to the right. In less than 0.1 mile, cross over a beautiful creek lined with colorful wildflowers.

0.5 At the end of the boardwalk, you'll leave the main pitcher plant bog and begin climbing a small hill into a longleaf-pine forest.

0.7 At the top of the hill, come to a T intersection with a wide sandy road. Turn right (northwest) onto the road.

0.8 The trail turns off the road to the southwest and onto a narrow, brushy path. From here you'll be walking downhill and into a large swamp.

1.1 Arrive at another bog with more pitcher plants. Expect to get wet; depending on rain, this could be very deep. Watch for snakes. Keep an eye higher up on the trees to find the trail markers. As you start coming out of the swamp, you pass through another seepage bog and more pitcher plants.

1.3 Arrive back at the road. Turn right (south) onto the dirt road.

1.7 It looks like the trail should go straight but don't (that's private property). Follow the road as it bends to the right (northwest),

1.8 Arrive at the beautiful, wide Dyas Creek. This is a great place for your dog to get a drink and splash around a bit on a hot day. When ready turn around and retrace your steps back the way you just came.

2.2 Pass the side trail to the bog at mile 1.3 but don't turn. Continue straight (north) on the dirt road.

2.4 Turn right (east) onto the original trail you came in on from the parking lot.

3.1 Arrive back at the trailhead.

OPTION: At mile 0.7, if you don't want to get wet and walk through the deep bog that's ahead, instead of making a right turn, turn left (south) onto the dirt road. In 0.6 mile you arrive at the intersection of that side trail through the bog on your right. You can climb down the trail a short distance to the outer edge of the bog to see the plants without hiking through it.

33 PITCHER PLANT LOOP

A second pitcher plant bog awaits you at the state's Splinter Hill Bog Complex on this easy loop through an area that was once heavily logged but is making a comeback. The trail takes you through some tight bogs, across a few creeks and wetlands that your dog will love to splash around in, and to a full 0.1-mile field of beautiful white-top pitcher plants.

THE RUNDOWN

Start: From the trailhead kiosk on the north side of the parking lot
Distance: 4.2-mile loop
Approximate hiking time: 3 hours
Difficulty: Easy with caveats (see The Hike)
Trailhead elevation: 198 feet
Highest point: 246 feet
Best season: Late Apr through late June; open sunrise to sunset
Trail surface: Dirt and grass footpath with bog crossings
Other trail users: Cyclists, hunters
Canine compatibility: Voice control
Land status: State preserve
Fees and permits: None
Trail contact: Alabama Forever Wild, State Lands Division, 64 N. Union St., Montgomery; (334) 242-3484; www .alabamaforeverwild.com
Nearest town: Perdido

Trail tips: Once again, you're going to want the camera to capture the beautiful pitcher plants. But remember that you'll be walking through a few boggy areas and in the warmer months, mosquitoes will be a nuisance, so bring your insect repellent. For at least half the hike there isn't any shade at all, so be prepared with a hat and put that sunscreen on both you and your pup.
Maps: USGS: Perdido, AL
Other maps: Online at www .alabamaforeverwild.com/sites/ default/files/Hunting%20Maps/ Splinter%20Hill%20Bog%20 Complex-Permit%20Map-2017-2018. pdf
Other: Hunting is allowed at the Splinter Hill Bog Complex. Please get in touch with the Trail Contact (above) for dates and restrictions

FINDING THE TRAILHEAD

From the intersection of I-65 and CR 47 in Perdido, take CR 47 north for 0.3 mile and turn right onto Splinter Hill Road. Travel 0.6 mile. Parking and the trailhead will be on the left. Trailhead GPS: N31 01.603' / W87 39.237'

THE HIKE

Only 2.0 miles east of the George W. Folkerts Bog Trail (Hike 32) there is yet another amazing pitcher plant bog and hike, this one at the Forever Wild Splinter Hill Bog Complex on the Pitcher Plant Loop trail.

In all, there are ten species of the carnivorous pitcher plant in North America, all of which live in bogs, swamps, pine savannas, or sandy meadows where the soil is saturated with water. Along the Gulf Coast and South Regions of the state, there is an abundance of longleaf-pine seepage bogs. The trees grow in sandy soil on top of rolling hills. Rainwater flows down the hill through the sand to low-lying land between the hills and accumulates just below the ground's surface. It's not standing water, but the ground feels mushy when walked on. A bog is born.

Tall longleaf pines are a good indication that the actual pitcher plant bog is not far away.

The fields at the Splinter Hill Complex come alive with pitcher plants.

The variety found along the Gulf Coast is the white-top pitcher plant, with its beautiful long, white-and-green tapered tubular stalk, narrow at the bottom and wide at the top, almost like a trumpet. The upper part is white with red or maroon veinlike patterns that is topped with a single large leaf, a flap, as it were. The plants don't actually "eat" the insects; rather they digest them. Insects are drawn in by the plant's nectar but they never get out and are dissolved by that nectar. Although you will see thousands of them along this hike, the plant is currently classified as rare and endangered.

The Forever Wild Splinter Hill Bog Complex is a 627-acre tract located at the headwaters of the Perdido River at Dyas Creek. As with many of their tracts, the state-managed program opened it for outdoor recreation, including horseback riding, mountain biking, and of course, hiking. The trail we will be walking is the Pitcher Plant Loop, a 4.2-mile loop trail that leads you directly to the bog.

For the most part, the trail is an old dirt road repurposed for hiking. For most of the hike, it is a wide, sandy path climbing up and down gently rolling hills. At one time the property was opened to logging, and from the moment you begin the hike, you will see remnants of that period. Most of the hills are without the tall longleafs that characterize the region. What is there, however, are beautiful young trees, a good 6 to 7 feet tall, that have been replanted by the state to bring the forest back.

There are only two drawbacks to this hike. The first is that lack of trees. There are stands of trees that will provide some shade for you and Fido, but between March and June, when the pitcher plants are starting to bloom or hitting their peak, it can be a hot walk. Plan accordingly, hike early in the morning, and bring plenty of water.

The other drawback are the bogs you will be walking through. Most of the time they are easy to navigate just by walking along their edge. But if you visit after one of the Gulf's well-known summer downpours, you could be wading in some deep water. But, in the same sense, your dog will love to cool its paws in these and in the three streams you will be crossing.

The trail is not heavily blazed but is very easy to follow. There are bright yellow diamond markers with black arrows pointing directions scattered along the hike, and key intersections or sharp turns are marked with large green wooden signs that point the way.

There are actually two trailheads. The Miles and Directions below start you at the eastern trailhead.

CREATURE COMFORTS

RESTING UP
Log Cabin Inn, 1819 S. US 31, Bay Minette, AL; (251) 494-0234; logcabininn.us

The Log Cabin Inn is a quaint, pet-friendly hotel only a few miles south of the trail. One dog of any size is allowed. An additional per night pet fee is charged. Contact the hotel for rates. Make your reservations online or by phone.

CAMPING
Live Oak Landing, 8700 Live Oak Rd., Stockton; (251) 800-7464; www.liveoakalabama .com

A great little campground located on the banks of the second largest river delta in the country, Live Oak has twenty-eight RV sites, twenty drive-in primitive campsites, plus backcountry and tree camping (actual tents in the trees). There's lots to do here, like disc golf, kayaking the delta, and hiking on the campground's 4 miles of trails. Primitive and backcountry sites are $20 per night. Book online at www.liveoakalabama.com/ accommodations.

FUELING UP
Sonic Drive-In, 205 McMeans Ave., Bay Minette; (251) 937-4472; www.sonicdrivein .com/

How can you go wrong with this iconic American drive-in? You and Fido can eat in your car or on the outdoor patio. The menu is quintessential Americana: burgers, hot dogs, breakfast burritos, and amazing hand-mixed shakes.

Pitcher Plant Loop

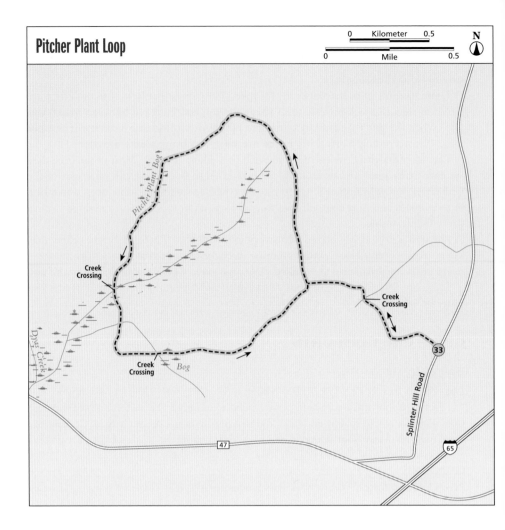

MILES AND DIRECTIONS

0.0 Start from the trailhead at the kiosk on the north side of the parking lot. Go around the yellow steel gate. The path is a wide, sandy road.

0.2 Pass another wide path coming in from the left (west).

0.4 Cross a small creek. This is your first oasis of shade on the first half of the hike.

0.7 Pass the return trail coming in from the left (southwest).

1.3 Climb a short hill lined with gravel to prevent erosion. Just after the hill, come to a T intersection with a sign that reads PITCHER PLANT LOOP. Turn left onto the wide grass/dirt/sand path.

1.4 A path heads off to the right. Keep going straight to the northwest.

1.5 Come to a Y with a sign showing the direction of the trail to the left. Take the left fork to the southwest.

1.6 Enjoy some nice shade through a section of hardwoods.

1.8 The pitcher plant bog begins on both sides of the trail and continues for the next 0.3 mile.

2.1 The fields of pitcher plants come to an end.

2.4 The trail turns grassy and with a good canopy to keep the sun off. In less than 0.1 mile, come to a bog. This could be very deep in mud and water after a rain, and the trail is a bit overgrown through here. Pick your way through it.

2.5 Come to the second bog. There will most likely be some standing water here, but after rain it can be deep in mud and water as it slogs through the mixed hardwood and pine forest. After the bog the trail is not so overgrown and grassy.

2.7 Pass a sign that points the direction of the trail to the left (southeast) and the West Trailhead to the right (south). Continue straight to the southeast. In less than 0.1 mile, come to a Y. Take the left fork to the east. The trail is very enclosed here with hardwoods and leaves covering the path.

2.8 Come to another deep bog with a creek flowing through it. This one is quite long, at least 0.1 mile, and you will have to pick your way around it.

3.5 Come to a Y and a sign that reads East Trailhead and points straight ahead to the northeast. Continue straight. In a few yards you will rejoin the route you came in on. Turn right (east) onto the trail and head back to the trailhead.

4.2 Arrive back at the trailhead.

34 GLENN SEBASTIAN NATURE TRAIL

Another great little college hiking trail system is the Glenn Sebastian Nature Trail on the campus of the University of South Alabama. Three trails intertwine to provide over 7 miles of possible loop combinations through a mixed hardwood and pine forest. On this 2.5-mile double loop, you'll pass a beautiful wetland and catch a glimpse of wildlife like box turtles and herons. There are alligators in these waters so keep your pup leashed here, but once you move into the woods, your pup is free to roam off leash if under voice control.

THE RUNDOWN

Start: From to the west at the trailhead kiosk
Distance: 2.5-mile double-loop
Approximate hiking time: 2 hours
Difficulty: Easy on dirt footpaths over rolling hills
Trailhead elevation: 36 feet
Highest point: 59 feet
Best season: Year-round; open sunrise to sunset
Trail surface: Dirt footpaths
Other trail users: Joggers
Canine compatibility: Leash required around wetlands and lakes due to alligators, off-leash under voice control away from these areas
Land status: College property
Fees and permits: None
Trail contact: University of South Alabama Department of Campus Recreation, 51 Stadium Blvd., Mobile; (251) 460-6065; http://www.southalabama.edu/departments/campusrec/facilityrental/naturetrail.html
Nearest town: Mobile
Trail tips: While the trail is mostly a wonderful walk in the woods, bring the camera for some amazing shots of the lily pad–filled lake and wetlands just past the trailhead. Be sure to heed the warnings. While your pup will want to take a dive into the lake, alligators have been spotted here. Keep dogs on the leash and out of the water.
Maps: USGS: Springhill, AL
Other maps: A large map is at the trailhead kiosk and scattered in kiosks along the trail; a map is also available online at www.southalabama.edu/departments/campusrec/facilityrental/explore.html.

FINDING THE TRAILHEAD

From exit 5A on I-65, head west on Springhill Avenue 1.8 miles. Springhill Avenue will become Ziegler Boulevard at Langan Park. Continue on Ziegler Boulevard 1.1 miles and turn left onto North University Boulevard. Travel 0.8 mile and turn right onto USA Drive N. Travel 0.1 mile and turn left onto Aubrey Green Drive. In less than 0.1 mile, turn right, and the trailhead will be in front of you. Trailhead GPS: N30 42.061' / W88 11.059'

THE HIKE

Alabama's colleges and universities have provided their students with some remarkable hiking trails on their campuses. There are the Lake Trail (Hike 20) at the University of West Alabama, the University of Alabama Arboretum, the Donald D. Davis Arboretum

A small cypress tree adds a burst of color to the wetland on the Glenn Sebastian Nature Trail.

at Auburn University, and this gem along the Gulf Coast, the University of South Alabama's (USA) Glenn Sebastian Nature Trail.

While the trails have been on the USA campus for over thirty years, the paths were not "official" until 2006, when they were mapped and several additions were made, including a trailhead kiosk, trail maps at intersections, the addition of interpretive signage, and the blazing of the trails themselves. The new trail system opened in 2011.

The trail was named in honor of Dr. Glenn Sebastian, a former national park ranger and professor emeritus who enlightened and excited USA students, myself included, for over thirty years about the study of geology. Dr. Sebastian often took his students to these trails for a little outside-classroom work. He retired from teaching in 2006 after chairing the Earth Sciences Department of the university's College of Arts and Sciences for twenty-five years.

But enough of the history. Let's hit the trails!

There are over 7.5 miles of trail at the USA campus: the Red, White, Blue (get it? USA?), and Yellow Trails. All of the trails intertwine so you can make a seemingly endless set of loops with varied lengths.

The route described here is only a small subset of the overall trail system. Once you get your feet wet (not literally), you will be able to find your own route and wander for hours along the hills. For this walk, we will be using the Blue and Yellow Trails to make a 2.5-mile hike.

Generally, all of the trails are easy walking on a dirt footpath over nice, rolling hills. There are no difficult climbs at all on any of the routes.

The trail takes you through a hardwood and pine forest. Even though you're in the heart of West Mobile, there is still plenty of wildlife to see, like foxes, coyotes, and turtles.

As you begin your journey at the main kiosk, you will be walking past a beautiful pond and wetland with white water lilies blooming on the banks and great—or American— egrets standing proudly in the water. Though not part of the trail described here, there is a long bridge that takes you across the pond. It's well worth the short detour for the view. A few benches are available near the wetland so you can sit and take in the tranquil scene.

The trail wanders through the compact space with wildflowers like red cardinal and butterwort gracing the path. You will cross a couple of seasonal creeks along the way.

The trails are well marked with paint blazes, as are the intersections that have either signs for the trails that intersect or a trail map in kiosks at the junctions, or both.

Dogs love simply roaming and exploring the forest understory. The trail's manager says that pets are allowed off leash here, but be considerate and leash them when others are hiking nearby. And be sure to clean up after them. This is a well-used trail system.

You should also keep them on leash around the wetland and pond. Alligators have been spotted here in the past, so keep them, and small children, close at hand.

An interesting rule posted at the trailhead says, "Consumption of plants and fungi is at your own risk." Apparently, others have tasted them with bad results.

CREATURE COMFORTS

RESTING UP

Quality Inn and Suites, 150 W. I-65 Service Rd., Mobile; (251) 343-4949; www .choicehotels.com/alabama/mobile/quality-inn-hotels

Make your reservations either by phone or online. Either way, be sure pet-friendly rooms are available before booking. Two pets are allowed per room with a $25 per pet, per night fee.

CAMPING

Chickasabogue Park, 60 Aldock Rd., Eight Mile; (251) 574-2267; www.mobile countyal.gov/living/parks_chickasabogue.html

Beautiful and secluded campsites await you at Chickasabogue. Every site is tucked away in the pines and oaks, or you can backpack a short distance to camp at one of the primitive campsites on the banks of the scenic and historic Chickasaw Creek. And while you're there, take a walk on one of the park's 17 miles of hiking trails. Improved tent camping and primitive backcountry sites are $10.40 per night. A $40 deposit is required but returned upon checkout if you've cleaned up the site before leaving. Make your reservations by phone or in person.

FUELING UP

The River Shack Restaurant, 6120 Marina Dr. S, Mobile; (251) 443-7318

Fresh Gulf seafood and a show. It's on the menu at the River Shack. Bring Fido along to this outstanding seafood restaurant located on Mobile Bay at—appropriately enough—Dog River. Start off with delicious hand-breaded fried pickles, then tuck into

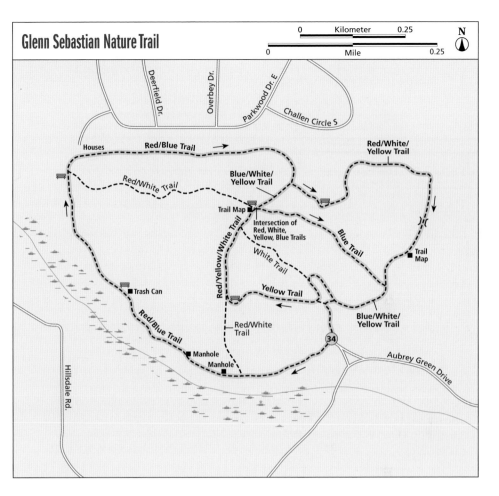

0 Kilometer 0.25 **N**

0   Mile   0.25

a shrimp, oyster, or catfish po' boy, or a mouthwatering sizzling rib eye. And the show? A dazzling sunset over Mobile Bay from the picnic-table seating on a pier overlooking the water.

MILES AND DIRECTIONS

0.0 Start from the kiosk at the trailhead parking lot. Head southwest where you will walk around a gate erected to keep cars off the first section of the trail. This is the beginning of the Blue Trail., which starts out paved but quickly turns into a wide dirt and gravel path. To your left (southeast), you'll be walking alongside a beautiful wetland with a variety of waterfowl and teeming with lily pads. Once again, heed the warnings about alligators and keep kids close at hand and dogs on leash.

0.1 A side trail forks to the right. Continue straight to the west.

0.2 Pass a drainage manhole cover in the middle of the trail. In less than 0.1 mile, come to a Y with a second manhole cover in the middle. Take the right fork to the northwest and start heading into the woods.

0.4 Pass a bench on the right with a trash can. The trail has merged with the Red Trail and is blazed blue and red.

0.6 Pass a bench on the left. In less than 0.1 mile, the trail bends to the right (east) and becomes a very wide grassy path. Houses from the neighborhood line the trail behind fences to your left.

1.0 As the trail swings to the south, you'll come to an intersection of the Blue, Yellow, White, and Red Trails. A trail map is located here. Continue on the Blue Trail to the southwest. In less than 0.1 mile, come to a bench and another trail map. The Yellow Trail (which we'll take in a moment) continues straight to the southwest. Turn right (east) here to continue on the Blue Trail.

1.3 Come to an intersection with the Yellow Trail. The Blue Trail joins with this path here for a short distance. Turn right (southwest) onto the Blue, White, and Yellow Trails.

1.4 Turn right (northwest) to continue on the Blue Trail.

1.5 The trail turns southwest then arrives at another intersection with the Yellow Trail. Turn right (west) onto the Yellow Trail.

1.6 Come to a Y with a bench in the middle of the fork. Take the right fork to the north to continue on the Yellow Trail.

1.8 Arrive back at the bench, trail map, and intersection with the Blue Trail you passed at mile 1.0. Continue on the Yellow Trail to the northeast.

1.9 Arrive back at the intersection with all 4 trails you passed earlier. Turn right (southeast) to continue on the Yellow Trail. In less than 0.1 mile, come to a Y with a bench. Take the left fork to the east to continue on the Yellow Trail.

2.2 Cross a 10-foot bridge over a creek.

2.3 Pass another trail map. In less than 0.1 mile, you'll arrive back at the intersection with the Blue Trail at mile 1.3. Continue straight to the southwest to continue on the Yellow Trail.

2.4 Arrive back at where the Blue Trail splits off at mile 1.4. Continue straight (west) on the Yellow Trail and in a few yards turn left (south). In less than 0.1 mile arrive back at the trailhead.

35 MUDDY CREEK INTERPRETIVE TRAIL

This is an easy and beautiful family- and dog-friendly hike over a series of boardwalks through a longleaf-pine forest. The trails lead you through some amazing wetlands and over the park's namesake creek. Kids and adults alike will learn about this fascinating ecosystem from its many interpretive signs, while Fido will enjoy exploring along—and in—the creek on the eastern side of the trail.

THE RUNDOWN

Start: From the north side of the parking lot at the kiosk
Distance: 2.2-mile loop
Approximate hiking time: 1.5 hours
Difficulty: Easy over dirt footpaths and boardwalk
Trailhead elevation: 44 feet
Highest point: 54 feet
Best season: Fall through spring when the creek and wetland is full; open sunrise to sunset
Trail surface: Dirt and clay footpaths, boardwalks, very short section of pavement
Other trail users: None

Canine compatibility: Leash required
Land status: State wetland preserve
Fees and permits: None
Trail contact: Alabama State Port Authority, 250 N. Water St., Mobile; (251) 441-7001; www.asdd.com
Nearest town: Theodore
Trail tips: You will be walking through a wetland and a slow-moving creek, so sure to bring the insect repellent. The gate to the parking lot may be locked if you arrive very early, but a worker will eventually show up and open it.
Maps: USGS: Theodore, AL

FINDING THE TRAILHEAD

From the intersection of US 90 and Bellingrath Gardens Road in Theodore, take Bellingrath Gardens Road south 2.2 miles. Turn left onto Industrial Road. Travel 1.0 mile. The paved parking lot is on the left. Trailhead GPS: N30 31.029' / W88 09.158'

THE HIKE

You wouldn't think that there would be a nice little hiking trail in the middle of an area that's called the Theodore Industrial Complex. As you drive down Industrial Road, visions of oil tanks, chemical plants, warehouses, and factories pop into your mind. Well, shake that thought right out of your head because you're in for a real surprise and a wonderful hike on the Muddy Creek Interpretive Trail.

We have to thank the Alabama State Port Authority for the amazing job they did in creating this 2.2-mile loop. The port authority is responsible for handling the shipping that sails into the state through the terminal facilities just up the road in Mobile.

The project began in 1998 as part of a mitigation brought about by the impacts construction had on the Theodore ship channel. Volunteers, employees, and work-release personnel from the Alabama Department of Corrections began by clearing out tons of trash and pulling out almost 100 acres of invasive plants—by hand! The project was the largest invasive-plant removal ever in the state.

A view down one of the long boardwalks that make up the Muddy Creek Interpretive Trail.

Once the land was readied, they replanted 20,000 native trees and shrubs, put up eighty bird-nesting boxes, and built this fun loop trail.

Five long, hard years later, the trail opened to the public. All of that hard work did not go unnoticed. Their efforts received national recognition and awards, and they won the biggest award of all—the impressive number of people who hike the trail each year.

Today, you and your pup will love walking the peaceful and quiet boardwalks and dirt paths through the longleaf pine, tupelo gum, sweet bay, red maple, pond cypress, and wax myrtle forest. The boardwalks take you over a beautiful cypress swamp and the trail's namesake, Muddy Creek.

Keep in mind that, as with most water features in the state, water in the creek, wetland, and swamp can be seasonal. The best time to visit is fall through spring, when the seasonal rains are plentiful along the Gulf and the creek is wide and flowing. During this time vibrant colors of wildflowers like red chokeberry and lantana line the path, and blooming magnolias brighten the way. But having said that, remember that as the weather warms, you can expect mosquitoes. Bring that bug spray.

The hike begins on a short 0.2-mile section of paved trail but then turns into a hard-packed dirt and clay path. The boardwalks along the hike are wide with tall handrails, making it safe for small children and your dog, and they sport occasional viewing platforms and benches so you can sit and soak in the solitude. And you might learn something from the signs sharing information on the importance of longleaf ecosystems and the species of trees and shrubs you will be seeing.

At the northern end of the hike you will learn about and see the handiwork of eager beavers who built their home here by damming the creek and its tributaries. At one time, landowners thought that such dams were detrimental to the wetland ecosystem, but with careful management, beaver ponds actual help wetlands flourish.

Finally, as you make your way back to the trailhead, the path is at ground level with the creek, which your dog will love to explore. Just be on the lookout for snakes. And for a short time, the hard-packed clay is covered with a soft, cushiony green moss that glows in the morning sun.

CREATURE COMFORTS

RESTING UP

Days Inn, 5472 A Inn Rd., Mobile; (251) 272-7976; www.wyndhamhotels.com/days-inn/mobile-alabama/days-inn-and-suites-mobile/overview

Make reservations online or by phone. If you're making them online, you should still call the hotel in advance to make sure there are pet-friendly rooms available. Two pets of any size are allowed. There is a $25 per pet, per night fee.

FUELING UP

The River Shack Restaurant, 6120 Marina Dr. S, Mobile; (251) 443-7318

You can't visit the Gulf without trying some seafood. Bring Fido along to the River Shack on Mobile Bay at—appropriately enough—Dog River. Start off with delicious hand-breaded fried pickles, then tuck into a shrimp, oyster, or catfish po' boy or a mouth-watering sizzling rib eye. You and your pup will love the outdoor seating at a picnic table on a pier with a great view.

MILES AND DIRECTIONS

- **0.0** Start at the parking lot trailhead on Industrial Road. A MUDDY CREEK INTERPRE-TIVE TRAIL sign is here that shows the route of the trail. Head north on a paved path a few yards and come to a Y. The right fork is a dirt road. Turn left (west) and continue following the paved path. You will soon see the first of many signs describing the habitat you will be walking through.

- **0.2** The paved path comes to a T intersection with another paved road. Cross the road to the north and enter the woods on a narrow footpath. Through this section you will be surrounded by longleaf pines.

- **0.3** Come to a Y in the trail. A map here shows where you are. The right fork is the route you will be returning on. Take the left fork (northeast). A long boardwalk begins in about 30 feet. The boardwalks are very nice with high railings. Through here you'll see tupelo gum, sweet bay, elderberry, red maple, and bald cypress trees.

- **0.4** The boardwalk crosses Muddy Creek.

- **0.5** The boardwalk ends at another trail map sign and turns to the right (north).

- **0.6** Cross a short 30-foot boardwalk.

- **0.7** The trail gets very dense with longleaf pines and wax myrtles.

- **1.1** Pass another trail map sign and in a few yards cross another boardwalk. This is the north end of the loop.

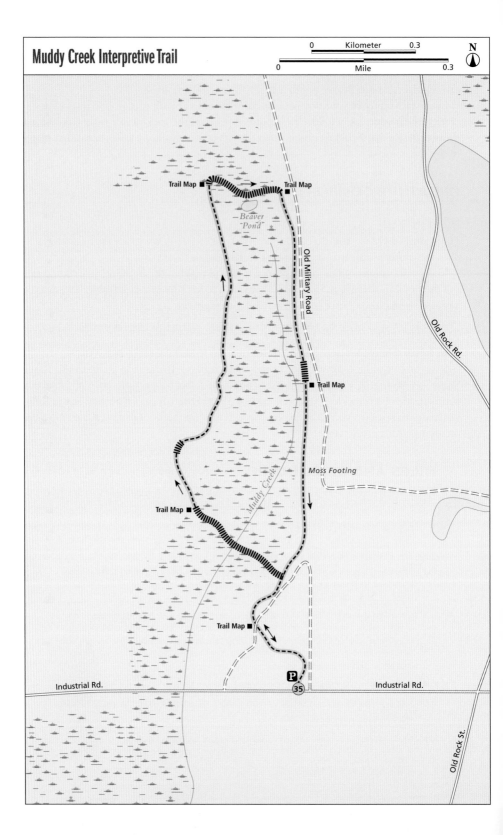

Muddy Creek Interpretive Trail

Kilometer
0   0.3

Mile
0   0.3

N

Trail Map

Trail Map

Beaver "Pond"

Old Military Road

Old Rock Rd.

Trail Map

Moss Footing

Muddy Creek

Trail Map

Trail Map

Industrial Rd.

P
35

Industrial Rd.

Old Rock St.

1.2 Pass a series of signs providing information on beavers and their importance to the wetland.

1.3 The boardwalk ends at another trail map sign and the trail turns to the right (south). The path begins following the creek at creek level, a good chance for your dog to explore; just watch for snakes.

1.6 Pass another trail map sign and cross another short boardwalk.

1.7 For a few hundred feet the trail bed is soft, green moss. Along this section you'll see a steel cable with yellow steel posts through the trees to your left (east). This is a barrier from a dirt road that parallels the trail.

1.9 Return to the Y at the southern end of the loop. Take the left fork to the south and retrace your steps to the trailhead.

2.2 Arrive back at the trailhead.

36 BLAKELEY DELTA WETLAND LOOP

Historic Blakeley State Park is well-known for the Civil War battle that occurred there in 1865, but this hike will give you a different perspective of the park as it rambles through wetlands and swamps, and along the banks of the second largest river delta in the country, the Mobile-Tensaw River Delta. For your pup there is plenty to explore through the forest of bigleaf and sweet bay magnolias and live oaks, plus a great little stream they'll love to splash in.

THE RUNDOWN

Start: From the west side of the narrow parking area at a closed metal gate
Distance: 4.9-mile double loop
Approximate hiking time: 2.5 hours
Difficulty: Moderate with some climbs up and down ravines
Trailhead elevation: 114 feet
Highest point: 121 feet
Best season: Fall through spring; open 8 a.m. to sunset
Trail surface: Dirt with several boardwalks
Other trail users: Cyclists, equestrians
Canine compatibility: Leash required
Land status: Historic state park
Fees and permits: Day-use fee: adults $4; children 6–12, $3; children under 6, free
Trail contact: Historic Blakeley State Park, 34745 AL 225, Spanish Fort;

(251) 626-0798; www.blakeleypark.com
Nearest town: Spanish Fort
Trail tips: Restrooms and vault toilets are scattered on the trail for your convenience. Bring along that insect repellent! You're walking through swamps and wetlands, and along the delta, where you will encounter mosquitoes in the warmer months. And then there are yellow flies with their nasty bites. As the weather warms, you will encounter them. See "Joe's Five Hiking Tips" for options.
Maps: USGS: Bridgehead, AL
Other maps: Available at the park's entrance gate or online at www.blakeleypark.com/Things-to-Do/Trails

FINDING THE TRAILHEAD

From the intersection of US 90 and AL 225 in Spanish Fort, take AL 225 north 4.4 miles. Turn left onto Upper Shay Branch Road. This is the well-marked park entrance. In 400 feet, come to the pay station, where you can pick up maps and brochures. After paying the entrance fee, continue straight for 0.3 mile. Continue straight at the fork in the road and travel 0.5 mile. The road ends at a chain gate. A FOREVER WILD sign is located here. Trailhead GPS: N30 43.934' / W87 54.710'

THE HIKE

There are two sides to Historic Blakeley State Park. Many visitors come to visit the battlefield where the last major clash of the Civil War took place, resulting in the surrender of the last Confederate port city, Mobile, to the Union army. But there is a different side that many people don't see: the amazing, tropical look and feel of the wetlands and swamps that fill the west side of the park, and the ecosystem of the second largest delta

One of many long boardwalks through picturesque swamps. Watch your step. The lack of sun from a thick canopy keeps the planks moist and a bit slippery.

in the country, the Mobile-Tensaw River Delta. You and your pup will get a chance to experience it on this hike that I call the Blakeley Delta Wetland Loop.

This is a fun double-loop hike that takes you through all of that beautiful scenery. You'll find yourself walking through a thick mixed hardwood forest of Darlington oaks, longleaf and slash pines, pignut hickory, American beech, and bigleaf and sweet bay magnolia trees with their large leathery leaves and white flowers. The canopy is very heavy through the forest, which is nice in the hot, subtropical summer months. From spring through summer the dark trail is brightened with the appearance of colorful flowering native azaleas.

The hike begins on the wide and sandy Forever Wild Trail but quickly narrows as the path turns into the Halletts Trail. Halletts will lead you down into an area that is known as the River Bottomland, where the swamps and wetlands will be found. The best time to hike through here over the boardwalks is in the spring or fall when rains fill the wetlands.

You will cross several long boardwalks along the Halletts and General Liddell's Trail that lead you through these swamps and wetlands. You may see the handiwork of beavers through here as you near the delta.

As I said earlier, the canopy along this hike is very thick, allowing only a little sun. Because of this, the boardwalks and bridges tend to be a bit slippery from the humidity that blankets the area in the summer with little time to dry out. Just cross carefully.

From here we join up with the Old Town Nature Trail that passes the Mary Grice Pavilion. The steeple on top of the pavilion came from a church that stood nearby in the mid-1800s. The pavilion itself is a popular location for events, including the annual Blakeley Bluegrass Festival.

Continuing on, the trail comes out to the E.O. Wilson Boardwalk. Named for the famous biologist and author of the book and documentary, "Lord of the Ants," the boardwalk takes you alongside the banks of the Mobile-Tensaw River Delta under cedar trees draped in beautiful Spanish moss, just like a picture postcard. You'll have wide views of the water and the many birds that call the delta home, including egrets, ospreys, and maybe even a bald eagle. On the horizon to the southwest you will see the city of Mobile.

There are a few viewing platforms with benches along the boardwalk where you and Fido can just sit and take in the solitude.

On the return trip, you will pass through the Harper Tent Campground, and what's labeled Tensaw Campsite #1 and #2, where you'll find a nice restroom, as well as walk along a portion of the Breastworks Trail, which parallels some of the best preserved Confederate breastworks in the South.

As you wrap up the trip on the Old Apalachee Trail, you'll cross Shay Branch again. It's a fun little creek where your dog will love splashing around and grabbing a quick drink.

As of this writing, the trails are not blazed at Blakeley but are easy to follow. Intersections do have nice signage to point the way. Having said that, the new management is making impressive improvements to the trail system, so that could change soon.

CREATURE COMFORTS

RESTING UP
La Quinta Inn, 8946 Sawwood St., Daphne; (251) 338-6555; www.lq.com

Two dogs of any size are allowed with no additional fee. If you leave your pet unattended in your room, you must leave your cell phone number with the front desk. You can make your reservation online, but it's recommended that you make them by phone to make sure that there is a pet-friendly room available.

CAMPING
Historic Blakeley State Park, 34745 AL 225, Spanish Fort; (251) 626-0798; blakeley park.com/Camping-Cabins

Blakeley has two nice tent camping sites, both with nice, new bathhouses. In a secluded section of the woods, the Bartram Campground features eight sites with water and electricity. These sites are $30 per night for two people, $10 extra for each additional person, $5 extra per child ages 6 to 12. Up to eight people are allowed per site. A $30 nonrefundable reservation fee is required. Primitive sites can be found in the Harper Tent Campground area. Sites are $10 per night for adults, $5 for children ages 6 to 12 with a $20 minimum reservation and a $20 nonrefundable deposit. Up to eight people are allowed per site. Reservations are taken by phone or at the park's entrance gate.

FUELING UP

Ed's Seafood Shed, 3382 Battleship Pkwy., Spanish Fort; (251) 625-1947; edsshed .com/menu

It's dinner and a show at Ed's. Dinner is fresh Gulf seafood "cooked the old Mobile way." Indulge in dishes like the Bayway Boiler with a pound of crab legs, ½ pound of peel-and-eat white shrimp, and ½ pound of royal red shrimp, or the local favorite, Yo Mama's Platter, with gumbo, garlic cheese grits, turnip greens, fish, oysters, shrimp, scallops, and crab legs. Wow! The show? A beautiful sunset over Mobile Bay from deck seating where you can dine with your pup.

MILES AND DIRECTIONS

0.0 Start on the west side of the trailhead by walking around the chain gate. In less than 0.1 mile, come to a Y. The Apalachee Trail is to the right (northwest). Take the left fork heading west on the Hallets Trail.

0.4 The trail narrows and becomes brushier.

0.6 Begin a long walk over a nice stream and wetland on a boardwalk. Be careful. It can be very slippery. Also, the stairs at the beginning are steep. I recommend you walk your dog to the right of the stairs and use a ramp that is here. In less than 0.1 mile, pass a bench on the deck to the right.

0.7 Come to the end of the boardwalk.

1.1 Come to the intersection with Squirrel's Nest Trail. You can turn left here onto the trail, which is a wide dirt road and pick up these directions at mile 1.5, but for a more natural hike, we will turn right (north) to stay on the Hallets Trail.

1.3 Come to an intersection. Thomas Byrne Lane heads straight to the north. The Breastworks Trail runs east and west. Later, we'll return on the Thomas Byrne and head east on the Breastworks, but right now turn left (west) onto the Breastworks Trail.

1.4 Cross a short boardwalk over a creek.

1.5 Come to an intersection. Turn right (west) onto Squirrel's Nest Lane.

1.6 The General Liddell's Trail splits off to the right (northwest) at a portable toilet. Turn right onto the trail. The trail at this point is a narrow 2-foot path atop a ridge with deep sloping sides.

1.7 As you climb a hill, a cypress swamp can be seen to your left surrounded by saw palmetto.

1.8 At the top of the hill arrive at a picnic pavilion. Turn right (east) and head steeply downhill. In less than 0.1 mile, cross a 60-foot bridge over a runoff. At

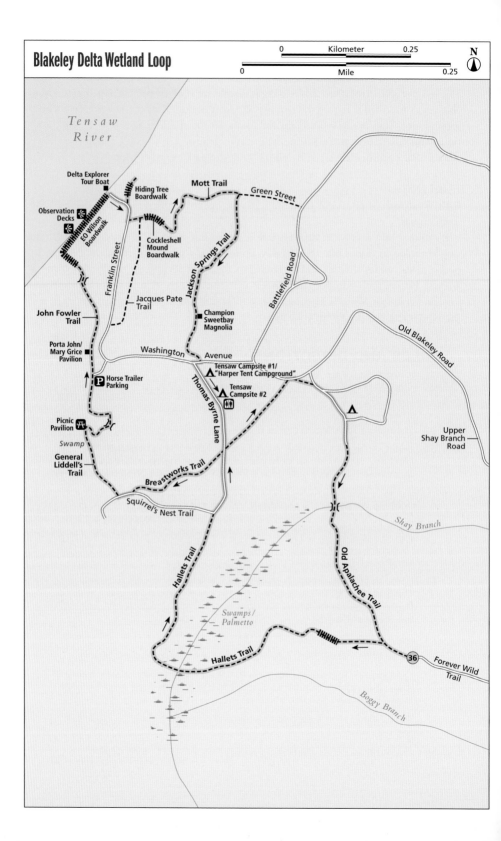

the end of the bridge, turn left (east). A dark blackwater swamp will be on your left.

1.9 Cross a 120-foot-long bridge over a creek. Once across, turn left (north). In less than 0.1 mile, climb a steep set of stairs made from 6x6 railroad ties uphill.

2.0 Arrive at the horse trailer parking lot. There are a couple of picnic tables here where you can take a break. Head straight across the field to the north and pick up the John Fowler Trail. The canopy thins out a bit through this section.

2.2 Pass a portable toilet on the left. The Mary Grice Pavilion and picnic area will be just ahead on the right. Continue straight to the north following the tree line.

2.3 Cross 2 short bridges back to back over a runoff. In less than 0.1 mile, come to an intersection. The main park road is to the right. Turn left (north). In a few yards come to the beginning of the E.O. Wilson Boardwalk.

2.4 Come to an observation deck on the left.

2.5 Pass a second observation deck on the left.

2.6 Turn right (southeast) to exit the boardwalk at the *Delta Explorer* tour boat. In less than 0.1 mile, turn right onto a boardwalk to visit the Hiding Tree. Be sure to hide.

2.7 At the end of the boardwalk turn around and return to mile 2.6. Exit the boardwalk and turn left (south) on what was once the main road of the old town of Blakeley, Franklin Street.

2.8 Look for a very small green sign to your left (east) in the trees. When you see it, turn left off the road toward the sign and begin your hike on the Jacques Pate Trail.

2.9 Turn left (east) onto the Cockleshell Mound Boardwalk over a wetland and stream. In less than 0.1 mile, come to the end of the boardwalk and turn left (northeast) onto Mott Trail. Cross a long footbridge over a stream and wetland.

3.0 At the end of the bridge, climb a steep set of stairs up a ridge. The stair fascia has been painted red so you don't trip. In less than 0.1 mile, head down a set of stairs. The stairs are very steep and the treads are spaced quite a distance apart. You should consider walking your dog down the embankment to the side of the stairs to keep them safe from injury. At the bottom of the stairs, the trail turns right to the east. The canopy is thinner here as you move away from the delta and the wetlands.

3.2 Arrive at Green Street .The Wehle Nature Center is just down the dirt road to your left. Cross the road to the south and pick up the Jackson Springs Trail.

3.4 Cross a bridge over a swampy area.

3.5 At the end there is a sign for the Champion Sweetbay Magnolia Tree. Turn left (southeast). In less than 0.1 mile, come to a short boardwalk that leads to the Champion Tree. The footing is more root strewn through this section. A small creek runs parallel on the left. In a dozen yards cross a 60-foot bridge over a runoff and almost immediately after exiting cross a 100-foot bridge over a swampy area followed by a steep set of stairs made from 6x6 railroad ties. At the end of the stairs, you'll come to the intersection with Washington Avenue. Cross straight across the road to the southwest and pick up Thomas Byrne Lane. Only a few yards in, you'll pass the Harper Tent Camping area and the first of two primitive campsites, Tensaw Campsite #1.

3.7 Pass Tensaw Campsite #2 on the left and a men's/women's restroom on the right.

3.8 Arrive back at the intersection with the Breastworks Trail. Turn left (northeast) onto the Breastworks Trail.

4.1 Arrive back at Washington Avenue. Turn right onto the road.

4.3 Arrive at the entrance to the Harper Tent Campground at the bathhouse. Turn right (southeast) into the campground and follow the tree line on the right (western) edge of the campground south. In less than 0.1 mile, pick up the Old Apalachee Trail, an old, wide dirt road. In a few yards pass a 6-inch round pole on the left (there used to be an old gate here). An old sign here reads, APALACHEE TRAIL ENTRANCE 0.6 MILE, SHAY BRANCH TRAIL N. 0.2 MILE.

4.5 Cross a small bridge over a stream. This is a great spot for dogs to drink and cool down. After the stream the trail becomes hard-packed dirt and steep. You may have to detour to the left of the trail to avoid deep ruts.

4.9 Arrive back at the intersection with the Hallets Trail. Turn left (southeast) onto Hallets. In less than 0.1 mile, arrive back at the trailhead.

PUPPY PAWS AND GOLDEN YEARS

Another fascinating hike to experience at Historic Blakeley State Park is the Breastworks Trail and the Blakeley Battlefield.

Blakeley was the site of the last major battle of the Civil War. After the Union took Fort Morgan and Gaines, which protected the mouth of Mobile Bay and the last Confederate seaport, Mobile, the Union army made a drive to this small outpost along the banks of the Mobile-Tensaw Delta.

The battle took place between April 2 and April 9, 1865. During that time, General Grant defeated Lee at Appomattox Courthouse, Virginia, effectively ending the war. The city of Mobile was the last major Confederate port to be captured.

The trail winds through wetlands formed by Baptizing Branch and follows one of the most complete hand-dug Confederate breastworks remaining in the South. The trail leads you to the battlefield itself where a self-guided tour tells you the history of the battle. Your dog will love roaming the large field dotted with pines.

37 PERDIDO RIVER TRAIL SECTION 1

Although Section 1 of the Perdido River Trail is only 3 miles in length, it packs in a lot. The trail uses a combination of abandoned logging roads and sandy footpaths that lead you through an Atlantic white cedar bog and towering pines; it culminates in a visit to the banks of the Perdido River, where a huge white sandbar awaits, the perfect spot to have lunch and take a swim in the cool waters of the river. This section is only a small part of the 20-mile-long trail that makes for a great backpacking trek.

THE RUNDOWN

Start: From the north side of the Blue Lake Landing parking lot
Distance: 3.0-mile out-and-back
Approximate hiking time: 2 hours
Difficulty: Moderate over dirt and sand paths and through a cedar swamp
Trailhead elevation: 52 feet
Highest point: 54 feet
Best season: Spring to early fall; open sunrise to sunset
Trail surface: Sand, dirt
Other trail users: Hunters
Canine compatibility: Voice control
Land status: State wildlife management area
Fees and permits: None; there is a fee to camp at a shelter (see Creature Comforts for details and restrictions).
Trail contact: 5 Rivers Delta Center, 30945 5 Rivers Blvd., Spanish Fort; (251) 625-0814; www.outdooralabama.com/5-rivers-alabamas-delta-resource-center
Nearest town: Robertsdale
Trail tips: Pack your swimsuit, bring along a beach towel, and take a dip in the cool, tannin-colored waters of the Perdido from the huge sandbar. Don't forget the bug spray, though, in the summer; to get to the sandbar, you'll be walking through a cedar swamp.
Maps: USGS: Barrineau Park, FL
Other maps: Large map at trailhead kiosk is also available online at www.alabamaforeverwild.com/sites/default/files/Perdido_Hiking_Map.pdf
Other: After a period of rain, the trail can be flooded not only locally but also farther north. Check the National Weather Service river stage page for the height of the river before heading out: https://water.weather.gov/ahps2/hydrograph.php?gage=BRPF1&wfo=mob. Flood stage is 13 feet. The Atlantic white cedar swamp you will be hiking through as you near the large sandbar is usually a boggy walk and holds water for a long period of time after rain; it could have water standing a foot deep.

FINDING THE TRAILHEAD

From the intersection of I-10 (exit 53) and CR 64 in Robertsdale, take CR 64 north 7 miles. Turn right onto AL 112 and head southeast 7.5 miles. Turn left onto Barrineau Park Road / Duck Road at the green STATE LANDS sign. Immediately after turning off the highway, there is a Y. Take the right fork onto the dirt and gravel Duck Road. From here to the trailhead it is a dirt and gravel road that could have potholes. In 0.4 mile, you will pass the Perdido River Wildlife Management Area Check Station on the right. Continue straight. In 1.3 miles, turn left onto Fairview Avenue. Travel 1.1 miles and carefully cross a set of railroad tracks; on the other side take

the right fork. Travel another 1.1 miles and you will see the first sign showing the direction to Blue Lake Landing. Travel 1.3 miles and turn left onto another dirt road at the
Blue Lake Landing sign. The trailhead is ahead in 0.1 mile. This is a dirt and gravel
parking area with a canoe landing and plenty of room for at least 50 cars. Trailhead
GPS: N30 39.466' / W87 24.255'

THE HIKE

Let's face it. The Alabama Gulf Coast is not a prime backpacking destination. Baldwin
County is one of the fastest-growing regions in the state, if not in the Southeast. Everyone wants to move to the white-sand beaches and turquoise waters of the Gulf that, like
most seaside towns, is rimmed with condos and beach houses. But today, add hiking and
backpacking to your list of outdoor activities near the beach because the 20-mile-long
Perdido River Trail is officially open.

The trail is located only a short distance from those Gulf beaches. Okay, as the crow
flies. The trail is well off the beaten path. The trip to the trailhead is over long, winding
dirt and gravel roads. It will take you a while to get there, but it's well worth it.

I'll talk about the backpacking options in a moment. Right now, though, let's talk
about this hike, which is a subset of the longer trail. The Perdido is broken down into
four sections. This hike is called the Southern Section or, more commonly, Section 1, a
3.0-mile out-and-back journey.

The Perdido River, which forms the border between Alabama and Florida, is your
quintessential Southern blackwater river. The waters are clear and cold as they relent-
lessly flow southward to the Gulf of Mexico but are tinted a tea color from the tannin
leeched from the trees that line the river's banks.

The trail takes a picturesque route along a dirt and sand footpath with some old dirt
logging roads. The path winds its way northward from the trailhead through a longleaf
pine forest with colorful wildflowers and bogs full of amazing Atlantic white cedar, the
trees' "knees" protruding through the murky green waters, and along the top of sandy
bluffs giving you nice views of the river.

On your journey you will undoubtedly spot whitetail deer and wild turkey, but when
you are near the river and have a clear view of the sky, keep your eyes turned upward.
Bald eagles frequent and nest in the area. The area is also known to have a substantial
black bear population, but they are rare to see.

Eventually the trail pops out of the woods to a beautiful—and huge—white sandbar.
This is the turnaround for this hike, but make sure you have plenty of time to linger here.
You and your dog will have a blast swimming and splashing in the water, eating lunch,
then drying off in the sun on the fine-grain sand landing before heading back.

The trail is blazed yellow, a tip of the hat to the state bird, the yellowhammer, and
where the path makes a sharp turn it uses what is affectionately known as the "dit-dot"
method of blazing: two dollar-bill-size paint blazes, one on top of the other. The top
blaze indicates the direction of the turn; if it's offset to the left, the trail turns left, to the
right, the trail turns right.

There are a couple of things to remember and consider before and during a hike of
the Perdido. First, you need to keep an eye on the river stages. A level over 13 feet is
flood stage, and with the trail this close to the river, it can go underwater. (See the Other
section above for the river stage website.) Also, bug out if there are signs of threatening
weather, like the well-known south Alabama summertime deluge of rain. The river can

Just before entering the cedar swamp you'll have a beautiful view of the end of this hike, a large white sandbar.

flash flood quickly, and pine trees are like lightning rods. I have seen people hike the trail in almost waist-deep water after a good rain. Not fun or a good idea.

Also be on the lookout for snakes as you walk through the bog section and remember that hunting is allowed here. Get in touch with the Trail Contact (above) for where to obtain information on dates and restrictions.

If you're looking for something a little more adventurous, then why not backpack the entire Perdido River Trail? The trail was completed in 2018 and offers either a 20-mile point-to-point hike or a 40-mile out-and-back. The trail has three trailheads, which are also launches for kayakers paddling the Perdido River Canoe Trail.

Camping is allowed along the route in four trail shelters that must be reserved in advance (see Creature Comforts, below).

Before leaving the Perdido, I need to commend the work of Alabama's state-run Forever Wild program for having the foresight to protect this beautiful wilderness from the burgeoning Alabama Gulf Coast tourist scene, and the volunteers of the Alabama Hiking Trail Society for building this remarkable little trail. It took many hours and a lot of hard work, much of it done in the heat of the Gulf Coast summer, to cut the path through the dense forest. They did a great job.

CREATURE COMFORTS

RESTING UP

Red Roof Inn, 3049 W. 1st St., Gulf Shores; (251) 968-8604; www.redroof.com/property/al/GulfShores/RRI946

The Red Roof in Gulf Shores knows that tourists who flock to Alabama's beaches want to bring their pets, and the hotel is very accommodating. They allow one well-behaved

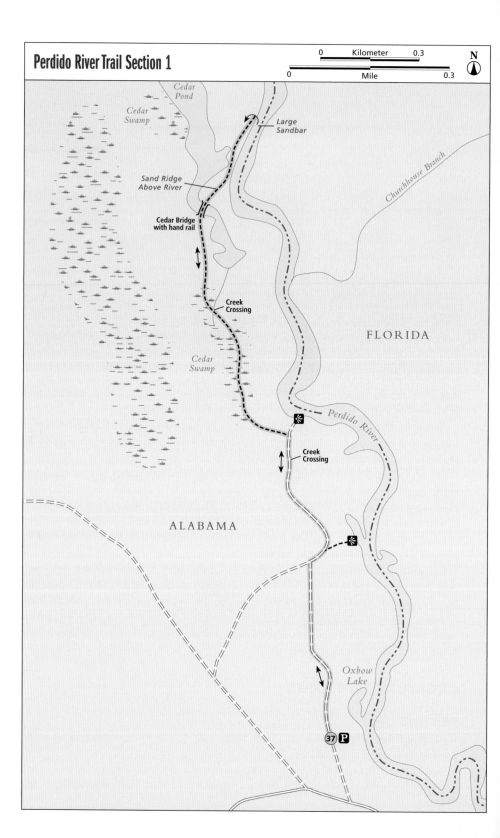

Perdido River Trail Section 1

Cedar Pond

Cedar Swamp

Large Sandbar

Sand Ridge Above River

Cedar Bridge with hand rail

Creek Crossing

Cedar Swamp

Creek Crossing

Churchhouse Branch

FLORIDA

Perdido River

ALABAMA

Oxbow Lake

37 P

of dog of any size with no additional charges. Make your reservations online and make sure to tell them you are bringing Fido.

CAMPING

Gulf State Park, 20115 AL 135, Gulf Shores; (251) 948-7275; www.alapark.com/Gulf-State-Park-Camping

Out of all of Alabama's state parks, Gulf State Park has arguably the most popular campground because you're only minutes from the state's sugary-white beaches. You'll need to make your reservations well in advance. The campground has 496 improved sites and 11 primitive sites, and all book up fast. Visit the campground website for rates and to make reservations. If you have trouble booking them online, then phone the campground.

FUELING UP

Pirate's Cove, 6694 CR 95, Elberta; (251) 987-1224; www.piratescoveriffraff.com

This is the most fun you and your dog will have dining in all of Alabama! Pirate's Cove is located on Arnica Bay, which is a cove along the Gulf in the tiny town of Josephine. Pirate's Cove features fantastic pizza, chicken wings, and what is touted as the best cheeseburgers around, all served up right on the beach where your well-behaved dog is welcome to visit and you, your family, and Fido can all swim right there in the bay.

MILES AND DIRECTIONS

0.0 Start at trail kiosk in the parking lot. The trail heads down a dirt road to the north. It is well marked with yellow paint blazes. In just a few feet, you will pass a second kiosk with a trail map showing the full Perdido River Trail.

0.3 Turn right (northeast) onto another dirt road at the double yellow blaze.

0.4 Come to a Y. Take the right fork a short distance for your first good look at the river. When done, turn around and return to the Y and proceed right (north) onto the original road.

0.7 Cross a creek. A few yards after the creek, there is another side trail on the right with an excellent view of the river and the large sandbar you're heading to. When done viewing turn around and return to the main trail heading north.

1.0 Come to a Y. Take the left fork (northeast) onto a much narrower 2-foot-wide pine-needle-covered path.

1.1 Come to a creek. You'll have to jump over it; it's not particularly wide, but it is a good 2 to 3 feet deep, so if you miss, you'll get wet (not that I've ever done that!). Following the creek, you'll begin your trek through an Atlantic white cedar swamp. The path stays boggy most of the time with water and mud, so you'll have to pick your way through. After a rain, however, it can be knee-deep in water.

1.2 Pass a grove of saw palmetto on the right.

1.3 Come to the end of the swamp. The trail moves slightly uphill onto a little sandy bluff above the river, which is to your right (east). You'll have a few good views through here using short side trails.

1.5 Arrive at the big sandbar. Feel free to explore, swim, eat lunch, even camp. When you're done, turn around and retrace your steps to the trailhead.

3.0 Arrive back at the trailhead.

PUPPY PAWS AND GOLDEN YEARS

While hiking on the Alabama Gulf Coast, you may want to take a short drive just across the border to hike these great Florida trails:

- Big Lagoon State Park

Five miles of trail to scenic beaches along the lagoon and Gulf and a three-story observation tower

- Fort Pickens: Gulf Islands National Seashore

A 2.2-mile out-and-back to the historic stone fortress

- Garcon Point

A 3.1-mile lollipop loop to Gulf prairies, pitcher plants, oak hammocks, and pines

Leashes are optional on some trails for well-behaved dogs.

38 BLUE TRAIL

A fun hike for you and a great romp for your pup are found at the Graham Creek Nature Preserve in Foley. Your dog will be able to splash in a wide creek near the start of the hike, and in season you will be treated to a rainbow of wildflowers, flowering magnolia and dogwood trees, plus fields of beautiful white-top pitcher plants. Keep your eyes peeled for gopher tortoises along the sandy paths.

THE RUNDOWN

Start: From the trailhead that is across from the parking lot to the west
Distance: 3.8-mile double loop
Approximate hiking time: 2 hours
Difficulty: Easy over mainly flat, wide dirt roads
Trailhead elevation: 0 feet
Highest point: 24 feet
Best seasons: Year-round; open sunrise to sunset
Trail surface: Sand, dirt, grass
Other trail users: Cyclists, disc golfers
Canine compatibility: Leash required
Land status: City nature preserve
Fees and permits: None
Trail contact: City of Foley, 407 E. Laurel Ave., PO Box 1750, Foley; (251) 952-4041; www.visitfoley.org

Nearest town: Foley
Trail tips: Restrooms are available near the trailhead. Your pup will find water in the creek crossings, but just in case there is a good old-fashioned hand water pump located at mile 1.4 (the intersection of Faust Lane and E. Pitcher Plant Lane trails). Be sure to bring the insect repellent; in the warmer months you will need to fend off those mosquitoes near bogs.
Maps: USGS: Orange Beach, AL
Other maps: Online at www .grahamcreekpreserve.org/ recreation/293/ or at the trailhead kiosk. You can also view maps posted on several kiosks located at major trail intersections

FINDING THE TRAILHEAD

From the intersection of US 98 and US 59 in Foley, take US 59 south 3.5 miles and turn left onto CR 12 E. Travel 1.0 mile and turn right onto Wolf Bay Drive. Drive 1.0 mile on Wolf Bay Drive. The road will make a sharp left-hand curve just before the park entrance. Turn right into the preserve; a large GRAHAM CREEK NATURE PRESERVE sign marks the turn. Follow the dirt road 0.2 mile. The parking area is to the left at a kiosk just before a kayak launch. The trailhead is directly across the road from the parking area to the west. Trailhead GPS: N30 20.783' / W87 37.465'

THE HIKE

There's more to a visit to Alabama's Gulf Coast than its beaches. There's also some great hiking at the Graham Creek Nature Preserve in Foley, only a few minutes north of those famous sugary-white beaches.

In total there are four trails that interconnect to form 5.9 miles of hiking opportunities. This trail, the Blue Trail, will lead you through much of the park's 484 acres and to many of the most beautiful areas and features found within its boundaries.

The centerpiece of the park is its namesake, Graham Creek, which begins flowing through the park as a narrow stream and gradually widens until it empties into Wolf Bay

The morning sun peeks over the trees and lights up a pond along the Blue Trail at Graham Creek Preserve.

and eventually the Gulf of Mexico. This mix creates a brackish environment where wildlife abounds, like the big, burly Florida manatee that occasionally makes its way inland up the creek. You may also spot the endangered gopher tortoise near its burrow in the sandy soil, in addition to coyotes, bald eagles, and ospreys.

You'll cross the creek a couple of times along the hike, including at the 0.3 mile mark where the reliable flow can be really wide and swiftly flowing after a good rain. Your pup will love frolicking in the cool, tannin-stained water.

You will also parallel the creek as it starts to really widen along a side trip on the Milkwort Trail (aka the Red Trail). The short, grassy bluff is a good place to sit and watch kayakers paddle the waterway, heading to the big water of Wolf Bay and the Gulf farther south.

The path is a nice, easy walking trail over flat dirt roads through a longleaf-pine forest that is decorated with rosebud orchids, lilies, sunflowers, and over 700 other plant species. The trail will lead you past a couple of large, grassy fields. On one, an obstacle course has been erected. In others, you'll find yourself paralleling an eighteen-hole disc golf course, so if your dog loves to chase Frisbees, watch out.

Eventually, at mile 2.8 you will come to a longleaf seepage bog and an impressive field of white-top pitcher plants that generally bloom from late April through June. Pitcher plants are rare carnivorous plants, much like a Venus flytrap, that grow in the bogs formed in a pine forest. Bugs are attracted into the plant's tubular stem by a sweet nectar, but, after entering, they never come out.

The trails are lightly marked with directional arrows, but intersections are marked with large signs almost like street signs, showing the names of the trails.

Even though there is water available in the creeks, your pup might still get thirsty. There is an old-fashioned hand water pump located at mile 1.4 (the intersection of Faust Lane and E. Pitcher Plant Lane) so they can get their fill.

There is a lot to do at Graham Creek besides hiking. As I mentioned before, there is disc golf, but you can also bike the trails and try your hand at archery. If you are traveling with your kids, there's a nice playground and clean restrooms near the trailhead.

A new addition is the park's Interpretive Center, where you can explore and learn more about the area's ecosystem, check out the native reptile exhibit and educational displays, and get more information about the park itself.

The city of Foley has also made this a very interactive park, hosting many tours and special events throughout the year. Visit Graham Creek's website for schedules (see Trail Contact, above).

CREATURE COMFORTS

RESTING UP

Staybridge Suites, 3947 Gulf Shores Pkwy., Gulf Shores; (251) 975-1030; www.ihg .com/staybridge/hotels/us/en/gulf-shores/pnssb/hoteldetail

Located only a few miles away from Graham Creek, the Staybridge allows pets weighing a total of 80 pounds, with a two-pet maximum. There is a $75 pet fee charged if you're staying between one and seven nights, $150 if you're stay more than seven days. Make your reservations online, then call the hotel to have them add a pet room to your reservation.

CAMPING

Gulf State Park, 20115 AL 135, Gulf Shores; (251) 948-7275; www.alapark.com/ Gulf-State-Park-Camping

Out of all of Alabama's state parks, Gulf State Park has arguably the most popular campground, because you're only minutes from the state's sugary-white beaches. You'll need to make your reservations well in advance. The campground has 496 improved sites and 11 primitive sites, and all book up fast. Visit the campground website for rates and to make reservations. If you have trouble booking them online, then phone the campground.

FUELING UP

Tacky Jack's Grill and Tavern, 27206 Safe Harbor Dr., Orange Beach; (251) 981-4144; www.tackyjacks.com/

You can't beat the view from the outdoor seating at Tacky Jack's in Orange Beach, and the food is great! Start with an appetizer like the Crispy La Hawg Bite—slow-roasted then deep-fried pork shank served with their Blowin' Smoke BBQ Sauce. Then dive in to the house specialty—the Tacky Shrimp—shrimp simmered for hours in a special blend of spices, seasonings, and herbs and served up with this spicy broth and French bread for dipping.

MILES AND DIRECTIONS

0.0 Start at the parking lot near the kayak launch. From the kiosk here that holds brochures and a large-scale map, cross the dirt road to the west. Follow the tree line along the south side of the wide disc golf course to the west.

0.2 The trail turns left (south) at hole #17 of the disc golf course into the woods and onto Spoonflower Lane. It is a wide dirt and grass path.

0.3 In less than 0.1 mile, cross an often wide and flowing creek. There is a wooden walkway to the left to help you across. Of course, Fido will probably

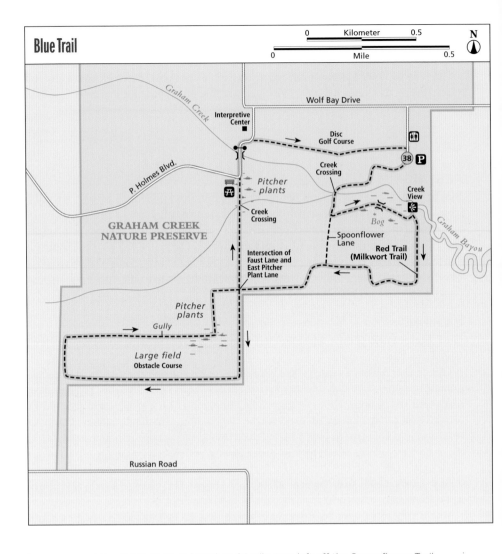

0   Kilometer   0.5

N

0   Mile   0.5

Graham Creek

Wolf Bay Drive

Interpretive
Center

Disc
Golf Course

38 P

Creek
Crossing

P. Holmes Blvd.

Pitcher
plants

Creek
Crossing

Creek
View

GRAHAM CREEK
NATURE PRESERVE

Bog

Graham Bayou

Spoonflower
Lane

Red Trail
(Milkwort Trail)

Intersection of
Faust Lane and
East Pitcher
Plant Lane

Pitcher
plants

Gully

Large field
Obstacle Course

Russian Road

want the direct route. In less than 0.1 mile, turn left off the Spoonflower Trail onto the Milkwort Trail.

0.4 Come to the first of several boggy areas on the trail that can be deep in mud or full of water after a rain.

0.5 Cross another boggy area. This one has a short footbridge; you'll cross at least 2 more in less than 0.1 mile.

0.6 Come to an excellent view of Graham Creek as it flows into Wolf Bay and eventually the Gulf of Mexico. With luck you'll get some good pictures of kayakers plying the waters. This is the end of Milkwort Trail. When done taking in the scene, turn right (south) to continue on the trail.

0.7 Pass an unmarked trail on your right. Continue straight (south).

0.9 Pass an unmarked trail on your right. Continue straight (west). In less than 0.1 mile, come to a large field. Turn right (north) and follow the tree line.

1.3	You'll pass the Spoonflower Trail that you originally came in on to the right (north).
1.3	At the southwest end of the field, turn right (west) onto E. Pitcher Plant Lane.
1.4	Arrive at the intersection of E. Pitcher Plant Lane and Faust Lane. An old hand water pump is here, so you can water your pup. Turn left (south) onto Faust Lane. This is a wide dirt and small-size gravel road.
1.5	W. Pitcher Plant Lane comes in from the right (west). Continue straight to the south and come out to a field that is used as an obstacle course. Follow the tree line to the south.
1.6	Continue to follow the tree line to the west.
2.1	Come to a gate. Turn right (north) onto Firebreak Lane.
2.3	Turn right (east) onto W. Pitcher Plant Lane at disc golf course hole #9. In less than 0.1 mile, come to hole #9 tee and hole #10. Keep left on the trail.
2.6	Cross a gully that can be deep in mud or under water after a rain.
2.7	Turn left (north) to stay on W. Pitcher Plant Lane.
2.8	Look for hundreds of white-top pitcher plants lining the trail. In less than 0.1 mile, come to a T intersection. To the left is a bench at a dead end. Turn right (east) onto the trail.
2.9	Arrive back at Faust Lane and the water pump. Turn left (north) onto Faust Lane.
3.1	Cross the creek. You'll also pass a nice wetland to your left and right.
3.2	A short side trail off to your left (west) takes you to some more pitcher plants. When done, return to Faust Lane and continue north. In less than 0.1 mile, pass the wide Philomene Holmes Boulevard on the left with benches and a picnic table at the intersection. Continue straight to the north on Faust Lane.
3.3	Cross a small creek as you walk through a gate. The Interpretive Center will be straight ahead. After crossing, turn right and cross the large field heading back to the trailhead.
3.8	Arrive back at the trailhead.

OPTION: The Milkwort Trail at mile 0.3 can be very boggy and deep in mud for days after it rains. If so, instead of taking the Milkwort Trail, continue straight south on the Spoonflower Trail to mile 1.2. At mile 0.9, instead of walking the north edge of the field, you can simply continue straight to the west on the south side of the field.

PUPPY PAWS AND GOLDEN YEARS

The city of Mobile on the Alabama Gulf Coast is known as the "Mother of Mystics" or the "Birthplace of Mardi Gras," that two-week period before Lent when anything goes.

Dogs have their own "mystic" society and parade as well. Across Mobile Bay in Fairhope, the Carnival season goes to the dogs with the Mystic Mutts of Revelry Parade. For one day during the season, and for a small fee, the streets are filled with over 500 pets, each escorted by their owner, both dressed in Mardi Gras regalia and parading to the rhythm of Mardi Gras music. All proceeds from the parade benefit the Haven, a nonprofit animal shelter whose mission is to be a sanctuary for animals who will be cared for no matter how long it takes to find them a loving home (www.havenforanimals.org/).

39 AUDUBON BIRD SANCTUARY

Here's your chance to stroll through a magnificent maritime forest past a shimmering lake and reptile-loaded swamp, and take in the beautiful view and the white dog-friendly beaches of the Gulf of Mexico on Alabama's barrier island, Dauphin Island. All along the route you and your dog will bathe in the soothing sounds of songbirds in this Audubon Society–sanctioned preserve and then frolic in the crashing waves of the Gulf.

THE RUNDOWN

Start: From the south side of the parking lot on Bienville Boulevard at the trail kiosks.
Distance: 2.5-mile double loop
Approximate hiking time: 1.5 hours (be sure to allow extra for beach time)
Difficulty: Easy over sand and dirt footpaths and boardwalks
Trailhead elevation: 60 feet
Highest point: 60 feet
Best season: Year-round, although June through early Sept is the hottest time of the year; open sunrise to sunset
Trail surface: Sand and grass, fine beach sand, boardwalk
Other trail users: None
Canine compatibility: Leash required
Land status: City preserve
Fees and permits: None
Trail contact: Dauphin Island Park and Beach Department, 109 Bienville Blvd., Dauphin Island; (251) 861-3607; www.dauphinisland.org/audubon-bird-sanctuary
Nearest town: Dauphin Island
Trail tips: All of the trails at the Audubon Bird Sanctuary are interconnected, so it's easy to mix

and match the routes you want to take. You can do as little as 1.0 mile on the Upper Woodland Trail or Lake Loop Trail, or hike all of the trails, weaving your way around the sanctuary for up to 3.3 miles. This interconnectivity also makes it easy to cut a trek short if you need to. Remember that while most of the trail has a good canopy and is very shady, there is no shade at the beach and along the section to the swamp overlook. Be sure to bring plenty of extra water and keep both you and your dog hydrated, wear a hat, and don't forget the sunscreen. Once on the beach you will want to take a dip in the Gulf. Remember that there are no lifeguards here. Check for warnings like dangerous rip currents on a weather radio or from local media. And don't forget your bug spray in the summer.
Maps: USGS: Fort Morgan, AL; Little Dauphin Island, AL
Other maps: Maps and birding brochure available online at www.dauphinisland.org/audubon-bird-sanctuary and on signs along the trail.

FINDING THE TRAILHEAD

From exit 17A on I-10 in Tillman's Corner, take AL 193 (Rangeline Road) south 6.8 miles. Turn left to continue on AL 193. Travel 0.8 mile and turn right to continue south on AL 193. Travel 17.9 miles; you will cross the Dauphin Island Bridge over the Intracoastal Waterway just before the island. Turn left onto Bienville Boulevard and travel 1.6 miles. The entrance on the right is a bit hidden from view. Trailhead GPS: N30 15.021' / W88 05.246'

THE HIKE

Dauphin Island is part of a chain of barrier islands that ring the Gulf of Mexico from Florida to Texas. The island itself is a popular retreat for "snowbirds," retirees who flee the harsh northern winters to spend time on sunny beaches. As you can imagine, as with any coastal island, Dauphin Island is a bustling little town, with people moving here to be near the sea and tourists flocking down in the summer.

The island's nickname is "America's Birdiest Town," and for good reason. The Audubon Society has recognized the island as one of the top four locations for bird watching, not just nationally but worldwide, calling it a "globally important location for [bird] migration."

With that in mind, the city of Dauphin Island and the Audubon Society set aside 164 acres of land to help protect and monitor the migratory birds that flock annually to this location, the Audubon Bird Sanctuary.

In this coastal forest of yaupon, wax myrtle, longleaf and slash pines, southern magnolias, and saw palmetto, you can spot over one hundred species of birds that either live here year-round or migrate in every year.

This secluded forest oasis on the island sports a wonderful trail system—five trails in all—that interconnect, forming just over 4.0 miles of paths that weave their way around this diverse environment. The hike I describe here is a good overall loop that takes in the best highlights of the sanctuary and one that has a nice surprise for your pup.

This loop uses a bit of each of the five trails—the Lake Loop, Campground Loop, Dune Edge, Swamp Overlook, and Upper Woodlands—plus a fun beach walk. The paths aren't blazed but are well maintained; you will have to try hard to get lost.

We begin the hike along the Nature Trail from the main parking area, then head east on the Campground Trail to the Banding Area, where during the migration season (which generally runs from mid-March through May and mid-September through October) volunteers and scientists capture, band, and monitor migrating birds.

From here the footpath turns to the south and becomes fine beach sand with scrub pine, oak, and thick saw palmetto lining the route. Blue flag (which are actually violet), beach heather, and sand hill rosemary add color to the trip.

Soon you will come to the Swamp Overlook Trail and visit an impressive observation platform that overlooks a shimmering pond and swamp, where many varieties of wintering and resident birds congregate, such as the yellow-crowned night heron, great egret, and belted kingfisher. Box turtles sun themselves in long queues on logs protruding from the water.

Then we come to the surprise for your pup: a visit to the only pet-friendly beaches on Alabama's Gulf Coast and the surf of the Gulf of Mexico. It's a beautiful stretch of white sand with an unlimited view of the Gulf and the historic Sand Island Lighthouse, built in 1873, on the horizon.

Be patient with Fido if you walk him into the surf. Many dogs haven't experienced waves like this before and can be intimidated. Also, there are no lifeguards here, so use caution when swimming, and before you head into the water, check with local media and officials about warnings for dangerous rip currents and such.

After strolling along the beach, head back north, passing an osprey nest at the Beach Overlook before heading east on the Dune Edge Trail that travels between Gaillard Lake and the Gulf of Mexico. Distorted sand live oaks line the path, providing a rugged landscape but little shade as the trail heads just behind the island's primary sand dunes.

A rarity in south Alabama—a dog-friendly beach along the Gulf of Mexico.

The path finally swings to the north on the Lake Loop Trail and the banks of Gaillard Lake. Several benches dot the banks, which are a pure joy to sit on and linger a bit when the wildflowers are in full bloom and the songbirds are serenading you. But a word of caution: Keep your dog close by, leashed, and out of the water. Alligators are known to live here.

The remainder of the hike back to the parking lot is a nice ramble through the beautiful and serene pine forest.

Summertime hiking along the Alabama Gulf Coast can be challenging. The subtropical climate and high humidity can be overwhelming for both of you. Keep an extra close eye on your pup for signs of stress and fatigue. Remember that there is no water available on this hike, so pack along extra. Also be sure that you use sunscreen and wear a hat.

Finally, remember that beach sand can be very hot in the summer. You may want to put boots on your pup during these months, or hike in the morning or late evening.

CREATURE COMFORTS

CAMPING
Dauphin Island Campground, 109 Bienville Blvd., Dauphin Island; (251) 861-2742; dauphinisland.org/camping/

There are 151 improved sites and plenty of primitive tent sites available at this cozy campground situated right in the heart of everything you want to see on Dauphin Island.

The park is located right next door to historic Fort Gaines, the Audubon Bird Sanctuary, and the beaches of the Gulf. This campground can be one crowded place—and not only in the summer. Call the campground to check availability and pricing and to make reservations.

FUELING UP

Miguel's Beach 'n Baja, 916 Bienville Blvd., Dauphin Island; (261) 861-5683; beach nbaja.com

As their slogan says, "West Coast flavor with Gulf Coast soul." That's what's served up at Miguel's: amazing burrito bowls or tacos served with shrimp, or mahimahi, or chicken, Baja pork, or ground beef quesadilla, all topped with Miguel's homemade salsa. Get there early for a seat for you and Fido in their outdoor eating area.

MILES AND DIRECTIONS

0.0 Start on the south side of the parking area. The trail begins at the informational kiosk. In less than 0.1 mile, come to a Y. A sign points the way to the Lake Trail to the right and the bird Banding Area to the left. Take the left fork to the east.

0.1 The trail is lined with saw palmetto as you pass a bench on the right. In a few yards pass a bench on left.

0.2 Come to a T intersection. A sign points the way to the parking lot and lake (back the way you came). Turn left (east) onto a wide, grassy path with a sand base. The foliage begins to open up as you get closer to the Gulf.

0.3 Pass a bench on the left. A wetland can be seen through the brush on the right. In less than 0.1 mile, arrive at the Banding Area and a bench on the right. You will see the campground straight ahead and a sign pointing right (south) to the Dune Edge Trail. Turn right and continue on the sandy path that is now lined with short pines.

0.4 Come to a Y. Take left fork to the southeast. In less than 0.1 mile, come to an intersection. The campground is to your left; a side trail comes in from the right (west). Continue straight to the southeast. *OPTION:* If it's not too buggy, turn right at the Y, and in less than 0.1 mile come to an overlook for a nice view of a swamp. Continue down this side trail to the southeast and you will return to the main path at mile 0.5.

0.5 Come to a T intersection. The campground is to the left. Turn right (south). The footing is now fine beach. In less than 0.1 mile, come to a boardwalk that will lead you over the dunes to the beach. Remember, don't walk on the fragile dunes!

0.6 Arrive at the end of boardwalk and the beach. Turn right (west) and follow the beach. Take your time and enjoy the view and the water before continuing west. (See Trail Tips for cautions.) Turn right (north) at the garbage cans to leave the beach.

1.1 Follow a boardwalk back up the sand dunes. In less than 0.1 mile, come to the Dune Observation Platform with benches, osprey nests, and beautiful views of the Gulf. When you're ready, continue north on the boardwalk.

1.2 At the end of the boardwalk turn right (east) onto the Dune Edge Trail. This is a very shady, palmetto-lined path. *OPTION:* To shorten the trip, instead of turning onto the Dune Edge Trail, continue heading north. This will take you to mile 1.7, where you can either continue on the Upper Woodland Trail or go straight to the parking lot.

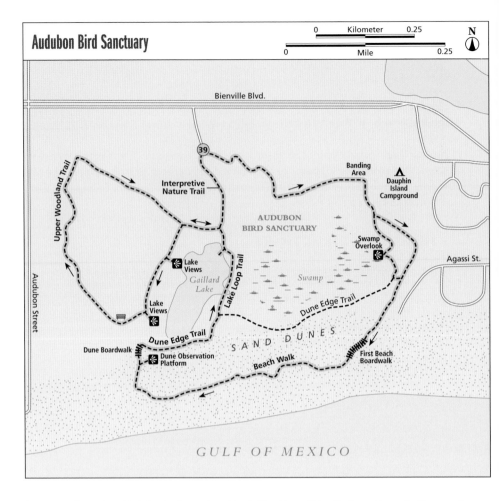

0   Kilometer   0.25

0   Mile   0.25

N

Bienville Blvd.

39

Banding
Area

Dauphin
Island
Campground

Upper Woodland Trail

Interpretive
Nature Trail

AUDUBON
BIRD SANCTUARY

Swamp
Overlook

Agassi St.

Audubon Street

Lake
Views

Gaillard
Lake

Lake Loop Trail

Swamp

Lake
Views

Dune Edge Trail

Dune Edge Trail

S A N D   D U N E S

Dune Boardwalk

Dune Observation
Platform

Beach Walk

First Beach
Boardwalk

GULF OF MEXICO

1.3 Come to a Y at the trail map in a kiosk. The Dune Edge Trail continues to the right; turn left (north) onto the Lake Loop Trail.

1.4 Come to a boardwalk on the Lake Loop Trail. Continue north. In less than 0.1 mile, a short section of the boardwalk turns to the right. In less than 0.1 mile, pass a side trail off to the right. Continue straight on the boardwalk and come to a ramp. Take the ramp for a beautiful view of the lake from its north end, where you'll see plenty of turtles and possibly an alligator. When ready, head back the way you came to the west.

1.5 The boardwalk ends, and in less than 0.1 mile, a trail comes in from the right (north). This will be used for the return trip. Right now continue to the west on the Lake Loop Trail.

1.6 Come to a Y. The Upper Woodland Trail comes in from the right (northwest). This will be the return for the second loop. Right now continue straight on the Lake Loop Trail. In less than 0.1 mile, there is a short side trail to the left (southeast) to the lake's edge and a bench with wonderful views of wildflowers and reptiles—including alligators! Keep your pet close at hand and out of the water and brush. When ready, continue to the southwest on the Lake Loop Trail.

1.7 Pass a bench on the right next to a sign showing the birds of prey you may see on the trail. In less than 0.1 mile, come to another side trail with views of the lake and a bench. When ready, return to the main trail. The Lake Loop Trail continues to the left (south). Cross the trail to the northwest to start hiking the Upper Woodland Trail.

1.8 Pass a bench on left with a small pond behind it.

1.9 The trail is lined with saw palmetto as you start to pass several side trails. Be looking for rectangular white signs tacked to the trees and marked TRAIL, with an arrow pointing the direction to head. In a few yards, pass a bench on the left.

2.0 Come to a T intersection at a trail map sign. Turn left (north). In 50 feet make a right turn. In less than 0.1 mile, come to a T Intersection. Turn right (north).

2.1 Come to another T Intersection with a bench and trail map. To the left a sign reads NO EXIT. Turn right to the southeast.

2.2 Pass a bench on the left.

2.3 Come to a Y with a sign showing the way to the parking lot. Take the right fork straight to the southeast. In less than 0.1 mile, turn left (east) onto the Lake Loop Trail.

2.4 Arrive back at the boardwalk from mile 1.5. Turn left (north) onto the Interpretive Nature Trail. A slow creek will be on the right.

2.5 Arrive back at the trailhead.

40 PELICAN ISLAND

Are you and your dog beach lovers? Then you know how difficult it is to find a dog-friendly beach. Look no further! Take a ride to Alabama's barrier island, Dauphin Island, for this 3.0-mile out-and-back hike on a beautiful white-sand peninsula that juts out from the island and is accented by the crashing waves of the Gulf of Mexico. Talk about the ultimate swimming hole!

THE RUNDOWN

Start: At the Dauphin Island Beach kiosk on the south side of the parking lot
Distance: 3.0-mile out-and-back (variable up to 3.0 miles, depending on tide)
Approximate hiking time: 2 hours
Difficulty: Moderate due to the entire trail being fine beach sand
Trailhead elevation: 16 feet
Highest point: 16 feet
Best season: Year-round; open 8 a.m.–6 p.m.
Trail surface: Fine beach sand
Other trail users: Fishermen, sunbathers
Canine compatibility: Leash required
Land status: Public beach
Fees and permits: $2 day-use fee for walk-ins or $5 parking for cars
Trail contact: Dauphin Island Park and Beach Department, 109 Bienville

Blvd., Dauphin Island; (251) 861-3607; www.dauphinisland.org
Nearest town: Dauphin Island
Trail tips: Restrooms are located on the pier that starts at the trailhead. Picnic tables are also located here. Don't forget the sunscreen for you and your dog. This is a beach walk, after all. The sun beating down on that sand can burn your pup's paws, so plan to visit either early morning or late evening, or consider putting booties on them. And with that heat, Fido can become dehydrated and fatigued very fast. Be sure to bring plenty of water and watch for signs that it's time to call it a day.
Maps: USGS: Fort Morgan, AL
Other: The sand dunes are protected habitat for nesting birds. Please stay off of them and follow the beaten path between them.

FINDING THE TRAILHEAD

 From exit 17A on I-10 in Tillman's Corner, take AL 193 (Rangeline Road) south 6.8 miles. Turn left to continue on AL 193. Travel 0.8 mile and turn right to continue south on AL 193. Travel 17.9 miles; you will cross the Dauphin Island Bridge over the Intracoastal Waterway just before the island. Turn right (west) onto Bienville Boulevard. Travel 0.9 mile. Beach parking and the entrance gate will be on the left. Trailhead GPS: N30 14.936' / W88 07.640'

THE HIKE

Our last hike is going to be different. Usually when you think of hiking, you think of mountains, rock outcroppings, wetlands—you know, all things woodsy. Not this one. This one is for beach lovers, along a stretch of sugary-white beach that is a rarity on the Alabama Gulf Coast: a pet-friendly beach. This is a hike along Pelican Island.

Actually, that name is a bit of a misnomer. The stretch of sand we will be walking isn't really an island. It's a peninsula of sand that juts out from Alabama's barrier island, Dauphin Island, into the Gulf of Mexico. At one time, this sand *was* a sand island just outside

The path that leads to the Gulf of Mexico. Remember to stay on the path! You will be walking between dunes that are federally protected.

of Mobile Bay, but due to the action of wind, rain, currents, and hurricanes, it slowly shifted to where it is today. As a matter of fact, when I coauthored the Falcon Guide *Paddling Alabama* back in 2001, it was still an island you could paddle around.

Today, that spit of land gives you and your dog a good 3.0-mile out-and-back hike into the Gulf, although that mileage is variable due to tides. It's also variable if you aren't used to walking in beach sand, which can get mighty tiring mighty fast. Pace yourself and don't push it on your first few trips with your dog.

This is a beautiful and fun hike, especially if this is your pup's first experience walking an ocean beach. Everything is new and exciting for them, but be patient. Those crashing waves can be frightening on their first visit. The worst thing you can do is force them into the water with you.

Your hike begins at the kiosk on the south side of the public beach parking area. There isn't a real trail here. It's pretty much a straight shot south to the water's edge. But, having said that, keep in mind that you will be walking through a set of primary sand dunes. These dunes help protect the north side of the island, and the mainland, from storm surges produced by hurricanes. It's also habitat for some endangered species of birds and wildlife. Don't walk on the dunes; instead, look for paths that have already been established by others and follow them.

Once at the water turn left (to the east) and follow the spit of land around. You will see men and women doing a little surf fishing and catch a show put on by the local brown pelican population. It's an amazing sight to see them dive-bomb and crash into the water, popping up with a tasty fish meal. You may also catch a glimpse of bottlenose dolphins frolicking in the surf just offshore.

Walking the beach is fun, but there are some common-sense things to keep in mind. One of the most important is that if you see lightening, even far off in the distance, get off the beach. Lightening can travel almost 25 miles from the actual storm!

Beach hiking also presents a new set of challenges when you have your dog along. First, there is no shade, and in the subtropical heat, that can be dangerous to your furry friend. And as most of you know from doing it yourself, walking barefoot on hot beach sand isn't any fun, so imagine what it does to your pup's paws. Consider hiking early in the morning or late in the evening to beat the heat. You might want to consider booties for your pet, not only for the hot sand but also to keep the sand out of their pads.

Remember, there is no fresh water out on the beach, so be sure to carry plenty for you and extra for your dog to avoid dehydration.

And finally, the city of Dauphin Island has allowed us to bring our best friends to this beautiful beach. Let's keep it that way by cleaning up after your pup.

CREATURE COMFORTS

CAMPING

Dauphin Island Campground, 109 Bienville Blvd., Dauphin Island; (251) 861-2742; dauphinisland.org/camping/

There are 151 improved sites and plenty of primitive tent sites available at this cozy campground situated right in the heart of everything you'd want to see on Dauphin Island. The park is located right next door to historic Fort Gaines, the Audubon Bird Sanctuary (Hike 39), and the beaches of the Gulf. This campground can be one crowded place—and not only in the summer. Call the campground to check availability and pricing, and to make reservations.

FUELING UP

JT's Sunset Grill, 1102 DeSoto Ave., Dauphin Island; (251) 861-2829; www.jtssunset grill.com/home.html

Seafood just doesn't get any fresher than right here on the Gulf beaches, and that's what the friendly staff at JT's serves up. Start things off with an order of fried crab claws, then tuck into a delicious whitefish po' boy, a blackened-shrimp taco (a local favorite), or one of a dozen seafood classics—oysters, calamari, you name it. And the setting is great at the picnic tables on the dock, where you and Fido can take in the view of the water and passing boats.

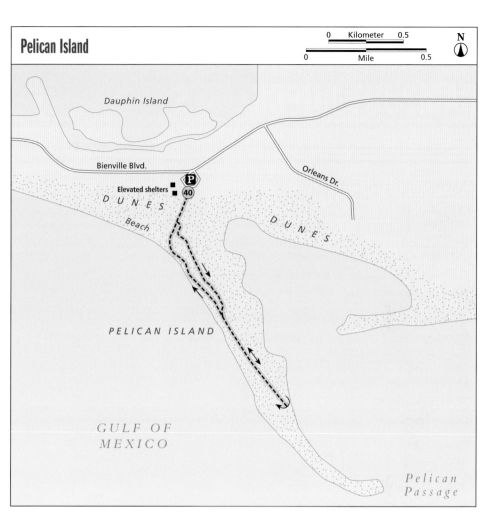

MILES AND DIRECTIONS

0.0 Start at the kiosk on a boardwalk on the south side of the parking lot. From here head straight south up a short set of stairs and a boardwalk over a short dune. In a few yards pass 2 elevated shelters with picnic tables to your right (west). You'll pass signs reminding you to keep off the dunes. Follow a narrow sand path through the dunes. The path is lined with various sea grasses.

0.2 Arrive at the beaches of the Gulf of Mexico. Turn left to begin walking out onto the peninsula. Meander as far as you like, or as the tides will let you . . . or as your stamina from beach walking lets you.

1.5 This is where I turned around and retraced my steps back to the trailhead. It was a really hot day for Archer T. Dog, but you can continue walking as far as you like, depending on the tide. Turn around when ready and retrace your steps.

3.0 Arrive back at the trailhead.

APPENDIX A: DAY HIKE AND CAMPOUT CHECKLISTS

DAY HIKE CHECKLIST

- ❒ Day pack
- ❒ Dog pack (optional)
- ❒ Health and vaccination certificate
- ❒ Collar, harness, leash, ID tag (with home/cell numbers), rabies tag
- ❒ Collapsible water bowl
- ❒ Water and metal or plastic (BPA-free) containers
- ❒ Water purifier, filter, or iodine tablets for long day hikes
- ❒ Kibble, snacks, and extra protein energy snacks
- ❒ Dog booties
- ❒ Hiking boots
- ❒ Bug repellent in sealed bag
- ❒ Sun hat
- ❒ Sunscreen for you and your dog (apply it to the tips of their ears)
- ❒ Biodegradable poop bags
- ❒ Wire grooming brush to remove burrs and stickers from your dog's fur
- ❒ Multifunction knife (i.e., Swiss Army knife)
- ❒ Flashlight
- ❒ Matches or lighter and fire starter
- ❒ Space blanket
- ❒ Whistle
- ❒ USGS maps and compass (and know how to use them)
- ❒ GPS (optional)
- ❒ Camera
- ❒ First-aid kit (see Appendix B)

HOW MUCH WATER?

For Humans:

- ❐ The general rule is 16 ounces (2 cups) of water per hour of walking for adults, 8 to 16 ounces (1 to 2 cups) for children
- ❐ In extremely hot or humid weather, increase your intake to 4 cups per hour

For Your Pup:

- ❐ 32 ounces for hikes under 4 hours (half-day hikes)
- ❐ 2 quarts minimum for hikes longer than 4 hours
- ❐ 8 ounces per hour or for every 3 miles of hiking

BACKPACKING CHECKLIST

Pack everything from the Day Hike Checklist plus the following items.

Dog Necessities:

- ❐ Extra leash or rope
- ❐ Sleeping pad
- ❐ Additional water
- ❐ Dog food (number of days on the trail × 3 meals per day)
- ❐ Chew toy
- ❐ Additional dog snacks (assume 6 rest stops per day)
- ❐ Nylon tie-out line for camp

Human Necessities:

- ❐ Tent with rain fly that will comfortably sleep you and your dog
- ❐ Clothes (moisture wicking socks and shirt; long pants; depending on season, gloves, fleece, and knit hat)
- ❐ Camp stove and fuel
- ❐ Food such as oatmeal, granola cereal, peanut butter, dried fruits; make it lightweight with plenty of nutrition, carbs, and protein

APPENDIX B: TRAIL EMERGENCIES AND FIRST AID

One of the most important things you can do is have your vet's phone number in your cell phone so you can reach them directly or at least their emergency after-hours contact.

Unfortunately, a cell phone often doesn't have a signal in wilderness areas. This is why it's important for you to sign the register at trailheads or complete the fee envelope when paying your day-use fee. This way, trail volunteers will know who is on the trail after hours and may need help.

And always let your friends and family know where you will be hiking. Tell them where you will be hiking, when you plan to start the hike, what trails you will be on, and when you plan to return. Provide them with trail contact information so that, in the event you are late returning and they haven't heard from you, they can call for help.

BEST DEFENSE

The number one tool to help prevent trail mishaps is the dog's leash. Of course, follow the leashing rules wherever you hike. If you're on an off-leash hike, snap it on when you are:

- Crossing fast moving streams
- Hiking narrow hillsides with drop-offs
- Hiking in wind and snow, which can disorient dogs
- Hiking in areas known to have wildlife that could pose threats (alligators, black bears, etc.)

FIRST AID

Here are a few first-aid basics for treating your dog until you can get them to the vet.

Bleeding Cuts and Wounds:

- Remove foreign objects.
- Rinse with warm water or 3% hydrogen peroxide.
- Place a nonstick pad or gauze over the wound and bandage it with vet wrap (also called gauze wrap).
- For a paw wound, cover with a bootie or an old sock cut to size and held on with duct tape.

Heatstroke

Dogs do not sweat, despite that old saying "sweating like a dog." They release heat through panting and their paws. When their temperature rises above 104 degrees, heatstroke could be next, so follow these tips:

- Get them out of the sun immediately and apply water-soaked towels to their head, chest, abdomen, and feet.
- If you're near water, let them stand in it while pouring water over them, but it cannot be icy water.

Hypothermia

The inverse of heatstroke, hypothermia occurs when a dog's temperature drops in cold weather to below 95 degrees.

- Get them to a shelter of some sort where you can build a fire.
- Wrap them in a blanket, your clothes, or sleeping bag, or wrap bottles of warm water in a towel and place it next to them—whatever you have to take the chill off.
- Hold them close to your body for heat.

Insect Bites

If your dog is stung by bees, bit by a spider, or any nasty bug, here's what to do:

- If it's a sting and the stinger is still present, use your fingernail to scrape it away from where it penetrates the skin.
- Apply a cold compress and apply an antihistamine spray like Benadryl. Ask your vet about carrying over-the-counter Benadryl just in case and the appropriate dosage for your dog's size and weight.

FIRST-AID KIT ESSENTIALS CHECKLIST

- ❏ Canine first-aid manual
- ❏ Paperwork in a waterproof bag: shot records and photos of your pet
- ❏ Contact information for your vet and ASPCA Poison Control Center (800-426-4435)
- ❏ Extra collar and nylon leash
- ❏ Any medications your pet is on
- ❏ Soft muzzle to prevent biting (do not use if they are vomiting)
- ❏ Vet wrap (the stretchy kind to hold bandages in place)
- ❏ Scissors
- ❏ Tweezers
- ❏ Digital rectal thermometer
- ❏ Petroleum jelly (to lubricate the thermometer)
- ❏ Absorbent gauze pads
- ❏ Adhesive tape

- ❑ Antiseptic wipes, spray, powder, or lotion
- ❑ Cotton balls or swabs
- ❑ Gauze roll
- ❑ Non-latex disposable gloves
- ❑ Sterile nonstick gauze pads for bandages
- ❑ Sterile saline solution
- ❑ Their favorite treats to help calm them and reward them for letting you treat them

OTHER USEFUL ITEMS

- ❑ "Space" (emergency) foil blanket
- ❑ Benadryl (*if* approved by your vet, who must provide you with dosage requirements)
- ❑ Small magnifying glass
- ❑ Disposable gloves
- ❑ Hydrogen peroxide: This is used to induce vomiting if they ingest something toxic, but it should be administered *only* after consulting with your vet
- ❑ Liquid styptic (to stop bleeding)
- ❑ An eyedropper or syringe to flush wounds and give oral medications

APPENDIX C: WILDLIFE CONFLICTS

There is one simple rule to remember when it comes to conflicts with wildlife on the trail: They should never happen in the first place.

Remember that this is their home, not yours. Respect their habitat, take care of it, and don't provoke an attack. Most of the time if you ignore the animal and give them their space, they will simply walk away. If they do become aggressive, it is usually because you were getting too close to their home or their nest, or you came up on them suddenly and scared them. Either way, they are simply protecting themselves and their offspring.

And an encounter doesn't have to be an attack. It could just be accidental. As a "for example," I was hiking one day with six other hikers, all walking single file down the trail. Little known to us, a doe and her fawn were sleeping in the brush, and our coming through scared them to death. The doe waited for the line to pass, but not long enough—she jumped up and ran across the trail, upending the last hiker in the line. By the way, that hiker's trail name is now "Dances with Deer."

PREVENTING ENCOUNTERS

- Don't surprise animals. Talk a little louder, walk a little heavier, and let them know you're coming.
- Keep your pet leashed. Leash laws are there to protect your dog and the wildlife.
- If you are in an off-leash area, do not let your dog run out of sight. Keep them close so they don't scare up trouble.

SNAKE ENCOUNTERS

The number one critter you will meet on the trail are snakes, but which ones are venomous and which ones are not? Whether or not you can tell the difference, use common sense. Stand back and normally they will slither away, then proceed, walking heavy to shoo them off.

The Alabama Extension Office has an excellent reference on the subject, "Venomous Snakes of Alabama," online at news.aces.edu/blog/2017/07/26/venomous–alabama–snakes/.

ALLIGATOR SAFETY

When hiking in the extreme southern region of the state, particularly along the Gulf Coast, you may encounter an American alligator on the trails near ponds, swamps, and wetlands. Alligators have an eclectic menu, anything from birds and frogs to small mammals, which includes children and dogs.

Help yourself, and others, by not feeding the gators, and that means not "unintentionally" feeding them by dropping food and food wrappers.

Keep your kids and dog close at hand. Follow the leash laws for your pet and heed warnings. If in doubt, don't take any chances.

ALLIGATOR FACTS
- There are two species: the Chinese and the one you'll find in Alabama, the American alligator.
- The largest alligator recorded in Alabama, and the world, was 15 feet long and weighed 1,101 pounds.
- Alligators are capable of running in short bursts up to 30 miles per hour on land.
- Alligators have no natural predators.
- Alligators are most active when temperatures are between 82 and 92 degrees. They stop feeding when the ambient temperature drops below 70 degrees and go dormant when it drops below 55 degrees.

BLACK BEAR

The black bear population in Alabama is growing exponentially, with the highest concentration found in the northeast, extreme south, and Gulf Coast parts of the state. Sadly, much of the bear's habitat is being destroyed and turned into subdivisions, so we are seeing more and more roaming through towns and looking for food.

Black bears look cute and cuddly, but they can be extremely dangerous, especially if they have cubs nearby. You may not see a bear in the woods but if you do, stop what you're doing. Stay calm and don't run. With your dog close to your side on its leash, make a wide upwind detour around the bear so they can smell you. Make a lot of noise by talking loud or clanging some gear like metal bowls. Be deliberate, move around them, and above all, avoid sudden movements that could spook or provoke them.

BLACK BEAR FACTS
- Black bears average 4 to 7 feet in length and 2 to 3 feet tall to their shoulders when on all fours.
- Their average weight is 200 to 600 pounds.
- Their average lifespan is 10 years, but they can live up to 30 years in the wild.
- The bear is very intelligent, adaptable, and curious but shy, tending to avoid confrontation.
- Black bears can run for short distances and can reach speeds of 25 to 30 miles per hour.

APPENDIX D: SOURCES FOR POOCH GEAR, USEFUL WEBSITES, AND BOOKS

WEBSITES

AlabamaOutdoors.com   Statewide outfitter for you and your dog

AlaPark.com   Online home of Alabama's state parks with info on camping, trails, and more

BringFido.com   Number one source to locate pet-friendly lodging and dining.

Chewy.com   National online dog-gear store

HikeAlabama.org   The official website of the state hiking and trail building group, the Alabama Hiking Trail Society

Kurgo.com   National online dog-gear store, featuring great packs and accessories

MountainHighOutfitters.com   North Alabama outfitter for you and your dog

NatGeoMaps.com   A source for trail maps

PinhotiTrailAlliance.org   Online source for info on Alabama's long path, the Pinhoti Trail

Recreation.gov   Public land campground reservations and trip planning

RedBeardsOutfitter.com   Gulf Coast outfitter for you and your dog

REI.com   National outdoor recreation outfitter

ReserveAmerica.com   Online camping reservations

Ruffwear.com   Online store for dog gear and accessories

SipseyWilderness.org   Information on Alabama's Sipsey Wilderness

Store.usgs.gov   Online site to purchase USGS maps

TheDogOutdoors.com   Online store for dog gear and accessories

Wilderness.net   Online source for topo maps and outdoor information

HELPFUL READS

Acker, Randy, DVM, and Jim Fergus. *Dog First Aid: A Field Guide to Emergency Care for the Outdoor Dog.* Belgrade, MT: Wilderness Adventures Press, 1994.

Backpacker Magazine. *Hiking and Backpacking with Dogs.* Guilford, CT: Falcon Guides, 2014.

Backpacker Magazine. *Trailside Navigation Map and Compass.* Guilford, CT: Falcon Guides, 2010.

Cuhaj, Joe. *Hiking Alabama,* 4th ed. Guilford, CT: Falcon Guides, 2014.

Cuhaj, Joe. *Hiking the Gulf Coast.* Guilford, CT: Falcon Guides, 2015.

Cuhaj, Joe. *Hiking Through History Alabama.* Guilford, CT: Falcon Guides, 2016.

Mullally, Linda. *Hiking with Dogs: Becoming a Wilderness-Wise Dog Owner.* Guilford, CT: Falcon Guides, 1999.

Wills, Kenneth M., and Dr. L. J. Davenport. *Exploring Wild Alabama: A Guide to the State's Publicly Accessible Natural Areas.* Tuscaloosa: University of Alabama Press, 2016.

1. Walls of Jericho

Start: From the trailhead on AL 79 to the west

Distance: 6.6-mile out-and-back

Approximate hiking time: 4 hours, but leave time to linger at the falls and canyon

Elevation gain: 1,348 feet

Best season: Year-round; open sunrise to sunset

Trail surface: Dirt and rock footpath

Other trail users: None

Canine compatibility: Leash required

Land status: State / Nature Conservancy tract

Fees and permits: None

Trail contact: Alabama Forever Wild, Alabama Department of Conservation & Natural Resources, 64 N. Union St., Ste. 468, Montgomery; (334) 242-3484; www.outdoor alabama.com

Nearest town: Hytop

Trail tips: Rocks can be slippery in the canyon at the falls. And you're walking down into a canyon. What goes down . . .

Other: The Walls of Jericho is probably the most popular hiking destination in the state with its bowl canyon and waterfalls.

Trailhead GPS: N34 58.62' / W86 4.82'

2. Pinhoti Trail / Cave Creek Loop

Start: At the Cheaha Trailhead on AL 281 to the northwest

Distance: 6.7-mile loop

Approximate hiking time: 5 hours

Elevation gain: 1,105 feet

Best season: Year-round; open sunrise to sunset, unless backpacking

Trail surface: Dirt and rock footpath

Other trail users: Hunters

Canine compatibility: Leash required

Land status: National forest

Fees and permits: None

Trail contact: Talladega Ranger District, Talladega National Forest, 1001 North St. / AL 21 N, Talladega; (256) 362-2909; www.fs.usda.gov/detail/alabama/about-forest/districts/?cid=fsbdev3_002555

Nearest town: Talladega

Trail tips: Check with the Trail Contact (above) for dates and restrictions during hunting season.

Other: This loop hike takes you to some beautiful views of the Talladega National Forest, including from atop McDill Point, which many say is the best view in the entire forest.

Trailhead GPS: N33 28.283' / W85 48.357'

3. Pinhoti / Skyway / Chinnabee Loop

Start: From Pinhoti Trail's Adam's Gap Trailhead at the intersection of the Talladega Scenic Highway, Adams Gap Road, and CR 600-2

Distance: 17.8-mile loop

Approximate hiking time: 2–2.5 days

Elevation gain: 2,904 feet

Best season: Year-round

Trail surface: Dirt and rock footpath

Other trail users: Hunters

Canine compatibility: Leash required

Land status: National forest

Fees and permits: None

Trail contact: Talladega Ranger District, US Forest Service, 1001 North St. (AL 21 N), Talladega; (256) 362-2909; www.fs.usda.gov/detail/alabama/about-forest/districts/?cid=fsbdev3_00255

Nearest town: Talladega

Trail tips: Check with the Trail Contact (above) for dates and restrictions during hunting season.

Other: A great weekend backpacking trip, this loop uses three trails—the Pinhoti, Skyway, and Chinnabee Trails—to make a circuit with views, several stream crossings, and waterfalls.

Trailhead GPS: N33 24.249' / W85 52.467'

4. Oak Mountain State Park White Trail / Blue Trail Loop

Start: From the North Trailhead on John Findley Drive.

Distance: 12.8-mile loop

Approximate hiking time: 1 long day or 2 days with overnight backcountry camping

Elevation gain: 1,824 feet

Best season: Year-round; open 7 a.m.–7 p.m.

Trail surface: Rock and dirt footpath

Other trail users: None

Canine compatibility: Leash required

Land status: State park

Fees and permits: Day-use fee: adults, 12 and over, $5; children 4–11 and seniors over 62, $2. If you plan to do backcountry camping, $6 per camper, per night plus taxes and fees

Trail contact: Oak Mountain State Park, 200 Terrace Dr., Pelham; (205) 620-2520; www.alapark .com/oak-mountain-state-park

Nearest town: Pelham

Trail tips: If you are going to do an overnight, be sure to pay and register for backcountry camping.

Other: This hike can be done in a full day, but it will be a long day. I recommend backpacking in for the night. There are great views from the Blue Trail and some pretty difficult sections heading up to the King's Chair on the Blue Trail and Shackleford Point on the White Trail. You will get to see Peavine Falls at the south end of the loop, where the two trails intersect.

Trailhead GPS: N33 21.443' / W83 42.298'

5. Smith Mountain Fire Tower Trail

Start: At the Smith Mountain Fire Tower parking lot on Smith Mountain Road

Distance: 0.9-mile loop

Approximate hiking time: 1.5 hours

Elevation gain: 216 feet

Best season: Sept through May; open sunrise to sunset

Trail surface: Dirt footpath but very rocky

Other trail users: None

Canine compatibility: Leash required

Land status: Deeded Alabama Power Company property

Fees and permits: None

Trail contact: Cherokee Ridge Alpine Trail Association, PO Box 240503, Eclectic, AL 36024; www.cherokeeridge alpinetrail.org

Nearest town: Dadeville

Trail tips: Do not climb the tower or stay on top of the mountain if thunderstorms are looming.

Other: A short hike but oh so satisfying, with beautiful views of Lake Martin from the rocky bluffs and from atop the rebuilt fire tower on top of the mountain.

Trailhead GPS: N32 48.692' / W85 50.119'

6. Perdido River Trail

Start: Start at either the Gravel Fork Landing and head south for a SOBO (southbound) hike or the Blue Lake Landing for a northbound hike.

Distance: 20-mile point-to-point (requires shuttle vehicle) or 40-mile out-and-back

Approximate hiking time: 2 days

Elevation gain: 314 feet

Best season: Sept through May; open sunrise to sunset

Trail surface: Sand and dirt footpath

Other trail users: None

Canine compatibility: Leash required

Land status: State preserve

Fees and permits: None. There are trail shelters along the route that can be reserved for $25 for one night, but dogs are not allowed in them. You can tent camp with your dog on the beaches in front of the shelters for free

Trail contact: Alabama Forever Wild, Alabama Department of Conservation & Natural Resources, 64 N. Union St., Ste. 468, Montgomery; (334) 242-3484; www.outdoor alabama.com; Alabama Hiking Trail Society, PO Box 691, Montgomery; hikealabama .org

Nearest town: Robertsdale

Trail tips: Hunting is allowed in the Perdido River Wildlife Management Area. Check with the Trail Contact (above) for dates and restrictions. Also, the river is prone to flooding, which may put the trail completely underwater. Watch the weather and visit the USGS water level gauge online (water.weather.gov/ahps2/hydrograph .php?gage=BRPF1&wfo=mob); 13 feet is considered flood stage, but don't let it get that deep before changing plans. Camping is allowed with your dog on the sandbars near the trail shelters. Bring the insect spray in the summer months.

Other: This is the entire 20.0-mile trail that we described a subset in Perdido River Trail Section 1 (Hike 37). You can do the hike as a point-to-point 20.0-mile hike, which would require a shuttle vehicle at the other end, or a 40.0-mile out-and-back. There is also a trailhead at the halfway point, so you can cut the hike distance in half. There are plenty of opportunities for you and your dog to swim the cool waters of the river along the way.

Trailhead GPS: Gravel Landing (North): N30 47.004' / W87 33.130'; Blue Lake Landing (South): N30 39.466' / W87 24.255'

APPENDIX F: LOCAL INTEREST TRAIL FINDER

BEST CANYONS
2 Cane Creek Canyon Preserve
9 Fall Creek Falls
10 Caney Creek Falls

BEST WATERFALLS
2 Cane Creek Canyon Preserve
7 Falls Loop Trail
9 Fall Creek Falls

BEST WILDFLOWERS
2 Cane Creek Canyon Preserve
4 Honeycomb Trail
5 Tom Bevill Loop
12 Chinnabee Silent Trail / Lake Shore Loop
15 Waterfall Loop
20 Lake Trail
32 George W. Folkerts Bog Trail

BEST BIRDING TRAILS
23 Wood Duck Trail
39 Audubon Bird Sanctuary

HIKES FOR HISTORY LOVERS
3 Plateau Loop
6 King's Chapel Loop
13 Ruffner Mountain Nature Preserve
14 Red Mountain Park
16 Tannehill Ironworks Historical State Park
19 Flagg Mountain Loop
31 St. Stephens Historical Park

BEST SWIMMING
8 Hurricane Creek Park
11 Turkey Creek Nature Preserve
12 Chinnabee Silent Trail / Lake Shore Loop
30 Little River State Forest
40 Pelican Island

BEST BEACH HIKE
37 Perdido River Trail Section 1
39 Audubon Bird Sanctuary
40 Pelican Island

BEST VIEWS
12 Chinnabee Silent Trail / Lake Shore Loop
22 John B. Scott Forever Wild Trail

INDEX